Reading
WOMEN
Writing

a series edited by
Shari Benstock and Celeste Schenck

Reading Women Writing is dedicated to furthering international feminist debate. The series publishes books on all aspects of feminist theory and textual practice. *Reading Women Writing* especially welcomes books that address cultures, histories, and experience beyond first-world academic boundaries.

Tainted Souls and Painted Faces: The Rhetoric of Fallenness in Victorian Culture
by Amanda Anderson
Greatness Engendered: George Eliot and Virginia Woolf
by Alison Booth
Talking Back: Toward a Latin American Feminist Literary Criticism
by Debra A. Castillo
Articulate Silences: Hisaye Yamamoto, Maxine Hong Kingston, Joy Kogawa
by King-Kok Cheung
H.D.'s Freudian Poetics: Psychoanalysis in Translation
by Dianne Chisholm
From Mastery to Analysis: Theories of Gender in Psychoanalytic Feminism
by Patricia Elliot
Feminist Theory, Women's Writing
by Laurie A. Finke
Colette and the Fantom Subject of Autobiography
by Jerry Aline Flieger
Cartesian Women: Versions and Subversions of Rational Discourse in the Old Regime
by Erica Harth
Narrative Transvestism: Rhetoric and Gender in the Eighteenth-Century English Novel
by Madeleine Kahn
The Unspeakable Mother: Forbidden Discourse in Jean Rhys and H.D.
by Deborah Kelly Kloepfer
Women and Romance: The Consolations of Gender in the English Novel
by Laurie Langbauer
Autobiographical Voices: Race, Gender, Self-Portraiture
by Françoise Lionnet
Woman and Modernity: The (Life)Styles of Lou Andreas-Salomé
by Biddy Martin
In the Name of Love: Women, Masochism, and the Gothic
by Michelle A. Massé
Reading Gertrude Stein: Body, Text, Gnosis
by Lisa Ruddick

Articulate Silences

HISAYE YAMAMOTO,
MAXINE HONG KINGSTON,
JOY KOGAWA

King-Kok Cheung

Cornell University Press

ITHACA AND LONDON

First published 1993 by Cornell University Press.

Library of Congress Cataloging-in-Publication Data

Cheung, King-Kok
    Articulate silences : Hisaye Yamamoto, Maxine Hong Kingston, Joy Kogawa / King-Kok Cheung.
        p.   cm. — (Reading women writing)
    Includes bibliographical references and index.
    ISBN 0-8014-2415-1 (cloth)—ISBN 0-8014-8147-3 (pbk.)
    1. American literature—Asian American authors—History and criticism.   2. Women and literature—United States—History—20th century.   3. American literature—Women authors—History and criticism.   4. Yamamoto, Hisaye—Criticism and interpretation.
    5. Kingston, Maxine Hong—Criticism and interpretation.
    6. Kogawa, Joy—Criticism and interpretation.   7. Asian Americans in literature.   I. Title.   II. Series.
    PS153.A84C48   1993
    810.9'9287—dc20   92-46452

⊗ The paper in this book meets the minimum requirements of the American National Standard for Information Sciences— Permanence of Paper for Printed Library Materials, ANSI Z39.48-1984.

To my parents

My mother has taught me the exigencies of talk;
my father, the nuances of silence.

Contents

Illustrations

Acknowledgments

This book could never have emerged without the aid of fellowships from the American Council of Learned Societies and the University of California Humanities Research Institute (UCHRI), which allowed me the time necessary to read, reflect, and compose. Research grants from the Academic Senate and from the Institute of American Cultures and the Asian American Studies Center of UCLA have made possible the indefatigable assistance of Brenda Kwon, Barbara Jung, Robert Ku, James Lee, Rachel Lee, Kristin Leuschner, Lisa Mortimer, Brian Niiya, and Sharon Park.

Celeste Schenck and Bernhard Kendler, who have shown interest in the project since its inception, have been astute and provocative critics. Barbara Smith, Shelley Fisher Fishkin, Elaine Hedges, Gordon Hutner, Kathryn Poethig, and Renate Stendhal generously lent their expert editorial counsel.

I learned much from the seminar "The Subjects of Feminist Criticism" (School of Criticism and Theory, Dartmouth, 1988), conducted by Nancy K. Miller, whose intellectual courage I admire and whose encouragement I treasure. The 1991–92 participants in "Minority Discourse" at UCHRI, Irvine, offered both warm fellowship and trenchant criticism; I thank in particular Anne Dannenberg and Abdul JanMohammed for their thoughtful readings.

The small size of the Asian American field makes exchange with specialists all the more precious. Stan Yogi and Sau-ling Wong have provided abiding intellectual companionship. I also thank Frank

Chin, C. Lok Chua, Donald Goellnicht, Elaine Kim, Amy Ling, Lisa Lowe, and Gayle Sato for sending me their works or commenting on mine; Teruyo Ueki for explicating the two ideograms for "love" in *Obasan*; and Shu-mei Shih for penning them.

Colleagues at UCLA have been magnanimous in diverse ways. Daniel Calder, Lucie Cheng, and Herbert Morris showed faith in my ability to explore an emerging terrain when I was a newcomer to Asian American literature; Mike Rose was protective of my time. Don Nakanishi provided untold moral and material support. Valerie Smith, Karen Rowe, and Stephen Yenser read portions of the manuscript and offered tonic suggestions. Kenneth Lincoln, who read more than his fair share, let me know when my prose waxed too rhetorical or waned to elliptical. Yuji Ichioka, Valerie Matsumoto, and Russell Leong enlightened me on several aspects of Asian American culture and history. Martha Banta spurred me on with her redoubtable example and kind regard; Henry Ansgar Kelly allowed me to pick his encyclopedic brain; Walter Anderson gave laconic advice. Jonathan Post, Departmental Chair, applied much-needed pressure by asking periodically, "So when is your book coming out?" Special thanks to Richard Yarborough, whose sparing compliments I have chosen to believe at all times.

Thanks too to my former mentors John Anson, James Atteberry, Stephen Booth, and Norman Rabkin; they never mistook my slowness of speech for imbecility. The interpretive strategies they taught me continue to enrich all my reading.

My students, to whom I owe an unceasing debt, keep my tongue, ears, and mind active; and they excite my scholarship by speaking, listening, and writing.

Friends have been palpably attentive. Rosalind Melis combed through the manuscript more than once and voluntarily did "fieldwork" for me at Slocan. Susan Brienza transmitted judicious briefings across the miles. Hide and Kana Ijiri sent me a fetching haiku for illustration. Elizabeth Kim, Jeff Spielberg, and Mei-Fan Tang put up with my litany of self-doubts.

My gratitude to Gerard is beyond words.

Portions of Chapter 2 have appeared in different forms in "Double-Telling: Intertextual Silence in Hisaye Yamamoto's Fiction," *American Literary History* 3.2 (1991): 277–93; and in "Thrice

Muted Tale: Interplay of Art and Politics in Hisaye Yamamoto's 'The Legend of Miss Sasagawara,'" *MELUS* 17.3 (1991–92): 109–25. Portions of Chapter 4 will appear as "Attentive Silence in Joy Kogawa's *Obasan*" in *Listen to Silences: New Essays in Feminist Criticism*, edited by Shelley Fisher Fishkin and Elaine Hedges (New York: Oxford University Press, forthcoming). They are used here by permission.

Pages from Maxine Hong Kingston's *China Men* containing her father's marginal notes are reproduced by permission of the author and the Bancroft Library at Berkeley.

I am grateful for permission to quote from the following works:

Maxine Hong Kingston, *China Men*. Copyright © 1977, 1978, 1979, 1980 by Vintage/Random House, New York, and Schaffner Agency, Inc., Tucson, Arizona.

Maxine Hong Kingston, *The Woman Warrior: Memoirs of a Girlhood among Ghosts*. Copyright © 1975, 1976 by Vintage/Random House, New York, and Schaffner Agency, Inc., Tucson, Arizona.

Joy Kogawa, *Obasan*. Copyright © 1981 by Joy Kogawa.

Hisaye Yamamoto, *Seventeen Syllables and Other Stories*. Copyright © 1988 by Hisaye Yamamoto. Reprinted by permission of the author and Kitchen Table: Women of Color Press, P.O. Box 908, Latham, N.Y. 12110.

K.-K. C.

Los Angeles, California

Terminology

In this book I use the term "Asian American" to refer to North American writers of Asian descent. Asians in the United States and Canada have had parallel experiences. After the bombing of Pearl Harbor, for instance, people of Japanese ancestry living along the Pacific coasts of both countries were forcibly removed from their homes; those who were U.S. and Canadian citizens were denied their constitutional rights.

The term "Asian American literature" generally describes works by writers of diverse national origins—Chinese, Japanese, Korean, Filipino, East Indian, Pakistani, Vietnamese, Thai, Cambodian, Laotian, and Pacific Islanders. My selection of only one Chinese American and two Japanese American authors is in no way meant to be representative. Nor are the attitudes toward verbal and non-verbal expression of the selected authors necessarily shared by members of their own—let alone other—nationalities.

Though dissatisfied with the terms, I use "minority," "race," and "ethnicity" more or less interchangeably to refer to persons of color. People of color are numerically no longer minorities in many parts of the United States; "race," as applied to Asian Americans, homogenizes highly distinctive national groups; "ethnicity" obscures the charged differences due to race, but the word does allow for greater flexibility when I discuss the three *creative* writers. Unlike race, ethnicity is "not something that is simply passed on from generation to generation" but something dynamic and constantly reinvented (Fischer 195).

Other terms used throughout the book include:

nikkei   Japanese Americans; literally, Japanese lineage
issei   Japanese immigrants; literally, first generation
nisei   children of the issei; literally, second generation
sansei   children of the nisei; literally, third generation
kibei   nisei raised or educated in Japan for a period before returning
to America; literally, return to America

Articulate Silences

1
Introduction

Articulate Silences engages, at times tacitly, in a three-way conversation. In analyzing the writing of Hisaye Yamamoto, Maxine Hong Kingston, and Joy Kogawa I am in dialogue with recent feminist theories about women's poetics, notably those regarding narrative gaps or ellipses, and with scholarship concerning ethnicity. My book builds on the work of feminist and Asian American critics but also modifies what I consider to be Eurocentric premises. I take issue with both Anglo-American feminists who valorize voice and speech indiscriminately and revisionist Asian American male critics who refute stereotypes by renouncing silence entirely. I also question certain tenets held by scholars on ethnicity: at one extreme the insistence on a unified (ethnic) self and on cultural "authenticity"; at the other, the urge to transcend ethnicity al together.

When speaking of Eurocentric premises I have in mind primarily the social norms concerning speech and silence in North America, especially the premium placed on assertiveness in educational institutions and in society at large. Silence, by contrast, has often been perceived negatively as absence, or as "an out-of-awareness phenomenon—the ground against which the figure of talk is perceived" (Tannen & Saville-Troike xi). Such a logocentric tendency obscures the fact that silence, too, can speak many tongues, varying from culture to culture.

But I do not mean to imply that overvaluation of speech is confined to Euro-Americans or characteristic of them all. Many women and members of racial minorities, growing up in an America where voice is tantamount to power and where they have been traditionally muzzled, have also forsworn silence in order to have a say in society. Moreover, what is commonly designated as the "West" encompasses conflicting notions and its own self-critiques. The Bible specifies that there is "a time to keep silence, and a time to speak" (Eccl. 3:7). In the theoretical-philosophical realm, many thinkers—among them Augustine, Nietzsche, Heidegger, Picard, Wittgenstein, Foucault, Dauenhauer, Derrida—have in their own ways valorized speechlessness or displaced logocentrism.[1] In literature, irony and understatement, as well as other modes of implicit communication, have always been appreciated (see, for example, Portch, Sontag, Stout, and J. A. Ward). Even in the social realm, situational and regional differences exist in North America. As J. Vernon Jensen puts it, "Silence can communicate scorn, hostility, coldness, defiance, sternness, and hate; but it can also communicate respect, kindness, and acceptance" (252; see also Hall). Canadians are said to be more terse than their U.S. counterparts; one also hears of New England reticence. Accurate or not, these comparisons seldom call for automatic moral assessment.

Much more susceptible to judgment is Asian American silence. Despite the many positions on speech and silence in the Western philosophical tradition, and despite regional variations within North America, attitudes toward Asian and Asian American reserve have been mostly critical or patronizing. The quiet Asians are seen either as devious, timid, shrewd, and, above all, "inscrutable"—in much the same way that women are thought to be mysterious and unknowable—or as docile, submissive, and obedient, worthy of the label "model minority," just as silent women have traditionally been extolled. And precisely because quietness is associated with the feminine, as is the "East" in relation to the "West" (in Orientalist discourse), Asian and Asian American men too have been "feminized" in American popular culture.[2]

[1] Although it is beyond the scope of this book to engage that literature fully, I will draw on a specific branch of inquiry that questions the mimetic power of language.

[2] Scholars such as Tong (1971), Suzuki, and Osajima have pointed out that the label "model minority" places Asian Americans above presumably less tractable minorities and conceals a divisive strategy of containment by the dominant culture. Although other racial minorities are no less discriminated against, Asian Americans, according to the editors of *Aiiieeeee!*, have been the most subdued because of

Such attitudes also color the reading of Asian American literature. General readers, as Paula Gunn Allen observes, "tend to see alien literature in terms that are familiar to them, however irrelevant those terms may be to the literature under consideration" (54). A work that seeks to illuminate the narratives of Asian American writers must simultaneously interrogate the ethnocentric and logocentric perspectives that still inform much of mainstream feminism, perspectives that result in attributing silence solely to patriarchal constructions of womanhood and in eliding the issues of silencing and being silent. Silence can be a direct consequence of prohibition. But it also carries other functions and meanings that vary with individuals and cultures.[3] Yamamoto, Kingston, and Kogawa show that verbal assertion for many Asian Americans— male as well as female—involves overcoming obstacles peculiar to gender, culture, and race. Yet they do not always perceive verbal and nonverbal modes in hierarchical terms.

Modalities of silence need to be differentiated. The works of all three writers reveal the multiple problems of speechlessness and stress the importance of breaking silence. Silence can be imposed by the family in an attempt to maintain dignity or secrecy, by the ethnic community in adherence to cultural etiquette, or by the dominant culture in an effort to prevent any voicing of minority experiences. But the works also challenge blanket endorsements of speech and reductive perspectives on silence. The writers question the authority of language (especially language that passes for history) and speak to the resources as well as the hazards of silence. They articulate—question, report, expose—the silences imposed on themselves and their peoples, whether in the form of feminine

---

their alleged tractability: "In terms of the utter lack of cultural distinction in America . . . the people of Chinese and Japanese ancestry stand out as white racism's only success" (Chin et al. xxvi).

The popular evaluation of silence in America, as I suggested earlier, is inflected not just by gender but also by race. Whereas the taciturnity of a "Western" hero such as John Wayne is very much in accord with his reputation as a man of vigilance, courage, and action, Asian American reticence has been construed as passive, secretive, and "utterly without manhood" (Chin et al. xxx). This knotty issue of "emasculation" is also discussed in Chin & Chan, Hwang 1989, Cheung 1990b, and Lee.

[3] The essays collected in Tannen & Saville-Troike look at silence from a cross-cultural and interdisciplinary viewpoint, yet none of them covers Asian or Asian American silence.

and cultural decorum, external or self-censorship, or historical or political invisibility; at the same time they reveal, through their own manners of telling and through their characters, that silences—textual ellipses, nonverbal gestures, authorial hesitations (as against moral, historical, religious, or political authority)—can also be articulate.

Feminist critics have discerned several common tendencies among, though not peculiar to, women writers which result from their exclusion from dominant discourse. First, women's writing is said to be characterized by silence, both as a theme and as a method. As a theme, silence speaks for the many barriers to female expression, such as those enumerated in Tillie Olsen's *Silences*.[4] The art of silence, on the other hand, covers various "strategies of reticence" (Janis Stout's term)—irony, hedging, coded language, muted plots—used by women writers to tell the forbidden and name the unspeakable.[5] Second, many women writers distrust inherited language and decline to assert themselves as *the* voice of truth.[6] Anticipating poststructuralists, they not only question re-

[4] Among Olsen's examples are conflicting demands of household responsibilities, rejection by the literary establishment, a lack of models, imposed repression, and self-censorship. The theme of female silence is also treated at length in Anzaldúa 1987, Bauer, Castillo 71–95, Christ, Griffin, Gubar, Rich, and Russ.

[5] Feminist critics who have examined the art of silence in women writers include Friedman, Gilbert & Gubar, Homans (1983, 1986), Johnson, Kammer, Kolodny (1980), Kristeva (1980), Lanser (1981, 1989), Miller (1981), Orenstein, Ostriker, Radner, Rainwater, Rayson, Rowe, Showalter, Stout, and Washington. Some of these critics are influenced by Marxist critics such as Macherey and Eagleton, who have also elaborated on narrative gaps and silences.

[6] The question whether language can represent feminine reality has divided French and American feminist theorists. Many French feminists (Cixous, Clément, Gauthier, Irigaray [1985a, 1985b], Kristeva [1980], and Wittig) consider the feminine to be unrepresentable by conventional language, a masculine construct that thrives on female absence; most American critics (e.g., Marks; Kolodny 1975, 1980; Ostriker; Yaeger) believe, on the contrary, that though language has traditionally served patriarchy, women can appropriate dominant discourse for their own purposes. In an attempt to mediate between the two schools of thought, Homans argues that although "there is a specifically gender-based alienation from language that is characterized by the special ambiguity of women's simultaneous participation in and exclusion from a hegemonic group," several North American novelists, including Marilyn French, Alice Walker, Toni Morrison, and Margaret Atwood, express this alienation by "representing their skepticism about representation" (1983, 205). The three Asian American writers, as we shall see, express similar skepticism in their works.

ceived knowledge but accentuate their own fictionality. To undercut narrative authority they frequently resort to such devices as
dream, fantasy, and unreliable point of view; or even project their
anxiety as authors onto demented characters.[7]

Third, skepticism about language and about textual authority
has led women writers to embrace open-endedness and multiplicity in their fiction. Instead of subscribing to any one "master-
narrative" (Lyotard), they exemplify what Rachel Blau DuPlessis
calls a "both/and vision" (1981/1985, 276), what Dale Bauer (taking
off from M. M. Bakhtin) terms "feminist dialogics," and what both
Gloria Anzaldúa (1981) and Mae Henderson describe as "speaking
in tongues." Paradoxically, verbal withholding or indirection often
goes hand in hand with multiplicity; as Joan Radner and Susan
Sniader Lanser observe, "multiple readings [are] made possible by
the ambiguity of coding" (423).

These theories about women's poetics open up exciting avenues
for analyzing the texts I have chosen to explore. But I must also
complicate and implicate some of the underpinning assumptions.
The silencing of women—a motif that runs through the works of
Yamamoto, Kogawa, and Kingston—takes on peculiar resonance
when we look at characters whose voicelessness is induced not
only by gender but also by culture and race. The writing career of
Mrs. Hayashi, the mother in Hisaye Yamamoto's "Seventeen Syllables," ends abruptly because of her husband's anger at her preoccupation with poetry. Yet even her chosen poetic form of seventeen
syllables bespeaks cultural constraints. Naomi, the narrator in
Kogawa's *Obasan*, recalls an old man who molested her when she
was a child; his injunction to secrecy has disrupted her bond with
her mother, and her sense of shame is greatly exacerbated by the
enforced political uprooting of her family during World War II. The
compounded impact of sexual and racial abuse ushers in twenty
years of repressed guilt. Maxine, the narrator of Kingston's *Woman
Warrior*, is gagged by misogynist proverbs while growing up in a
Chinese immigrant community.[8] But her silence becomes "thick-

---

[7] For a discussion of women's "anxiety of authorship," see Gilbert & Gubar; for an
analysis of women's use of fantasy, see Nancy Walker.

[8] I refer to the narrator of *The Woman Warrior* as Maxine for critical convenience. In
fact, like her ostracized aunt, the narrator remains unnamed throughout the book.
In withholding her name, Kingston not only links the narrator and her aunt sym-

est" when she enters an "American" school, where she is branded as retarded because she is unable to speak English. Having internalized the norms of her schoolteachers, Maxine later tries to torture another mute Chinese girl into speech.

This last episode enacts the Asian American psychological trauma of trying to live up to a dominant norm and points to the danger of excessive emphasis on vocalization. Monocultural criteria of competence and even feminist antipathy toward silence may run roughshod over the sensibilities of some ethnic groups. While the importance of voice is indisputable, pronouncing silence as the converse of speech or as its subordinate can also be oppressively univocal. *The Woman Warrior* does undoubtedly chart the narrator's progression from tonguelessness to expression, yet young Maxine's acceptance of the dominant culture's equation of "talk" with "brain" and "personality" is no less disturbing than the black girl Pecola's pathetic desire for the "bluest eye" in Toni Morrison's novel.

The negative social assessment of silence isolates and baffles many an Asian American. Verbal restraint, often inculcated in both Chinese and Japanese cultures and reinforced as a survival strategy in the face of racism in the corresponding immigrant communities, hardly prepares a child for vocal assertion, especially when she is perceived as the Other.[9] Reticence, however, lends credence to the

---

bolically but also suggests the indeterminate identity of the young narrator, who moves between different subject positions rather than manifesting a stable identity.

[9] Sucheng Chan observes that Asian American students "who were verbally reticent could slowly learn to express themselves" in classes where they were in the majority, but remained quiet in classes in which they were "numerically overwhelmed" by white students (1989, 270, 272); her observation is borne out by my own teaching experience. Chan further notes that these students must overcome a "double repression"—"Asian traditions that train the young (and especially the female) to be quiet, submissive, and obedient *and* American racism that threatens members of minority groups with harm unless they 'stay in their place.' Staying in their place means keeping silent" (276–77). Kikumura suggests another reason for Japanese American silence: "Papa [her issei father] also taught his children to be quiet and observant in situations when one was in doubt of the proper action or behavior" (94). Asian and Asian American silence does not necessarily signify submission or evasiveness, however, though it is often *perceived* as such in American society.

The reductiveness of ascribing putative Chinese American traits, such as obedience to authority, inhibition, and meekness, to Confucian influence alone has been pointed out by the psychologist Benjamin R. Tong, who argues that these

already ingrained Western notion of the inscrutable Oriental. It also allows the "other(s)" to speak for the race. According to the editors of *Aiiieeeee! An Anthology of Asian-American Writers*—one of the first works to reclaim and define Asian American literature— the "partly real and partly mythical silence" of Asian Americans has bolstered racism and perpetuated cultural invisibility:

> One measure of the success of white racism is the silence of the minority race and the amount of white energy necessary to maintain or increase that silence. The Chinese-American is told that it is not a matter of being ignored and excluded but of being quiet and foreign. . . .
>
> The deprivation of language in a verbal society like this country's has contributed to the lack of a recognized Asian-American cultural integrity (at most, native-born Asian-Americans are "Americanized" Chinese or Japanese) and the lack of a recognized style of Asian-American manhood. . . . Language coheres the people into a community by organizing and codifying the symbols of the people's common experience. Stunt the tongue and you have lopped off the culture and sensibility. (Chin et al. xxv–xxvi, xxxviii, xlviii)

Because "Orientals" have for too long been voiceless in American cultural and political spheres, Asian Americans today are tempted to dispel stereotypes by repudiating silence entirely.[10] "Silence is not inherent in Hawaii's local . . . Asians, as if they em-

---

traits were in fact cultivated in America in response to white racism, and that the uneducated Cantonese peasants who made up the majority of early Chinese immigrants were not steeped in Confucian ethics but were instead venturesome and rebellious (1971; see also Suzuki 35–38). Chin (1985) further attributes the submissive traits of Chinese Americans to Christianity. While Tong and Chin are right in distinguishing the Cantonese folk culture of the early immigrants from the "Great Traditions of Cathay" (Tong 1971, 4), I believe they underestimate the extent to which mainstream Chinese thought filters into folk imagination, in which the heroic ethos coexists with Buddhist beliefs and Confucian teachings (which do counsel self-restraint and obedience to parental and state authority). To attribute the "submissive" traits of Chinese Americans entirely to white racism or to Christianity is to discount the complexity and the rich contradictions of the Cantonese culture and the necessary flexibility and adaptability of the early immigrants.

[10] Titles of such works as *Breaking Silence: An Anthology of Contemporary Asian American Poets*, edited by Joseph Bruchac; *Too Long Silent: Japanese Americans Speak Out*, by Roger W. Axford; and *Shedding Silence: Poetry and Prose*, by Janice Mirikitani, attest to the prevailing impulse to forswear silence.

body the noble savage and the noble sage, one of them strong and silent, not possessing words, the other wise and silent, not needing words," Stephen H. Sumida argues. "But silence has been forced upon these people of Hawai'i by authority and circumstance, in punishment, perhaps, for someone's having spoken out in insubordination. . . . Silence in the . . . Local works and vignettes is not a virtue but an adversary" (1991, 227). Other critics go further in suggesting that Asian Americans who do exhibit reserve have simply internalized white imperatives (e.g., Chin et al. xxvi–xxvii; Rose 1987, 293).

While I address the adversarial aspects of silence, I also champion its virtues. I believe that many revisionist critics have unwittingly accepted the vocal mandate in America, an acceptance that blinds them to the positive cultural and aesthetic manifestations of reticence.[11] The privileging of speech has led, for instance, to tendentious readings of Joy Kogawa's *Obasan*. Those reviewers who see Obasan's quietude as no more than a mark of her passivity and victimization fail to register what Gayle K. Fujita calls the "sensibility of silence," validated in the novel as part of the nikkei legacy.

This legacy is not just social but also literary. Traditional Chinese and Japanese literature, no less and indeed much more than Euro-American literature, generally value the implicit over the explicit, so that even political writing is often coded.[12] But many younger

[11] It is worth noting that the Chinese and Japanese character for "silence" is antonymous less with "speech" than with "noise," "motion," and "commotion." I elaborate on this point in chap. 4. According to Kunihiro, "One characteristic of the Japanese attitude toward language is the comparatively light emphasis placed on overt linguistic expression. To the Japanese, language is *a* means of communication, whereas to the people of many other cultures it is *the* means. Japanese tend to be taciturn, considering it a virtue to say little and rely on nonlinguistic means to convey the rest. Verbal expression is often fragmentary and unsystematic, with emotional, communal patterns of communication" (56). In Kunihiro's opinion, "The Chinese . . . who valued empty space in the sparse beauty of their brush painting, are [nevertheless] given to exhaustive expression and endless argument" (57). I believe Kunihiro's contrast between the Japanese and the Chinese is somewhat exaggerated.

[12] Suggestiveness and allusiveness have been the hallmark and ideal of traditional Chinese poetry. The "typical Japanese dislike of the verbal" has been underscored by Miyoshi: "It might be said that the culture is primarily visual, not verbal, in orientation, and social decorum provides that reticence, not eloquence, is rewarded. Similarly, in art it is not articulation but the subtle art of silence that is

Asian Americans have come to favor a more strident tone as a means to combat social invisibility. Furthermore, views on cultural politics have spilled over into aesthetic criteria. In their attempt to advocate a "masculine" language, for instance, the editors of *Aiiieeeee!* valorize such novels as Louis Chu's *Eat a Bowl of Tea* and John Okada's *No-No Boy,* both of which are written in vociferous styles. The masculinist preference gives short shrift to works that communicate indirectly through the consummate play of silences. (Perhaps the very distinction between "masculine" and "feminine" styles is little more than a sociocultural construction.) To counterbalance these editors' ongoing attempts to reclaim an Asian Heroic Tradition and a "manly" style, I have chosen to give "feminine" poetics its due.[13]

Also missing from most feminist discussions and from the editors' treatise in *Aiiieeeee!* is an awareness of the whole gamut of male silences. Although sexual asymmetry surfaces—at times fiercely—in the works of Yamamoto, Kogawa, and Kingston, patriarchal dominance, manly fortitude, and emasculation all take specific forms of silence in these texts. Governed by the Japanese code of stoic behavior, the fathers in Yamamoto's "Seventeen Syllables" and "Yoneko's Earthquake" repress their jealousy and insecurities till their bottled-up emotions explode in violence. Racism further squelches expression. In *Obasan,* Naomi's uncle, who has endured the ravages of the internment camp, becomes as impenetrable as the "stone bread" he regularly bakes. In *China Men* the narrator's great-grandfather is literally forbidden to speak on the Hawaiian plantations where he works.

Male silence also manifests itself as the suppression of an Asian past. As traditional breadwinners, many early male immigrants put physical survival in the new country above cultural niceties.

---

valued. *Haiku* is the most perfect embodiment of this spirit but it is visible elsewhere as well" (xv). On the poetics of haiku see Ueda and Yasuda; see also Chin (1985) on the coded style of Sun Tze's *Art of War.*

[13] But it would be inaccurate to conclude that Asian American men invariably prefer open expression whereas Asian American women favor ellipsis. Janice Mirikitani is surely much more vociferous than Toshio Mori, Jessica Hagedorn more so than Bienvenido Santos, and Maxine Hong Kingston more so than David Wong Louie. The first two pairings, in which the women are a generation younger than the men, also suggest that generational characteristics impinge on style. See also Kolodny 1975 on the danger on presuming a "feminine style" (77).

Thus while Mrs. Hayashi's interest in writing haiku—her specific artistic expression and connection to the old world—threatens her husband in several ways, the only explicit reason given for his angry outburst at the end of "Seventeen Syllables" has to do with the exigencies of the family's tomato harvest. Male immigrants were, moreover, the ones who had to interact with white society, which often demanded deference from them and spurned their foreignness. In this context, women (especially mothers), operating under the relatively secure and secluded environment of home and ethnic community, were frequently the transmitters of culture for the second generation (Goellnicht 1991, 123; see also Yanagisako and Kikumura on this point). While Maxine's mother "funnels China" into the daughter's ears, her father—transformed from a poet-scholar in China to an "illiterate" laundryman in America—is almost mute: "No stories. No past. No China" (1980/ 1989, 14).[14]

The obliteration of an Asian past was not compensated by recognition in America. Early immigrants found their "presence" annulled by legalized discrimination (for example, Orientals could not testify in court) and their contributions consigned to oblivion. The withdrawal of the narrator's father in *China Men* prefigures the enforced invisibility of Chinese American men at large; at certain periods during the past century they were stripped of their constitutional rights and rendered voiceless by unjust laws. Cultural

---

[14] Comparing her female and male characters in an interview, Kingston says: "I wrote the characters so that women have memories and the men don't have memories. They don't remember anything. The character of my father, for example, has no memory. [H]e is so busy making up the present, which he has to build, that he has no time for continuity from the past" (Rabinowitz 180). She discloses in another interview that many of the men's stories were "originally heard from women" (Kim 1982, 208).

Other reasons why women rather than men were agents of cultural continuity might be rooted in the double standard of traditional Asian cultures and in the relatively late arrival of Asian women in America. Speaking of the no-name aunt in *The Woman Warrior*, Kingston writes: "She was the only daughter; her four brothers went with her father, husband, and uncles 'out on the road' and for some years became western men. . . . They expected her alone to keep the traditional ways, which her brothers, now among the barbarians, could fumble without detection. The heavy, deep-rooted women were to maintain the past against the flood, safe for returning" (8). In addition, the various immigrant mothers I discuss—Brave Orchid, Mrs. Hayashi, Obasan—all came to North America years after their husbands' arrival. The women may therefore remain closer than their spouses to Asian cultures.

history was brutally wrested from the nikkei. When the FBI and American soldiers searched Japanese American homes in the wake of the Pearl Harbor attack, nikkei had to burn just about everything associated with their national origin, from letters and pictures to literary manuscripts and heirlooms. It is, in part, the lost annals of Asian Americans that Yamamoto, Kogawa, and Kingston seek to recoup through memory, imagination, and scattered records.

Since minority experiences have so often been distorted or altogether undocumented in mainstream "history," these writers have even greater reason than most women authors and poststructuralists to be leery of language as the purveyor of objective knowledge.[15] In "The Legend of Miss Sasagawara," set pointedly in an internment camp, Yamamoto uses the story of a putative madwoman as an "ironic mirror" that magnifies the insidious effects of gossip, rumor, name calling   those practices that indirectly led to the unjust incarceration of Japanese Americans (Yogi 1988, 116). In *Obasan* Kogawa underscores the duplicitous nature of discourse that could whitewash prisons as "interior housing projects." Kingston emphasizes the difficulty of conveying reality by pointing out the omissions in received information and the lapses or discrepancies in her own memory.

Yamamoto, Kogawa, and Kingston repeatedly dramatize the elusiveness of "truth" as linguistically transmitted, but their texts are praised or censured almost exclusively according to historical or anthropological criteria. Yamamoto's *Seventeen Syllables and Other Stories* is hailed as "a literary time capsule—an intimate slice of Japanese American history" (Tajiri 257). Reviewers of *Obasan* laud the novel for furnishing the "true" story about Japanese Canadians. But many critics fault Kingston for altering Chinese myths and for falsifying Chinese American experience. Though these authors share other women writers' skepticism about language and received knowledge and call attention to their own fictionality, the

---

[15] Valerie Smith points out how literacy in the dominant language similarly poses a danger for African American writers: "Literacy has been a tool of social organization and control, inspiring in the learner a respect for authority. The ability to read and write thus does not in and of itself guarantee freedom and sophistication of expression; the very structures of discourse themselves embody values and assumptions that may elude one's control" (4). Hayden White argues that history itself must be considered as verbal fiction, shaped by various tropes (1978).

majority of their critics regard the works as either mirroring or obfuscating Asian American realities.

These critical responses indicate the peculiar burden imposed on ethnic—in this case Asian American—writers. Precisely because Asian American history has so often been eclipsed and manipulated, readers tend to look to biological insiders for "authentic" accounts.[16] In view of the general ignorance and diehard stereotypes to which Asian Americans have been subjected, together with the previous lack of nationally published writers of Asian descent, the ones currently receiving literary acclaim are quickly construed to be spokespersons for the ethnic group as a whole. (Brian T. Niiya and E. San Juan, Jr., discuss other problems related to the publishing industry.)

Inarguably, elements in the works of the three authors invite mimetic analysis. All three have freely incorporated historical material and even official documents in their fiction or memoirs. And certainly their narratives draw on actual experience. "I didn't have any imagination," Yamamoto modestly insists. "I just embroidered on things that happened, or that people told me happened" (Crow 1987, 74). Critics frequently call attention to the autobiographical or historical details in *Obasan*. Kingston's *Woman Warrior* has long been classified exclusively as autobiography and *China Men* as nonfiction. (The additional label "Literature" now appears on the back covers of the Vintage International editions of the two books.)

I do not want to discount these authors' ability to reproduce reality or to achieve verisimilitude. But their revisions of the past must not be confused with definitive history. It is impossible to retrieve an unadulterated past, one not always already mediated by language. According to Foucault, "The origin lies at a place of inevitable loss, the point where the truth of things corresponded to a truthful discourse, the site of a fleeting articulation that discourse has obscured and finally lost" (1977, 143). The opening chapter of *The Woman Warrior*, in which the narrator struggles to figure out

[16] The trouble with criteria involving authenticity is exemplified most dramatically in the cases of *Famous All over Town* by Danny Santiago (1983), presumed to be an authentic Chicano novel but in fact written by Daniel James, a Caucasian; and more recently *The Education of Little Tree* by Forrest Carter (1991), thought to be the autobiography of a Cherokee but actually written by Asa Earl Carter, a "Ku Klux Klan terrorist" (Gates 1991, 26).

what *actually* happened to her no-name aunt by creating several *imagined* versions, fleshes out this point nicely. But skepticism concerning discursive neutrality or transparency is shared by all three Asian American writers, whose methods of rewriting "history" can be understood in terms of both feminism and Foucault.[17]

Yamamoto, Kingston, and Kogawa implicitly or explicitly question the possibility of restoring an authoritative minority history and shy away from a complacent return to the past. Instead of presuming to replace a dubious official history with another imperative one, these authors willingly undermine their own authorship—authority—with allegorical or surrealistic devices. Works such as "The Legend of Miss Sasagawara," *China Men*, and *Obasan* fall nicely into what Linda Hutcheon calls "historiographic metafiction," whose "theoretical self-awareness of history and fiction as human constructs . . . is made the grounds for its rethinking and reworking of the forms and contents of the past" (1987, 12).[18] History is not rejected but rethought, refocused, and re-presented. Larry McCaffery's characterization of Gabriel García Márquez's *One Hundred Years of Solitude*—"self-conscious about its literary heritage and about the limits of mimesis . . . but yet managing to reconnect its readers to the world outside the page"—may be applied to the Asian American texts as well (264; quoted in Hutcheon 1987, 12). To read them as purely mimetic beclouds the authors' artistry and obscures their alternative "historiography."

I have attempted throughout this book to account for both sociohistorical contexts and each author's distinctive narrative strat-

---

[17] See Diamond and Quinby for other convergences between feminism and Foucault. Remarking on the false dichotomy between formalist and historical approaches in literary criticism, Carroll cautions: "Rather than posing as an alternative to the various formalisms vying for dominance today, a truly critical return to history must question itself in the same terms it uses to question the various formalisms it opposes itself to. That is, it must question itself as a . . . narrative form as it situates and undermines the notion of form as a closed, integral, autonomous, and self-reflexive entity. . . . A critical return to history in this sense is an unending process that can never reach its destination, that never quite returns, not because there is no ground at all but because there is no one, ultimate, totally determining ground, no ground of all grounds" (66; see also Bhabha, Butler, Lentricchia, Radhakrishnan).

[18] Hutcheon herself included *China Men* in her elaboration of historiographic metafiction (1987). Both Goellnicht (1989, 288) and Jones (214) have affixed that generic label to *Obasan*.

egies. Fredric Jameson notes that Third World texts, no matter how private they seem, "necessarily project a political dimension in the form of a national allegory: the story of the private individual destiny is always an allegory of the embattled situation of the public third-world culture and society" (1986, 69).[19] Similarly, the editors of *Aiiieeeee!* assert: "The distinction between social history and literature is a tricky one, especially when dealing with the literature of an emerging sensibility. The subject of minority literature is social history" (Chin et al. xxxv). In weaving historical and cultural background into my textual analysis, I try to show that these conventional categories are themselves unstable, and that the texts analyzed deliberately blur the distinction.

Crucial as the writers' background is to our understanding, it is equally important not to drown Asian American texts in contexts, lest we perpetrate what Henry Louis Gates, Jr., calls the "anthropological fallacy" (1984, 5). Since the formal and figurative aspects of Asian American literature have been relatively neglected in current criticism, I have chosen to elaborate on narrative strategies. While historical and cultural elements are everywhere discernible in the works of the three writers, each exhibits singular vision and invention. After all, as Michael Fischer points out, ethnicity is also "something reinvented and reinterpreted in each generation by each individual" (195). We must not bridle literary imagination in the name of historical authenticity or generic distinctions. The strategy of covering in one book texts as heterogeneous as the novel, autobiography, nonfiction, and short story reflects my own suspicion of conventional generic boundaries. The three Asian American authors interlace life and art. Contextualization gauges not simply how well (or how poorly) they mirror "experience" but also, conversely, how they reconfigure "reality."

Whether through multiple re-presentations or through the use of what feminists call "palimpsest" techniques, Yamamoto, Kogawa,

---

[19] Jameson's pronouncement has been criticized by Ahmad for reinforcing the binary opposition of First World and Third World and for homogenizing the literatures lumped together as Third World. Nevertheless, Jameson's observation about national allegory does provide a valuable angle for a view of emergent literatures. As we shall see in chap 2, "The Legend of Miss Sasagawara" welds a private and a public story together seamlessly.

and Kingston insistently subvert a monologic reality. Their dialogic visions are rooted in their marginal position as women and as members of ethnic minorities. To reckon with both, I locate my analysis in the interstices of three modes of "double-voiced discourse." First, I use the term to subsume the various methods by which the three authors circumvent authoritarian narration and signify the instability of "truth" and "history"; these methods include the juxtaposition of juvenile and adult perspectives and the interposing of the journalistic and the poetic, of "memory" and "counter-memory."[20]

Second, the term is directly associated with women's writing, which is often "coded" (Radner & Lanser) or made up of a "dominant" and a "muted" story: "The orthodox plot recedes, and another plot, hitherto submerged in the anonymity of the background, stands out in bold relief like a thumbprint" (Showalter 34).[21] A number of black feminists (Hazel Carby, Deborah McDowell, Valerie Smith) have further shown how African American women writers exploit ambiguous language to deliver covert messages. Of the three authors I discuss (all of whom in some fashion employ coding strategies), Yamamoto is especially given to muted plots. Her textual silence, like the double-voicing of black women writers, has to do with gender and cultural sensibility as well as with the politics of race.

The third form of double-voiced discourse—one propounded by critics of multicultural literature—refers specifically to the dual lineage of hyphenated writers. Gates notes that "in the case of the writer of African descent, her or his texts occupy spaces in at least

[20] As I understand Foucault's use of the terms, "memory" is in the service of "traditional history," of knowledge as transmitted, inscribed, sanctioned, and possessing the unmerited status of "truth." Conversely, "counter-memory" is in the service of "effective history," which resists official versions of historical continuity, "opposes history as knowledge," and unmasks "knowledge as perspective" (1977/1980, 160, 156).

[21] Showalter imputes the phenomenon to female literary identity, which is often shaped by a dominant male culture and an obscured female culture, and which may also be compounded with a muted ethnic culture. Her paradigm has its genesis in the cultural model outlined by Shirley Ardener and Edwin Ardener in *Perceiving Women*, ed. Shirley Ardener. Other feminist critics who have explored women writers' palimpsest techniques include Miller (1981), Gilbert & Gubar, and Washington. Yogi (1988, 1989) uses the term "buried plot" to describe parallel phenomena in the works of Hisaye Yamamoto and Wakako Yamauchi.

two traditions: a European or American literary tradition, and one of the several related but distinct black traditions. The 'heritage' of each black text written in a Western language is, then, a double heritage, two-toned, as it were" (1984, 4).[22] What Gates calls "two-toned" language is, I believe, especially apparent in the writing of immigrants' offspring, many of whom are not only bicultural but also bilingual. For this reason I have confined myself to second-generation writers. I study Yamamoto, Kogawa, and Kingston in particular because silence is at once a pervasive theme and a rhetorical strategy in their works. As minority women these writers are subject not only to the white gaze of the larger society but also to a communal gaze. Mediating between a dominant culture that advertises "free" speech (but maintains minority silence) and an ethnic one that insists on the propriety of reticence, all three writers have developed methods of indirection that reflect their female, racial, and bicultural legacies.

Yet amplifying the "double voice" of Asian Americans presents certain dangers, among them the temptation to reinforce the age-old East-West distinction and the concept of the dual personality. Edward W. Said has expatiated on the pernicious effect of splitting peoples into Orientals and Westerners:

> When one uses categories like Oriental and Western as both the starting and the end points of analysis . . . the result is usually to polarize the distinction—the Oriental becomes more Oriental, the Westerner more Western—and limit the human encounter between different cultures, traditions, and societies. In short, from its earliest modern history to the present, Orientalism as a form of thought for dealing with the foreign has typically shown the altogether regrettable tendency of any knowledge based on such hard-and-fast distinctions . . . to channel thought into a West or an East compartment. (1979, 45–46)

Such distinctions, when applied to Asian Americans, cast doubt on their wholeness and status as Americans:

> Thus, fourth-, fifth-, and sixth-generation Asian-Americans are still looked upon as foreigners because of this dual heritage, or the con-

---

[22] Other scholars of polyethnic literature who have examined the cultural duality of hyphenated writers include Baker (1–26), Castillo (esp. 260–92), Kim (1982, 23–57), Krupat, Lincoln (1983, 24–40), Ling, Lionnet, Saldívar, Valerie Smith (esp. 13–28), and Sollors (249–54).

cept of dual personality which suggests that the Asian-American can be broken down into his American part and his Asian part. . . . This sustaining inner resource keeps the Asian-American a stranger in the country in which he was born. (Chin et al. xxiv–xxv)

Acute awareness of the a priori assignation of Asian as alien has led many Asian(-)Americans to accentuate the right-hand (i.e., "American") side of the compound and then to eliminate the hyphen altogether. Kingston expresses a similar view: "We ought to leave out the hyphen in 'Chinese-American,' because the hyphen gives the word on either side equal weight, as if linking two nouns. . . . Without the hyphen, 'Chinese' is an adjective and 'American' a noun; a Chinese American is a type of American" (1982, 60).

The desire to be recognized as American is understandable, but such rightful recognition should not have to be achieved at the expense of Asian affiliation. The impulse to claim America has resulted not only in "mutual exclusion" of immigrant and American-born Asians but also in the dismissal of anything associated with the country of origin as a form of Orientalism.[23] Admittedly, it is all too easy to exaggerate cultural differences when in fact the range of behavior is far broader than stereotypes about the "Other" would allow. Despite the contradictory attitudes toward speech and silence in both American and Asian cultures, when it comes to contrasting the two, the opposition between the outspoken American (white or black) and the quiet Asian or Asian American often emerges. Lest I crystallize the image of the inscrutable Oriental, I must point out that reticence by no means characterizes all Asians. Within the texts analyzed, Brave Orchid in *The Woman Warrior* is a "champion talker," Bak Goong in *China Men* is a "talk addict," and Aunt Emily in *Obasan* is a "word-warrior." Wittman Ah Sing, the Chinese American pro-

[23] The mutual disdain between American-born and immigrants is discussed in Hom 1984 and dramatized in Hwang's *FOB* (Fresh off the Boat). See also Ching & Chin. The editors of *Aiiieeeee!* argue that "Asian-American sensibility is so delicate at this point [c. 1974] that the fact of Chinese or Japanese birth is enough to distinguish you from being American-born [and hence from being Asian-American], in spite of the fact that you may have no actual memories of life in Asia" (Chin et al. ix). These same editors are currently reclaiming an Asian heroic tradition and promulgating Chinese and Japanese epics; by so doing they prod the reading public to confront non-Western classics that have shaped Asian American literature. They continue, however, to dismiss Asian (American) traits that are less than "heroic" (i.e., militant) as resulting from white indoctrination or from Christianity.

tagonist of Kingston's *Tripmaster Monkey,* stands as one of the most garrulous figures in all American literature.

Though mindful of the pitfalls in magnifying Asian American silence because of its proximity to stock images, I believe a more subtle danger lies in reversing the stereotype. Categorical negation of silence contracts the range of "permissible" behavior among Asian Americans and blots out part of their distinctive cultural legacy. When an interviewer asked Kogawa about the "language of silence" in *Obasan,* she responded: "It's not to say that it's a Japanese characteristic but . . . there are cultures that are more silent, less verbal, that perhaps rely on intuition, that have a whole series of body language" (Redekop 17).

Similarly, I do not want to reify silence as an Asian trait but wish to explore its myriad guises and senses in the chosen texts, to demystify the stereotype, and to suggest that there are many ways of being American and Canadian. "So much writing by Asian Americans is focused on the theme of claiming an American, as opposed to Asian, identity that we may begin to wonder if this constitutes . . . the fervent wish to 'hide our ancestry,'" Elaine Kim muses. "Or is it in fact a celebration of our marginality and a profound expression of protest against being defined by domination?" (1987, 88). To my mind, celebration of our marginality requires precisely that we adopt aspects of both cultures, that we not "hide our ancestry."[24] As Aunt Emily in *Obasan* forcefully points out, "Momotaro [a Japanese fable] is a Canadian story. We're Canadian. . . . Everything a Canadian does is Canadian" (57). Asian Americans should not have to *prove* their Americanness by distancing themselves as far as possible from their ancestral cultures. Trying to be American by going against what is stereotypically Asian only reinforces the norm dictated by the dominant culture. Hypersensitivity to the white gaze—whether it results in the inter-

[24] Other racial minorities have increasingly asserted their diverse heritage. The recent shift in terminology from "Afro-American" to "African American," for instance, reflects a growing pride among blacks in their African ancestry. Mexican Americans who identify themselves as Chicanos similarly affirm a tripartite legacy. Historical trauma (most notably the internment of Japanese Americans during World War II) resulting from the unjust conflation of racial, cultural, and political affinities has made it especially difficult for some Asian Americans to reclaim their ethnic heritage. But one must resist rather than accept the racist equation of cultural persistence with political loyalty.

nalization or the deliberate reversal of imposed definition—could shrivel the self.

While I agree with the editors of *Aiiieeeee!* that Asian American sensibility is "neither Asian nor white American" (Chin et al. xxi), surely it can partake of both. I am especially uneasy about the hard-line distinction Frank Chin draws in *The Big Aiiieeeee!* between the "fake" and the "real" Asian American literature. He considers works emanating from an American missionary tradition as fake, and the ones faithful to "Asian childhood literature and history" as real (1991, 9). In his concern for cultural purity, he ignores one of the most defining characteristics of Asian American literature and ethnic American literature generally: hybridity. (Asian and Western classics mingle in Kingston's works; Christianity and Buddhism exist side by side in "The Legend of Miss Sasagawara" and *Obasan*.)[25] In their vehement insistence on "Asian-American integrity," the editors may have themselves given in to the Western conception of a unitary self and underestimated the potential of a multiple consciousness—one that is neither schizophrenic nor bisectable into East and West, neither merely preserving the ancestral culture nor dissolving into the mainstream.

The three women writers belie the template both of the dual personality and of the unitary self. The intricate sensibilities shown in their work result from multivalent attitudes toward both Asian and white American norms, such as those regarding speech and silence. One finds at once an incisive critique and a sympathetic grasp of the various forms of Asian American silence, a profound skepticism toward dominant discourse and a pressing need to be heard. Their own manners of telling temper the authority of words. They interweave speech and silence, narration and ellipses, autobiography and fiction in a way analogous to their recasting of Asian and Anglo-American cultural lore and practices. The web of perceptions makes their writings all the more dialogically "New World."

To avoid mere dichotomous opposition, I emphasize the *different*

[25] While Kingston tops the editors' blacklist of fake authors, "The Legend" is included and *Obasan* excerpted in *The Big Aiiieeeee!* (Chan et al. 1991); the editors' literary judgment often gets the better of their ideological statements. See also Lim 1990 and Ling for explicit and implicit critiques of the editors' refutation of cultural duality.

manifestations of both speech and silence. Language can liberate, but it can also coerce, distort, and regulate, as is widely recognized today. I foreground the silence depicted in the Asian American texts because it is a theme still often subject to reductive interpretations. I am not tempted to romanticize or exoticize it, however, or to place it above speech, thereby inverting the existing hierarchy. Like language, silence has many ugly faces. But even what I construe to be undesirable silences—the speechlessness induced by shame and guilt, the oppressive or protective withholding of words in the family, or the glaring oversight in official history—have all too scrutable motivations. Far from being pure Asian attributes, moreover, they are often overdetermined by both ancestral mores and exclusionary forces in North America. Then there are the enabling silences, such as the listening in Kingston, the elliptical telling in Yamamoto, and, above all, the breathtaking rendition of soundless but "accurate and alert knowing" in Kogawa. These silences, demanding utmost vigilance from writers and readers alike, are the very antitheses of passivity.

Many of these silences also have cross-cultural inspirations. Yamamoto's oblique narration is influenced by Japanese literary concision and nisei preference for indirection as well as by modernist experimentation with limited point of view. Kogawa fuses the Japanese legacy of attentiveness and intuitive knowing with Buddhist and Christian meditations. Hence, in my usage, "double-voicing"—which encompasses the discourse(s) of silence—designates "more than one" rather than specifically "two," if only for the reason that neither "Asian" nor "American" represents one fixed, homogeneous, or exclusive sensibility. This qualification is especially needed at a time when Americans of diverse extraction are remolding the traditional conception of "American" to accommodate different peoples. Writers intent on realizing the multicultural potential of America are increasingly claiming multiple heritages and practicing polyglot textualization.

My belief in the fertile possibility of a dynamic and polyphonic self accords well with Werner Sollors's espousal of "cultural syncretism." But I stop short of sharing his critique of the "ethnic perspective":

Taken exclusively, what is often called the ethnic perspective—the total emphasis on a writer's *descent*—all but annihilates art movements. . . . If anything, ethnic literary history ought to *increase* our understanding of the cultural interplays and contacts among writers of different backgrounds, the cultural mergers and secessions that took place in America, all of which can be accomplished only if the categorization of writers as members of ethnic groups is understood to be a very partial, temporal, and insufficient characterization at best. (14–15)

I am all for "cultural interplays" and "cultural mergers." But the traffic of ideas in America has been predominantly one-way. Despite the constant striving for democratic "consent," the primacy of the Anglo-American perspective persists. As Trinh T. Minh-ha puts it, "The form of cultural and sexual ascendancy that once worked through direct domination . . . now often operates via consent" (1989, 49). Cultural hegemony can be so overriding that an "inside" view by a person of color may at times come perilously close to one dictated from outside (a point I elaborate on in Chapter 3). While the situation does not always prevent a minority member from attaining a dialogic vision, it does diminish the quality of interplay. Until we cease reading from the exclusive vantage point of the hegemonic culture and stop reducing diversity to uniformity, we will not be ready to venture "beyond ethnicity."[26] Nor would a reversal of flow lead to a genuine two-way traffic. The three Asian American writers have found their voices by negotiating cultures. Non-Asian readers may learn from their writing that silence can also be articulation.

Articulate Silences is not, however, intended as an introduction to Asian American female poetics; nor do I even advocate such a "field." Asian American sensibilities vary in accordance with nationality, birthplace, age, social background, and individual endowment. My aim rather is to show that each of the three authors has developed her own unique bicultural idiom and that "Western" suppositions must occasionally be suspended to catch its nuances. As someone who grew up in a British colony and at-

[26] As Yarborough points out, "If it were not for descent-oriented scholars, many aspects of various cultures that are now finally being recognized and treated with some degree of objectivity would remain neglected or, worse still, misinterpreted" (865). Boelhower puts it another way: "All the while ethnic subjects were constantly and quickly reinterpreting the official American sign according to local cultural needs, the global culture was merrily unaware of its own internal colonies, of its own graphic richness" (83–84). See also Wald for a critique of the "Ethnicity School."

tended American universities, I too must struggle to "unlearn" certain presuppositions and allow my Asian upbringing to bear upon my critical work without claiming what Sollors calls "biological insiderism" (13). I am situated liminally in relation to the texts in question. My descent—broadly defined as Asian—has me a veritable insider, but as an immigrant from Hong Kong, I view Cantonese culture quite differently from American-born Kingston. Being Chinese American, I cannot know nikkei culture at first-hand, though I discern common linguistic denominators in Chinese American and Japanese American cultures. Owing to the historical antagonism between China and Japan, I was in fact taught to look on people of Japanese descent as the inimical "other."

A background such as my own illustrates the complexity in the "Asian American" position. If, as Elaine Kim contends, the term is "an externally imposed label that is meant to define us by distinguishing us from other Americans primarily on the basis of race rather than culture" (1982, xii), it also provides an opportunity for dissolving historical differences among formerly antagonistic national groups over conflicts played out on another soil.[27] Entering the fictional landscape of authors such as Yamamoto and Kogawa not only "exorcises" the ghosts of my Chinese past (to borrow C. Lok Chua's [1981] use of the term) but also allows me to see connection where there was only division. The move from being exclusively Chinese to being Asian American is thus for me at once a psychological, geographical, and political relocation.

Intellectually I situate myself somewhere between advocates of diverse feminisms, between those of feminism and nationalism, and between those of ethnicity and race. This position derives from my multiple allegiances and a deep ambivalence toward certain persuasions. I eschew the agonistic modes of discourse currently prevalent in feminist and Asian American arenas and in academia at large.[28] Because I neither readily ally myself with nor reject out of hand any one school of thought, my own voice may come across

---

[27] The strongest motive for Asians to subordinate their respective national identities to the collective designation is a political one: they would otherwise be even more invisible in the U.S. political arena. See also Lowe and San Juan on the limitation and possibility of the term "Asian American."

[28] On the schisms among feminists, see Hirsch & Keller; on gender antagonism in Asian American literature, see Cheung 1990b, Kim 1990.

as evasive or subdued. But I believe an attentive and collaborative engagement fits my argument better than insistent or vociferous confrontation. Hence I opt for a conversation in which no one is hushed and to which everyone can listen.

In sum, the purpose of my book is fourfold: (1) to unsettle the Eurocentric perspective on speech and silence, which I see as polarized, hierarchical, and gendered, especially in regard to Asians and Asian Americans; (2) to reexamine and redeploy current feminist theories in the light of the double-voicing of three Asian American women; (3) to propose a multivalent approach to Asian American literature which steers away from the "East-West" or the "dual personality" model and stresses instead a synergistic vision; and (4) to reconcile historicism and formalism by uncovering both the plural heritage and the individual talent of ethnic writers.

The execution is far less discrete than the fourfold purpose suggests, however. I consciously avoid separating "theory" from "text" and try to be true to each author's distinctive strategy, to what Barbara Christian calls "theorizing . . . in narrative forms" (52). Instead of applying an overarching theory to all the works, I have allowed the texts to generate their own. I realize that the notion of an individual author is suspect these days, especially after Foucault's rhetorical question "What is an author?" anticipated by Roland Barthes's rhetorical answer: "The author is dead." For an author to be "dead," she or he must first have lived. Asian American writers are just beginning to breathe.[29]

The titles of the three main chapters—"Rhetorical Silence," "Provocative Silence," and "Attentive Silence"—are convenient markers only. Each chapter examines a variety of silences, some of which overlap with those investigated in the other two. In addition to exploring modes of inarticulateness, these chapters harken to meanings muffled in the narratives. The telling ellipses often undercut cocksure voices—whether they be the voice of history, the voice of authority, or even "the voice in the margin."

"Rhetorical Silence" expands the scope of prevailing feminist

[29] My sentiments concerning Asian American writers are similar to those of many feminist critics concerning women writers who, as Miller insists, do not yet have "the luxury of flirting with the escape from identity" (1986, 274). See also Brodzki; Schenck 288.

criticism on both thematic and structural grounds. Thematically it attends to male as well as female repression; structurally it demonstrates that the "muted plots" in Yamamoto's stories pivot no less around culture and race than around gender. The first part of the chapter, focusing on "Seventeen Syllables" and "Yoneko's Earthquake," examines prohibition and inhibition in two Japanese American families. It shows how Yamamoto uses naive narrators to conceal and reveal unsettling stories, and through them to indict, *sotto voce*, sociocultural conventions. The second part, on "The Legend of Miss Sasagawara," demonstrates how the author constructs a "Chinese box" interfacing domestic, communal, and political repression. It argues against the strict opposition between art and politics, literature and social history. Close reading and historical knowledge about the Japanese American internment must go hand in hand to unfold the layers of significations tucked into "The Legend" and to uncover Yamamoto's cumulative "anxiety of authorship."

In addition, I caution against interpreting narrative gaps in women's texts solely in terms of response to external pressure. It seems unfair to view indirection as virtuosity in such male writers as William Faulkner, Henry James, and James Joyce and to attribute the same feature in female writers to necessity. Without denying the particular obstacles faced by female and minority writers, I show how Yamamoto taps the rhetorical—persuasive—power of silence. Whatever cultural and political constraints she may have felt are transformed into aesthetic restraint. Along the same line, we need to separate sociocultural critique prompted by the texts themselves from narrative technique. Yamamoto's authorial silence closely replicates the suppression of her characters, but the two must not be conflated. We can feel sorry for her mute characters and at the same time applaud the muted art of the author.[30]

"Provocative Silence" refers to the paradox in Kingston's *Woman Warrior* and *China Men* whereby parental and historical silence spurs creativity. In reaction to Brave Orchid's injunction against telling the no-name aunt's story and to her deliberate withholding of information, the narrator in *The Woman Warrior* fabricates several versions of that story. In *China Men*, it is the father's taciturnity that

[30] For a different response to an authorial replication of a character's silence, see Washington.

goads the narrator to invent his life story. Similarly, the lacunae surrounding Chinese men in American official records prompts her to create a national epic. In each instance the absence of information is used as a pre-text for artistic license, allowing the author both to give voice to the voiceless and to subvert patriarchal and historical orthodoxy.

Yet "rhetorical silence" also informs Kingston's seemingly effusive texts, both of which can be viewed as variations on the models of double-voicing advanced by feminist critics. *The Woman Warrior* openly and even stridently expresses feminist messages said to be often veiled in women's fiction. What remains untold is the juvenile narrator's internalization of the dominant way of thinking, which casts her own people as deviant and herself as retarded. This text implies that the hidden injuries to race are even harder to bring to the surface than female repression. Furthermore, insofar as the vision of a so-called insider can be shaped and distorted from the outside, the narrator's stated point of view should not be taken for an objective exegesis of her culture. The reader must instead attend to the incongruent positions of the narrator and the author and to the contradictions within the text. Kingston appropriates as her narrative method the mode of talk-story the narrator openly deplores in her mother. By putting "Chinese" and "American" teachings side by side, she implicitly undercuts the authority of both. Likewise, she uses feminist strategies to disrupt simultaneously Chinese and white patriarchy in *China Men*, which draws unspoken parallels between the racist persecution of Chinese male immigrants in America and the traditional subjugation of women by these very men. The author enacts a double political move in braiding racist and sexist abuse. She expands her feminist horizon to include men who have been voiceless in historical records, but she resists subordinating her feminist concerns in the name of nationalism.

"Attentive Silence" takes exception to critiques that equalize and denounce the silences portrayed in Kogawa's *Obasan*. The critical tendency reflects what Chandra Talpade Mohanty calls discursive colonialism vis-à-vis the Third World, resulting from "the implicit assumption of 'the West' (in all its complexities and contradictions) as the primary referent in theory and praxis" (334). To disregard the many gradations of silence in the novel would "colonize" those very differences Kogawa meticulously depicts and perpetuate the kind of cultural and linguistic imperialism she deplores. The multiple and distinctive forms that nonverbal behavior assumes in this novel must not be lumped together for condemnation as submissive, nor should they be upheld in toto as attentive. I differentiate oppressive, inhibitive, protective, stoic, and attentive silences and evaluate them separately.

As "historiographic metafiction" *Obasan* navigates between voice and voicelessness in both content and form. It invites the reader to listen at once to a voice for justice, embodied in Aunt Emily, a vocal political activist, and to an "underground" language of love and forgiveness, exemplified by Obasan, the narrator's guardian aunt. The text incorporates chunks of Emily's journals, which spell out explicitly the linguistic and political abuses of the Canadian government that led to the internment of Japanese Canadians. At Emily's urging, the narrator also tries to record her own past, but she does not adopt the sure voice of this aunt. Mindful of the distortions of traditional historians who define and objectify their subjects in a seamless narrative, Naomi offers in contrast a truncated memoir—a microscopic worm's-eye view of her family's experience before, during, and after World War II. The reader is forced to read between the lines, to make connections between dreams, fairy tales, and events, and between "fragments of memories."

Yamamoto, Kingston, and Kogawa differ markedly in their narrative strategies. They are linked, however, by their awareness of the difficulty of utterance, their skepticism about official records, their engagement with historiographic metafiction, and their ability to render the voiceless audible. Of particular note in their works is the inverse relation between spoken and written expression. Many of their characters (and perhaps also the authors themselves) distill onto the page what they cannot say out loud. Mrs. Hayashi in "Seventeen Syllables," Miss Sasagawara in "The Legend," and the narrators in both *The Woman Warrior* and *Obasan* all have trouble speaking or *telling* their life stories. Yet they all excel on paper: their unspoken emotions break into print as poetry, autobiography, and novel. As a bridge between silence and speech, the texts speak to the necessity for both, in art as in life.

2

Rhetorical Silence: "Seventeen Syllables," "Yoneko's Earthquake," and "The Legend of Miss Sasagawara"

The silences I speak of here are unnatural; the unnatural
thwarting of what struggles to come into being, but cannot.
                                   Tillie Olsen, *Silences*

Women writers are both prompt to hide in (their) writing(s)
and feel prompted to do so. As language-stealers, they must
yet learn to steal without being seen, and with no pretense of
being a stealer, for fear of "exposing the father."
                        Trinh T. Minh-ha, *Woman, Native, Other*

My throat chokes in reverent wonder
At the unfurled glory of a flag—
        Red as the sun
        White as the almond blossom
        Blue as the clear summer sky.
                Hisaye Yamamoto, "Et Ego in America Vixi"

Feminist scholars have discussed various methods of indirection
employed by women writers. I have referred to Joan Radner and
Susan Lanser's study of the strategies of coding used by women
and to Elaine Showalter's argument that women's fiction can be
read as a "double-voiced discourse." More recently Susan Stanford
Friedman has proposed a "psycho-political hermeneutic" for reading women's narratives as the "return of the repressed" (Freud's
phrase), an insistent if masked record of what is censored by the
patriarchal social order: "Operating within the dialectic of speech
and silence, women (or women's texts) often consciously or uncon-
sciously negotiate a compromise between revelation and conceal-
ment of the forbidden through textual disguise" (142).[1] Though I
find these interpretive strategies helpful as analytical tools, I feel

---

[1] The six coding strategies proposed by Radner and Lanser are appropriation,
juxtaposition, distraction, indirection, trivialization, and incompetence. Yogi (1988)
uses the term "buried plot" to describe parallel phenomena in Yamamoto and
Yamauchi.

also a strong need to go beyond feminist theories to account for the multiple levels of silence embedded in the fiction of Hisaye Yamamoto, a nisei writer who excels in coding through muted plots and innocent disguise.

Feminist critics explicitly or implicitly acknowledge that a woman of a racial minority may be doubly stifled, but they make little allowance for differences in cultural manifestations of speech and silence. According to Patricia J. Wetzel, what some American linguists (e.g., Lakoff; O'Barr & Atkins) regard as "women's language" or "powerless language" is in fact the "Japanese norm" (555–58). Nonverbal communication and indirect speech remain quite pervasive in traditional Japanese American families, at least among the first two generations, whose cultural reticence was further deepened by the trauma of internment (Fujita 34; Kikumura 98; Miyamoto 1986–87, 35; Chan et al. 1981, 26). Hence the use of silence and indirection by a nisei woman writer must not be attributed to gender alone. Furthermore, in focusing exclusively on female silence under patriarchy, feminist scholars generally overlook the degree to which men, too, must repress their emotions because of conventional definitions of manhood, especially in cultures that associate silence with fortitude.

Born of immigrant parents in 1921 in Redondo Beach, California, Yamamoto started writing when she was a teenager and contributed regularly to Japanese American newspapers. During World War II she was interned for three years in Poston, Arizona, where she served as a reporter and a columnist for the *Poston Chronicle* (the camp newspaper) and published "Death Rides the Rails to Poston," a serialized mystery. Awarded a John Hay Whitney Foundation Opportunity Fellowship in 1949, Yamamoto was one of the first Japanese American writers to gain national recognition after the war, when anti-Japanese sentiment was still rampant. Several of her short stories ("The High-Heeled Shoes," "The Brown House," and "Epithalamium") appeared in Martha Foley's lists of "Distinctive Short Stories," and "Yoneko's Earthquake" was included in *Best American Short Stories: 1952*. In 1986 she received the American Book Award for Lifetime Achievement from the Before Columbus Foundation. *Hot Summer Winds,* a film based on "Seventeen Syllables" and "Yoneko's Earthquake" and directed by Emiko

Omori, was first broadcast in May 1991 as part of PBS's *American Playhouse* series.[2]

Because of her extensive reading and her own experience, Yamamoto writes out of both an Anglo-American and a Japanese American literary tradition. Her method of double-telling—conveying two tales in the guise of one—involves an intertextual use of a familiar narrative technique: unreliable point of view. Three of her most haunting stories, "Seventeen Syllables," "Yoneko's Earthquake," and "The Legend of Miss Sasagawara" (henceforth "The Legend") contain manifest and veiled plots. In the first two stories, the overt "action" is narrated from the perspective of a young girl; the covert drama concerns the conflict between the girl's issei parents. Unreliable narration assumes strategic as well as thematic significance in "The Legend," a story that interrogates rumors and questions societal definitions of insanity. Though undoubtedly influenced by modernist experimentation with limited point of view, Yamamoto tailors the method to the Japanese American context.

Her stories capitalize on the infrequent verbal communication between issei spouses (see Yanagisako 105, 122) and between issei parents and nisei children. Issei parents (especially fathers) tend to be authoritative and protective toward the young, so that free verbal exchange between parents and children is frequently suppressed (Kikumura 98). By playing the naive nisei point of view against the pregnant silence of the issei in "Seventeen Syllables" and "Yoneko's Earthquake," Yamamoto constructs hidden plots and deflects attention from unsettling messages.[3] Suspense develops in part because the parents refrain from disclosing their problems to their children; only through the ingenuous telling of the nisei daughters do we catch dark nuances of the adult silence. Through the characters we experience the pain and frustration of silence; through the narration we feel its rhetorical power.

Yamamoto's elliptical style also circumvents social and political silencing. As Friedman observes, "textual repression can reflect cultural and political oppression" (145; see also Lauter). As a wom-

---

[2] See Kim 1982, 122–72, on the relationship between Japanese American history and literature; see Ichioka 1988, Matsumoto, and Takaki 179–229 for further historical background.

[3] Yamamoto's technique is reminiscent of the way Henry James dramatizes social relationships between the New World and the Old, as in *Daisy Miller*.

an writing at a time when feminist sensibilities were scarcely pub-
lishable, the nisei author couches her sympathy in a disarming
style that keeps alarming subtexts below the surface. We may infer
her self-consciousness as a woman writer and her awareness of her
verbal power from the telling pseudonym—Napoleon—she once
adopted, purportedly "as an apology for [her] little madness"
(Yamamoto 1976b, 128).

Belonging to a racial minority may further heighten her "anxiety
of authorship," especially in the face of the anti-Japanese sentiment
that broke into the open after the bombing of Pearl Harbor. Though
the incarceration of over 110,000 people of Japanese ancestry ended
with the war, political and social constrictions imposed by the
dominant culture necessitated textual constraints beyond the dura-
tion of the physical confinement.[4] In "The Legend" Yamamoto
skillfully couples a realistic depiction of a "mad" woman with underground reference to the insanity of the internment. The degree
to which the political subtext is muted may have something to do
with its original appearance in Kenyon Review in 1950, only five
years after the war ended.

Finally, as a nisei brought up to observe Japanese etiquette,
Yamamoto may remain influenced by the "interpersonal style"
(Frank Miyamoto's term) of her own ethnic community, which
tends to discourage verbal confrontation and open protest. She
herself, in commenting on the small number of nisei writers, has
noted that "something in the nature of the Nisei" works against
the impulse to write: "For a writer proceeds from a compulsion to
communicate a vision and he cannot afford to bother with what
people in general think of him. We Nisei, discreet, circumspect,
care very much what others think of us" (1976b, 126). If American
women in general have been brought up to be more polite than
men in their speech and writing, as Robin Lakoff argues (see also
Stout 10–11), Japanese American women whose feminine reserve
is reinforced by the cultural decorum of yet another tradition are

----

[4] Susan Schweik has convincingly argued for such "sociotextual constraint" (a
term she borrows from Ann Rosalind Jones) in the work of another nisei writer,
Toyo Suyemoto (89). Camp publications were rigorously censored by external authority, but self-censorship by many Japanese Americans continued long after the
war. Yamamoto's use of a naive narrator may also be seen as an "innocent disguise"
that deflects attention from the authorial self.

likely to be even more guarded in expressing themselves—at least on the surface.

The actual range of human behavior, however, is much wider than any given culture prescribes. In making the point about nikkei etiquette I risk accentuating the stereotype of the "inscrutable Oriental" and blurring the distinction between Japanese and Japanese Americans. My intention is quite the reverse: I wish to explode the stereotype by demystifying rather than denying the Japanese American preference for nonverbal or indirect communication, and to emphasize that continuities between ancestral and ethnic cultures (especially in the first two generations) do exist—important as it is to differentiate Japanese and Japanese Americans.[5]

To this question of cultural influence Yamamoto replies indirectly: "Since I was brought up like most Nisei, with Japanese ideas of *gaman* and *enryo* and that whole etiquette structure, I imagine my writing has been influenced by such behavior patterns—it would be strange if it wasn't" (letter to the author, June 1988; quoted by permission).[6] *Enryo* and *gaman* are Japanese terms associated with proper behavior. The rules related to *enryo* (often translated as "deference," "reserve," or "diffidence") are imparted early in a Japanese family: "A child quickly learns the importance of reticence, modesty, indirection, and humility and is punished for boastful, aggressive, loud, and self-centered behavior" (Kikumura & Kitano 54). In the interaction between Japanese subordinates and their superiors or between Japanese Americans and whites, "one of the main manifestations of *enryo* was the conscious use of silence

---

[5] Sylvia Junko Yanagisako observes that "at the same time that Japanese American families were formed through Issei marriage, Japanese family relationships were transported to the United States. Far from creating the first Japanese American families in isolation from Japanese ones, Issei marriages were from the beginning embedded in families that crossed national boundaries" (29).

[6] Yamamoto made a similar disclosure in April 1979: "I'm sure the Japanese tradition has had a great influence on my writing since my parents brought it with them from Japan and how could they not help but transmit it to us? I even wonder if I would have been a writer at all without this tradition to go by, since most of the stories seem to deal with this interaction of the Japanese tradition with the American experience. And even while I have come to look upon the American experience with a jaundiced (yellow) eye, I appreciate being able to communicate in the English language and just plain being alive at this time and in this place" (quoted in McDonald & Newman 23).

as a safe or neutral response to an embarrassing or ambiguous situation" (53). *Gaman*, meaning "internalization . . . and suppression of anger and emotion" (Kitano 136), is further associated with dogged perseverance: "The *Issei*'s ability to *gaman* (stick things out at all costs) was often what carried them through times of hardship, disillusionment, and loneliness" (Kikumura & Kitano 55).

Yamamoto parlays cultural precepts into literary gambits and transforms social rituals into a subtle rhetoric. She makes strategic use, for instance, of a conversational technique noted by the sociologist Stanford Lyman:

> Bluntness of speech is not a virtue among *Nisei*. . . . Among the *Nisei* as among their forebears in Japan, the main point of a conversational episode is not approached immediately. . . . Indeed, conversations among *Nisei* almost always partake of the elements of an information game between persons maintaining decorum by seemingly mystifying one another. It is the duty of the listener to ascertain the context of the speech he hears and to glean from his knowledge of the speaker and the context just what is the important point. (1971, 53)[7]

"Seventeen Syllables," "Yoneko's Earthquake," and "The Legend" all engage us in decoding the ostensibly random observations of the storytellers. The narrator in each of the first two stories confides to us matters of utmost concern to the young protagonist— events that constitute the manifest plot—while observing in passing her family's "routine." Between the lines lurks another plot that focuses on the child's parents, whose repressed emotions grip us as in an undertow. "The Legend" weaves together numerous reports concerning the title character, regarded by everyone as deranged. Toward the end, however, we are offered additional information that challenges both the popular interpretation and our own. The reader is left to ferret out the "main point" of the story.

[7] Lyman's article has sparked considerable debate. Frank S. Miyamoto, who basically agrees with Lyman's description of the nisei interactional style, takes Lyman to task for allegedly characterizing the style as "negative" (1986–87, 40), a charge that Lyman vehemently denies (see Lyman 1988a, 1988b; Miyamoto 1988). One reason for reticence is nicely articulated by Yuko Tsushima, a contemporary Japanese woman writer: "Silence is essential. As long as we maintain silence, and thus avoid trespassing, we leave open the possibility of resuming negotiations at any time" (43).

Feminist critics tend to see indirection in women writers as primarily a means to avert the masculine gaze. No less determining for Yamamoto are cultural orientations and the severity of the white gaze. Yet I differ with those critics who view verbal restraint as necessarily a handicap stemming from social restrictions. I view it more as a versatile strategy in its own right.[8] While Yamamoto's style may reflect special external constraints at the time of writing, her stories are the more compelling for being tacit and indirect.

"Seventeen Syllables"

The opening of "Seventeen Syllables" is deceptively merry and straightforward:

> The first Rosie knew that her mother had taken to writing poems was one evening when she finished one and read it aloud for her daughter's approval. It was about cats, and Rosie pretended to understand it thoroughly and appreciate it no end, partly because she hesitated to disillusion her mother about the quantity and quality of Japanese she had learned in all the years now that she had been going to Japanese school every Saturday. . . . Even so, her mother must have been skeptical about the depth of Rosie's understanding, because she explained afterwards about the kind of poem she was trying to write. (8)

Right from the start we witness and participate in an "information game." The anecdote about the mother's new hobby introduces us to both the motif and the technique of indirection. Mother and daughter are tactful and evasive: they refrain from acknowledging or confronting the problem of communication. Rosie conceals her limited knowledge of Japanese; her mother avoids embarrassing the daughter by not challenging her understanding.

The author, likewise indirect, grants us the daughter's impres-

---

[8] After an illuminating discussion of coding strategies, Radner & Lanser conclude that "the need for coding must always signify a freedom that is incomplete" (423). Yaeger, in contrast, has urged critics to see women's writing as a site of "play" (37). The "information game" in Yamamoto's fiction certainly has a ludic quality, which may be traced to her penchant for mystery (she is, after all, author of a mystery serial in *Poston Chronicle*).

sions while teasing us with the mother's unknown thoughts. We know that although Rosie responds enthusiastically to her mother's literary effort by saying "Yes, yes, I understand" and "How utterly lovely" (8), she feigns her appreciation to gloss over her linguistic deficiency. She has read a haiku written in English and would like to share it with her mother, but she finds the task of translation daunting: "It was much more possible to say yes, yes" (9). The mother's musings, by contrast, are presented only in speculative terms. We are told that she "must have been skeptical" about Rosie's comprehension and that she resumed composing, "either satisfied or seeing through the deception and resigned" (8). Along with the daughter, we share the uncertainty implied by "must have been" and the either–or phrase. Nevertheless, the daughter's quandary prompts us to imagine the mother's parallel predicament: Rosie's inability to share what she reads (in English) points to her mother's even greater frustration at being unable to share what she writes (in Japanese). The mother's creative activity must be largely a lone venture, for she cannot discuss her writing with either her daughter or, as we soon learn, her husband. Rosie's explicit responses will serve throughout the story as oblique analogues to her mother's hidden sentiments.

The daughter's immediate perspective and the mother's removed one set in motion the two parallel plots of this story. One recounts Rosie's adolescent experiences, particularly the joys and fears of incipient sexuality. The other describes the mother's increasing impulse to write and discuss haiku—a drive almost as insistent as sex. While we know from the beginning that the mother, under the pseudonym Ume Hanazono, has become "an extravagant contributor" to a Japanese American newspaper (9), the narrator's tone, which reflects the "rosy" temperament of the daughter, diffuses the gravity of the suspended plot. (There is little distance between the breezy discourse of Rosie and that of the narrator.) Rosie looks on her mother's new interest as a detached observer, amused but not excited:

> So Rosie and her father lived for awhile with two women, her mother and Ume Hanazono. Her mother (Tome Hayashi by name) kept house, cooked, washed, and, along with her husband . . . did her ample share of picking tomatoes out in the sweltering fields. . . .

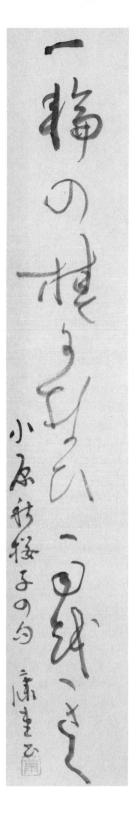

一輪の梅もとよりの寒さかな

小原鈴櫻子の句

　康生

A haiku

> Ume Hanazono, who came to life after the dinner dishes were done, was an earnest, muttering stranger who often neglected speaking when spoken to and stayed busy at the parlor table as late as midnight scribbling with pencil on scratch paper or carefully copying characters on good paper with her fat, pale green Parker. (9)

Tome Hayashi and Ume Hanazono apparently lead a peaceful coexistence: the formidable amount of housework and fieldwork Hayashi performs does not deter Hanazono from writing (cf. Olsen 34–40). Only in retrospect do we register innuendoes. The adjective "extravagant" hints that the family considers her poetic contribution to be a luxury incompatible with the exigencies in the "sweltering field."[9] "Muttering stranger" implies that her poetic self is alien to father and daughter, both of whom feel excluded from her artistic activity. The mother's poetry is remote from her husband's practical concerns; to the daughter, the very words she mutters sound foreign.

Under such circumstances, use of a pseudonym, though common among Japanese poets, suggests a separate personality for Mrs. Hayashi: she writes only when she can assume an identity independent of her husband's. Ironically, the pen name itself carries ominous overtones. Zenobia Baxter Mistri observes that "in Japanese, the name *Ume* stands for an exquisite flowering tree which blossoms in early spring and bears fruit by the end of spring—that is, in three months. *Hanazono* means 'a flower garden'" (198). The flowers of this namesake tree thus forecast Ume Hanazono's "life span," which, we are told, is "very brief—perhaps three months at most" (9); it too lasts only a season.

The reader is left wondering about the cause of the mother's aborted creativity, but is "distracted" by Rosie's adolescent concerns. The parents are mentioned only when they impinge upon the child's life. When the Hayashis visit the Hayanos, for instance, the new coat of one of the teenage daughters becomes the center of the discursive attention. The adults remain very much in the background, with Mr. Hayano and Mrs. Hayashi discussing haiku, Mr. Hayashi reading a magazine, and Mrs. Hayano sitting by herself.

[9] I am indebted to Sau-ling Wong's analysis (1988) of the incompatibility of "extravagance" and "necessity" in another rural context. Takaki also discusses Asian American immigration in these terms.

The evening proceeds in an anodyne way for Rosie, who gravitates toward her peers. We share her puzzlement when Mr. Hayashi leaves abruptly, without a word to his wife or to his hosts.

The episode exemplifies what Radner and Lanser call "distraction"—the muffling of a "feminist message [by] some kind of 'noise,' interference, or obscurity that will keep the message from being heard except by those who listen very carefully" (417–18). In this case the "noise" is the girls' hoopla over clothing, a fittingly feminine preoccupation that provides an unspoken contrast to Mrs. Hayashi's "abnormal" obsession, one that incurs her husband's displeasure.

Where others try to build up suspense in the shortest time possible, Yamamoto diverts our attention with apparently irrelevant details and then fastens it with sudden tension. Because of the young girls' noisy gaiety over the new coat, the anger simmering in Mr. Hayashi (which leads to his sudden exit) takes us unawares. Taken aback herself, Mrs. Hayashi not only apologizes to the Hayanos for her husband's rudeness but also excuses herself upon joining her husband: "You know how I get when it's haiku . . . I forget what time it is" (11–12). The inner thoughts of the couple are inaccessible to us. One says nothing; the other speaks only to placate.

The author, however, directs our response through the daughter's reaction. Watching her parents, Rosie feels "a rush of hate for both—for her mother for begging, for her father for denying her mother" (12). Yamamoto suggests that inexpressible feelings similar to Rosie's lurk beneath her mother's abject excuse and that the father's sway is no less absolute for being silent. Furthermore, when Rosie, in her anger, fantasizes a car collision leaving "three contorted, bleeding bodies, one of them hers" (12), we are given a sidelong glance at the friction between her parents that will culminate in a real act of violence in which the three lives will indeed be enmeshed. Rosie, for all her internal agitation at this point, remains demure outwardly. Like her parents, who refrain from speaking their minds in the child's presence, she has learned to contain her emotions.

The author also shies away from disclosure. No sooner has the parental friction been intimated than it is upstaged by the child's adventure. The next two sections focus almost exclusively on

Rosie's first brush with the opposite sex. During the rendezvous in which Rosie meets Jesus Carrasco (the son of a Mexican couple who work for her family), she swoons by the book: "kissed by Jesus, Rosie fell for the first time entirely victim to a helplessness delectable beyond speech" (14). At work here is the coding strategy of juxtaposition: "An item that seems unambiguous in one environment may develop quite tendentious levels of meaning in another" (Radner & Lanser 416). In itself the meeting between the youngsters heralds the beginning of love, but when we view it in retrospect against the adult plot, Rosie's budding romance is foreboding, even foredoomed. A moment will come when an intense emotion cannot be vocalized by the "victim"—the mother.

Rosie returns to the house after her newfound experience and finds her mother talking with her relatives about a haiku competition. When she runs into her father on her way to the bathhouse, he brushes her off. She assumes his gruffness is directed at her. Knowing better, we suspect that the father's churlish behavior results from the mother's continuing interest in haiku. But since Rosie is our source of information, we do not yet know the extent of his unstated disapproval. Daughter and mother pay little, if any, attention to Mr. Hayashi's moodiness. They are absorbed alike in self-discovery, preoccupied with love or art.

The two plots finally come together in the final section. Rosie daydreams about Jesus in school, feeling "grave and giddy by turns" (15). Her father comes to pick her up and tells her that she must help sort tomatoes when they get home: "This heat's not doing them any good. And we've got no time for a break today" (15). This is the only time Mr. Hayashi speaks more than one sentence. Unremarkable as his words are, they prove portentous. For the pressing tomato harvest is interrupted by the arrival of Mr. Kuroda, a newspaper editor who comes to inform Rosie's mother that she has won the first prize in a recent haiku contest and who brings her the award—a print "sketched with delicate quickness" (17), by Hiroshige, a *ukiyo-e* print artist (1797–1858). When Mrs. Hayashi invites him into the house for tea, the father emits his first explicit comment about his wife, or rather about her artistic fervor: "Ha, your mother's crazy!" (17). He soon asks Rosie to go in and remind Mrs. Hayashi about the tomatoes. Finding her mother absorbed in the editor's exposition of a haiku theory, Rosie merely relays the message and returns to the field, where she and her father work on in silence. "But suddenly, her father uttered an incredible noise, exactly like the cork of a bottle popping, and the next Rosie knew, he was stalking angrily toward the house" (17).

Also "like the cork of a bottle popping," the hitherto muted plot explodes in a wrenching epiphany:

> Soon Mr. Kuroda came out alone. . . . Next her father emerged, also alone, something in his arms (it was the picture, she realized), and, going over to the bathhouse woodpile, he threw the picture on the ground and picked up the axe. Smashing the picture, glass and all (she heard the explosion faintly), he reached over for the kerosene that was used to encourage the bath fire and poured it over the wreckage. I am dreaming, Rosie said to herself, I am dreaming, but her father, having made sure that his act of cremation was irrevocable, was even then returning to the fields. (18)

Rosie rushes to the house and finds her mother appearing "very calm" (18), watching the fire through the window. The frightening calm reveals the depths of her misery; the incinerated picture speaks for the way rage and despair consume her. The word "cremation" links object and person: the burning of the art object mirrors the expiring artist. We now understand why the mother's life span as a poet is so brief. In keeping with a tale spare in dialogue among the principal characters, the climax consists not in verbal confrontation but in a devastating action: the reader, like the mother and daughter, is forced to gaze in horror. More effective than angry screams or plaintive wails, the tableau expresses the husband's wrath and the wife's desolation.[10]

The two plots are then deftly conjoined. As mother and daughter watch the dying fire together, their lives—separate strands at the outset—are intertwined. Rosie, still throbbing from her first kiss, must look squarely at her mother's chastening marriage and re-view her rosy adolescent world through the smoky lens of Mrs. Hayashi's hindsight. When the mother asks, "Do you

[10] The incineration reminds me of the many poignant accounts (e.g., Sone 155–56, Uchida 63) of issei who burned or discarded everything associated with their country of origin after Pearl Harbor so as to avoid being suspected of subversion by the War Relocation Authority.

know why I married your father?" Rosie dreads hearing the explanation, having a premonition that "the *telling* would combine with
the other violence of the hot afternoon to level her life, her world to
the very ground" (18; my emphasis). Before, the mother has with-
held her tale of woe; now it is the daughter who wishes to be
protected from this verbal disclosure and its power of disenchant-
ment. But the telling proceeds. No longer condensing her private
thoughts into a haiku, the mother divulges her secret past to the
reluctant listener in a torrent of words. Inasmuch as her verbal
outpouring, like the father's brash act, deviates from the code of
emotional and verbal restraint observed thus far in the story (by
both the characters and the author), it takes both Rosie and the
reader by surprise.

Mrs. Hayashi's confession traces her heartaches back to a dire
romance and spells a cautionary tale for Rosie. As a young woman
in Japan, she became pregnant out of wedlock. She could not marry her lover because of their unequal social status (a factor that also
potentially divides Rosie and Jesus, whose parents work for the
Hayashis). Spurned by her family, she married Mr. Hayashi as an
alternative to suicide. Her child, had it not been stillborn, would
have been seventeen. The number connects past and present
losses. The mother may have tried to distill her grief into her night-
ly scribbles. But her art—poetry within seventeen syllables—is
also prematurely doomed.

The mother's regrets run counter to the daughter's dreams and
desires. The contending emotions are skillfully superimposed in
the dramatic last paragraph of the story:

> Suddenly, her mother knelt on the floor and took her by the wrists.
> "Rosie," she said urgently, "Promise me you will never marry!"
> Shocked more by the request than the revelation, Rosie stared at her
> mother's face. Jesus, Jesus, she called silently, not certain whether
> she was invoking the help of the son of the Carrascos or of God, until
> there returned sweetly the memory of Jesus' hand, how it had touch-
> ed her and where. Still her mother waited for an answer, holding her
> wrists so tightly that her hands were going numb. She tried to pull
> free. Promise, her mother whispered fiercely, promise. Yes, yes, I
> promise, Rosie said. But for an instant she turned away, and her
> mother, hearing the familiar glib agreement, released her. Oh, you,
> you, you, her eyes and twisted mouth said, you fool. Rosie, covering

her face, began at last to cry, and the embrace and consoling hand
came much later than she expected. (19)

The passage poignantly double-tells. The mother's request, so "unnatural" in light of the Japanese conception of marriage as *giri*
(obligation toward others) and as "a natural stage in the course of
one's life" (Yanagisako 95), underscores her thorough disillusionment with men. Deserted by her lover and stifled by her husband,
Mrs. Hayashi tries to prevent her daughter from meeting the same
fate. Yet her sudden kneeling, anxious clutching and reiteration of
"promise" oddly and ironically correspond to the posture, gesture,
and entreaty of an ardent suitor proposing marriage.

One suspects that the ironic correspondence flickers across the
daughter's mind as well. Though not deaf to her mother's appeal,
Rosie drifts into a romantic reverie at the very moment Mrs. Hayashi implores her to remain single. Her reaction to the demand is
couched in words that recall her recent sexual awakening. "Jesus"
is (in print at least) both a spontaneous exclamation and an invoca-
tion of her friend, whose titillating grip contrasts with Mrs. Hayashi's tenacious clutch. "Yes, yes" recalls not only the double affirmative at the beginning of the story, when Rosie pretends to
understand the workings of haiku, but also her date with Jesus:
"When he took hold of her empty hand, she could find no words
to protest; her vocabulary had become distressingly constricted
and . . . all that remained intact now was yes and no and oh, and
even these few sounds would not easily out" (14). The affirmative
answer also extends the proposal analogy: it is an answer many a
suitor wishes to hear and many a woman in love has uttered, for
better or worse (cf. Molly Bloom's famous response at the end of
Ulysses). Here it is a hollow acquiescence extorted by the mother
and given reluctantly by the daughter. As an earnest plea against
marriage and as a travesty of a proposal, the passage pits Mrs.
Hayashi's cynical wisdom against Rosie's dampened but inex-
tinguishable hopes.

Rosie has at last been jolted out of childhood. The syllables "yes,
yes" (at first so easily proffered as a white lie covering up linguistic
incompetence) have become increasingly problematic for her to
vocalize: one needs only to contrast the emotions behind the iden-
tical answer in the first and last paragraphs to gauge her develop-

ment. Although her "familiar glib agreement" and Mrs. Hayashi's temporary withdrawal hark back to the story's opening (when Rosie is considered too young to grasp the intricacies of Japanese poetics), the unspoken reprimand suggests that she is now expected to face life's muddles. The carefree narrative voice that opens the story is, at the end, gravid with adult cares.

Through Yamamoto's sleight of "hand," Mrs. Hayashi's embitterment and Rosie's transformation are together encapsulated in the delicate understatement that concludes the story. The tactile images—"the embrace and consoling hand"—once more recall Rosie's encounter with Jesus, but the timing here tells much more. The disconsolate mother, taking umbrage at Rosie's insincere reply, cannot bring herself to hug her sobbing daughter immediately. But the image of delayed embrace, as Stan Yogi observes, also "suggests the maturity that Mrs. Hayashi now expects of her daughter, who has been initiated into the excitement, pain, and disillusionment of adult life" (1989, 174). The effect of the ending, and of the entire story, is achieved through double-telling and through the dramatization of nonverbal interaction.

"Yoneko's Earthquake"

"Yoneko's Earthquake" likewise juggles parallel plots and summons our detective faculties. The manifest plot recounts a young girl's passing crush on a farmhand and her short-lived Christian faith. The latent plot hints at her mother's secret love affair with the same man and eventual conversion to Christianity. But unlike the submerged plot of "Seventeen Syllables," which flows along with the story and swells up at the end, the second plot in "Yoneko's Earthquake" is persistently and completely masked. A third-person limited point of view makes possible the opaqueness: we see the story through the eyes of ten-year-old Yoneko Hosoume, the eponymous protagonist. By imitating the haphazard manner of the child, the narrator can drop pertinent hints as though they were random digressions. For instance, the seemingly trivial opening anecdote, in which Yoneko's brother, Seigo, mistakes his sister's praying position for a display of grief, reminds us that a child's perception often falls short of the entire reality. Just as Seigo misreads his older sister's religious posture, Yoneko misinterprets adult gestures.

The reader, to cull and combine each piece of the hidden plot, must attend to every hint and hush. Through Yoneko's evaluations of her mother and Marpo (the Filipino farmhand who works for her family), we learn that both adults are remarkably attractive. Mrs. Hosoume is apparently a rare beauty: "When [Yoneko] herself was younger . . . she had at times been so struck with her mother's appearance that she had dropped to her knees and mutely clasped her mother's legs in her arms. . . . She also remembered she had once heard someone comparing her mother to 'a dewy, half-opened rosebud' " (53). The seductive Mrs. Hosoume surely has other admirers besides her daughter. Yoneko also idolizes Marpo and enumerates at length his multiple accomplishments as Christian, farmworker, athlete, musician, artist, and radio technician. We suspect that such a versatile man is irresistible not only to little Yoneko but also to older members of her sex. We never see Mrs. Hosoume and Marpo alone together or hear them comment on each other, but through Yoneko's adoration of the two we infer the likelihood of mutual attraction between the adults. An affair between them presumably begins, or is consummated, around the time of an earthquake during which Mr. Hosoume is injured in a car accident and apparently rendered impotent.

Neither the affair nor Mr. Hosoume's impotence is explicit in the story; the sexual dynamics in the adult world are beyond Yoneko's comprehension. For Yoneko, whom Marpo has converted to Christianity, the greatest consequence of the earthquake is her loss of faith in God: her belief is permanently shaken when her fervent prayers seem unheeded during the prolonged heaving. Because of her high-strung reaction, the whole household refers to the disaster as "Yoneko's earthquake."

Both the point of view and the title of the story lead us to see the earthquake and its impact on Yoneko as the epicenter of interest. Only toward the end do we discover that the temblor has also had physical and emotional aftershocks for Yoneko's parents and Marpo. Mr. Hosoume, unable to farm since the accident, is confined to the house while Marpo and Mrs. Hosoume work in the field and run errands together. We get our first inkling of intimacy between the two when Mrs. Hosoume gives Yoneko a ring that is too big for the child, saying: "If your father asks where you got it, say you found it on the street" (52). Another hint surfaces when the parents quarrel over Yoneko's right to wear nail polish. When Mr. Hosoume slaps his wife, Marpo—who used to be "a rather shy young man meek to the point of speechlessness in the presence of Mr. and Mrs. Hosoume" (49)—intervenes by reminding his boss of the children's presence. His intervention signifies not only paternal concern but chivalry.

We can see the key events that follow only darkly, as through an ill-lit scrim, by connecting the isolated details furnished by the naive narrator. One day Marpo disappears abruptly "without even saying good-bye to Yoneko and Seigo" (54). On that day the Hosoumes, quite out of their weekday routine, go to the city. Driving at top speed, Mr. Hosoume hits a collie: "The car jerked with the impact, but Mr. Hosoume drove right on" (54). When they arrive at a hospital, the children are told to wait in the car. A long time passes before the parents return, and the mother is "obviously in pain," which she attributes to "some necessarily astringent treatment" (54). The father admonishes the children to keep the excursion a secret.

No explosive scene analogous to Mr. Hayashi's burning of the prize picture takes place in "Yoneko's Earthquake," but the description of the trip to the hospital reverberates with the parents' untold agitations. The father's unblinking crushing of the collie evinces his fury at the liaison between Marpo and Mrs. Hosoume and his indifference to the life about to be quashed at the hospital. By contrast, Yoneko's unspoken pity for the animal reflects her mother's untold grief, for the collie's fate foreshadows that of her unborn child. As in the picture-burning scene, extreme emotions are conveyed by remarkable verbal economy: we are made to react to what has not been said.

The pregnant silence remains unbroken to the end in "Yoneko's Earthquake." Yoneko never learns about the abortion; nor does she link Marpo's departure with the visit to the hospital. Like Rosie, who has been too absorbed in her own romance to notice the discord between her parents, Yoneko is too hurt by Marpo's "abrupt desertion" (55) to discern her mother's forlornness. Only after Seigo has suddenly died of illness does Yoneko notice that her mother, who has "swollen eyes in the morning for weeks afterwards," is "inconsolable" (55). Yoneko attributes her mother's distress to Seigo's death, but the author has intimated additional causes. Yoneko's pique against Marpo—concealed from the other characters but revealed to the reader—refracts the endless remorse of her mother, who mourns now for not one but two lives and perhaps also for her absent lover.

At the end Mrs. Hosoume, seeking to teach Yoneko a lesson, adumbrates a causal link between the two premature deaths. But her cryptic moral is lost on her daughter:

> "Never kill a person, Yoneko, because if you do, God will take from you someone you love."
>
> "Oh, that," said Yoneko quickly, "I don't believe in that, I don't believe in God." . . . She had believed for a moment that her mother was going to ask about the ring (which, alas, she had lost already, somewhere in the flumes along the cantaloupe patch). (56)

Both Mrs. Hosoume's "Never kill a person" and Mrs. Hayashi's "Promise me you will never marry" are at once direct imperatives to the daughters and oblique indictments of the husbands. The verbal constructions fall under the category of "hedging," or strategies "for equivocating about or weakening a message" (Radner & Lanser 420). While Mrs. Hayashi and Mrs. Hosoume avoid explicitly referring to their husbands, they also heighten the blame, the one by denouncing men categorically if circuitously, the other by viewing her presumably involuntary abortion as an act of killing by the husband. Though Mrs. Hosoume seems to be referring to herself as the killer, she is acting in accordance with patriarchal injunction. The phrase "someone you love" is likewise equivocal, for it could refer to either Seigo or Marpo (Crow 1984, 202). Mrs. Hosoume, despite her contrition, seems to see her loss as divine punishment for the abortion rather than for her adultery.

Like the conclusion of "Seventeen Syllables," this ending adroitly welds the juvenile and adult plots. Yoneko has been converted by Marpo to Christianity, though she loses her faith soon enough; her mother, a nonbeliever at the beginning, becomes a devout Christian after Seigo's death. That the mother's conversion, too, may have been brought about by Marpo is left implicit. Marpo's departure affects both mother and daughter, but Mrs. Hosoume's sorrow outlasts Yoneko's fleeting sadness. Yoneko's dismay at her inadvertent loss of the ring reflects for us the mother's concealed privation. The ring, which earlier symbolizes the mother's sharing of her lover with her daughter, has become an absent reminder of a shared loss. But whereas the unhappy ending of "Seventeen Syllables" is softened by the delayed embrace—which intimates a connection, however tentative, between mother and daughter—here the image of the lost token given to the daughter by the mother suggests instead a "severed link" (Yogi 1989, 178). To the daughter the ring is a trinket; to the mother it signifies an inner tumult as intense as the earthquake that shattered Yoneko's faith.

What Showalter calls "double-voiced discourse" certainly informs Yamamoto's texts, constructed to "make the invisible visible, to make the silent speak" (31). In both "Seventeen Syllables" and "Yoneko's Earthquake" the muffled suffering of the mothers emerges belatedly. But Yamamoto's plots also monitor male silences, which, contrary to prevailing feminist beliefs, can be even thicker than female inhibition. If mothers and daughters in the two stories often talk at cross-purposes, communication between fathers and daughters and between husbands and wives is altogether restricted. In the few instances in which the fathers do speak to the daughters, they often sound peremptory or critical. Interaction between the spouses is scarcely better. Elaine Kim, describing gender relations in Yamamoto's fiction, sees the women as generally "imprisoned with well meaning but weak and insensitive husbands . . . [who] remain in the shadows as guardians of the prison doors, for the most part conventional and colorless" (1987, 99). Though ostensibly guarding the prison doors of the house, these tight-lipped husbands are themselves caught in loveless marriages, marooned within the larger society, and, above all, constrained by the patriarchal code of masculinity.

Since Japanese American patriarchy, no less than Japanese American silence, is inflected by both history and culture, we must trace the paternal contour of each muted plot against the historical and cultural background. The first waves of Japanese immigrants (1885–1910) consisted mainly of single men, who, after establishing themselves in the new country, sought wives either by returning to Japan or by exchanging photos across the Pacific.[11] The "picture brides" who came to America (mostly between 1910 and 1920) were generally ten to fifteen years younger than their husbands (Ichioka 1980, 347). Though we do not know the circumstances of the Hosoumes' marriage, Mrs. Hosoume, likened to a "half-opened rosebud," is probably closer in age to thirty-six-year-old Marpo than to her husband, who finds a regular gaming partner in the new fieldhand—"an old Japanese man who wore his gray hair in a military cut" (54). Trickery through long-distance marriage was not uncommon: men often "forwarded photographs taken in their youth or touched up ones that concealed their real age" (Ichioka 1980, 347). But women could perhaps also hide certain "blemishes." Judging from Mrs. Hayashi's confession at the end of "Seventeen Syllables," Mr. Hayashi—who "was never told why his unseen betrothed was so eager to hasten the day of meeting" (19)—was himself a victim of conjugal deception.

We can also see that while the husbands strictly abide by the Confucian code, according to which implicit respect is required from wife to husband and from children to parents, their young wives and children have begun to demand greater freedom and independence in the New World. The difference may be due to disparity in age and temperament, or to the influence of the American environment on women and children, but it may also be traced to the lowered status of Japanese males in America, which was intensely anti-Oriental at the time.[12] As farmers preoccupied with survival in a hostile environment, Mr. Hayashi and Mr. Hosoume are resolutely earthbound. This predilection is reflected in Mr. Hayashi's overwhelming concern for the tomato harvest and Mr.

---

[11] The practice, an extension of social customs in Japan, was denounced as immoral by American exclusionists and was terminated in 1921 (Ichioka 1980, 342–43). Today we may find a marriage between strangers puzzling, but many marriages in Asia and elsewhere have been similarly arranged. Since traditional Japanese marriage was rooted in *giri* (binding obligation), a couple was bound by duty rather than romantic love, though affection might develop in the course of the marriage (Yanagisako 96–97).

[12] The Alien Land Acts of 1913 and 1920 in California and similar statutes in other western states made Japanese and other Asians ineligible for citizenship and prevented them from owning land. Some immigrants bought land under the names of their American-born children.

Hosoume's humorless refusal to let Yoneko and her friends make fudge ("saying that fudge used too much sugar and that sugar was not a plaything") (51–52). Unsurprisingly, the writing of poetry appears "extravagant" and the application of cosmetics "gaudy." Marginalized by race in the host society, these men seem to feel an even greater need to assert their authority at home and overreact accordingly when they suspect themselves to be losing ground in the domestic sphere as well. Seen against the historical emasculation of Asian American men in white America—whether through legislation or popular representation (Chin et al. xxx–xlviii)—Mr. Hosoume's sexual impotence takes on symbolic significance.[13]

Governed by a code of masculinity that calls for rigorous self-restraint, the two men initially keep their disquiet to themselves. While reticence is traditionally inculcated in both Japanese men and women, men in particular have been taught that any "outward appearance that is boisterous, excessively emotional, visibly passionate, obviously fearful . . . is distasteful and itself shameful, fit perhaps only for children" (Lyman 1971, 52; see also Miyamoto 1986–87, 31–32, 40–42). Wakako Yamauchi, a contemporary of Yamamoto, alludes to this masculine code when she illustrates the socialization of Benji, the nine-year-old nisei protagonist in "Handkerchief":

> It had occurred to Benji to talk to Papa about . . . his unhappiness, his loneliness . . . no, not that. Loneliness was a weakness, a man didn't expose that soft underside. Papa was a man, airtight, strong . . . a man of few words, fewer emotions. You asked him only for things: a nickel, a dime, a ride to the library. The communication was simple: yes, no, later . . . not of multiple words or explanations. Tidy. The untidiness was underneath—just below the surface of the skin, under the twitch of an eyelid, under a clammy palm. And if you said, "I hurt," it had to be something Papa could see—a ragged wound. (146–47)

[13] Louis Chu's *Eat a Bowl of Tea* also addresses the theme of literal and symbolic impotence. Given the stereotypes prevalent at the time, according to which Japanese men were "unsexed" and Filipinos and Mexicans were dangerously "oversexed," it is perhaps no mere coincidence that Rosie and Yoneko, as well as Mrs. Hosoume, are romantically attracted to such non-Japanese males as Jesus and Marpo. (I thank Sucheng Chan for this suggestion.) Class differences further complicate interethnic dynamics. As poor farmhands, both Jesus and Marpo, who presumably is fired by Mr. Hosoume, are at the mercy of their Japanese bosses.

This notion of manhood is not specific to Japanese and Japanese Americans, and Japanese and Caucasian male mores seem to differ only in degree in associating emotional display with weakness. The British author Kazuo Ishiguro notes, "In British and Japanese society, the ability to control emotions is considered dignified and elegant" (Venant E18). Nevertheless, outward reserve is much less pervasive among Anglo-Americans, who are also more wont to speak their minds, whether or not they display emotions.[14] The taciturn manners of Mr. Hayashi and Mr. Hosoume do seem inordinately reinforced by the politics of race as well as by cultural rules that require men to be "more aloof and less emotionally demonstrative" than women (Yanagisako 118), that socialize them to practice "silent protest" (Lebra & Lebra 43). Bearing in mind that the two men may also find it easier to acknowledge (or even inflict) external injury than to confess psychological pain, one begins to detect the clues planted by the author to signal their hidden tribulations.[15]

The fathers' stories are even more obliquely told than the mothers'. Whereas the daughters' responses stir our awareness of the mothers' muffled passions, only their offhand observations insinuate the fathers' woes. Still, Yamamoto punctuates both narratives with sufficient hints to indicate that mounting masculine anxiety, not habitual insensitivity, sparks violence. The seemingly hard boiled Mr. Hayashi may in fact be plagued by loneliness, inadequacy, and sexual jealousy, though none of these feelings have been openly admitted by the character or noted by the narrator. Once again we must read beneath the narrator's straightforward description for the author's coded discourse. We are told that Mr. Hayashi and his wife used to play cards together before retiring jointly and that as a result of Mrs. Hayashi's new interest, he has to "resort to solitaire" (9). Since Mrs. Hayashi composes late into the night, we may assume that her husband now also goes to bed

[14] The psychologists Diane M. Sue and David Sue explain the contrast: "In Chinese and Japanese cultures restraint of emotions is emphasized because emotions are viewed as potentially disruptive forces on the family structure. Because of this restraint, emotional expression is considered a sign of immaturity and is suppressed. Most Americans, however, feel that the expressing of emotions is indicative of individuals who are mature and accepting of themselves" (253).

[15] In an interview, Yamamoto said that Mr. Hayashi "was only acting the way he'd been brought up to act, the way men were supposed to be" (Crow 1987, 80).

alone. His annoyance during the visit to the Hayanos undoubtedly emanates from his feeling of exclusion from the intellectual conversation. But the reader may deduce additional provocation. Mrs. Hayashi discusses poetry with Mr. Hayano "at the little table." Mr. Hayashi, "sitting at one end of the sofa," reads a copy of *Life* (significantly, a magazine consisting mostly of photos), saying a few words now and then to his hostess. While the "little table" makes for animated (and perhaps intimate) dialogue, the "end of the sofa" is secluded. Mr. Hayano (whose wife, we have been told, has already lost both health and beauty) is in Rosie's eyes "handsome, tall, and strong" (10). Buzzing through the elisions is the suggestion that not fatigue (the reason put forward by Mrs. Hayashi) but pique and jealousy have driven Mr. Hayashi to his abrupt departure. Mrs. Hayashi's former lover, we recall, was a man of a higher social class than she; by contrast, Mr. Hayashi—a farmer— is of a lower class than his wife's family. He may feel troubled by Mrs. Hayashi's verbal sophistication, which must remind him of their disparate class origins. Above all, he has probably sensed a compatibility—physical and intellectual—between his wife and Mr. Hayano which is absent from both of the marriages.

Hints of inferiority and sexual jealousy are repeated in the fateful visit of Mr. Kuroda, which finally unhinges Mr. Hayashi. Kuroda, the editor, is "a good-looking man" who speaks "in a more elegant Japanese than [Rosie] was used to" (16); in his presence Mrs. Hayashi shifts "easily into his style." The switch in manner once more bespeaks her earlier station. The announcement by the handsome and urbane editor of Mrs. Hayashi's artistic triumph then no doubt intensifies her husband's envy and sense of shame, feelings that trouble Mr. Hayashi more than the need to have the tomatoes packed in time (though the manual labor may be the symbolic activity of *his* adequacy). The simile that introduces his outburst of rage—"like the cork of a bottle popping" (17)—indicates the pressure of his pent-up resentment (and perhaps also the degree of his sexual frustration). Equally revealing is the soundless hysteria with which he wrecks the Hiroshige. If the stylish editor galls the lower-class Mr. Hayashi, the delicate print also mocks his poverty of artistic talent. (Mrs. Hayashi's confession at the end suggests that there have been grounds all along—albeit unrecognized—for her husband's emotional insecurity.)

The author effects a similar double take in "Yoneko's Earthquake," for only in retrospect can the reader fathom the psychological impact the earthquake has on Mr. Hosoume. "After the earth subsided . . . life returned to normal, except that Mr. Hosoume stayed at home most of the time. Sometimes . . . he would have supper on the stove when Mrs. Hosoume came in from the fields. Mrs. Hosoume and Marpo did all the field labor now" (51). The traditional roles of husband and wife have become reversed. The reversal, as Yogi observes, is especially significant in the context of issei families (1989, 176), in which the division of labor between husbands and wives was unusually strict: "wives took care of things 'inside' the house . . . and husbands took care of things outside it" (Yanagisako 97). Unable to perform outside duties, Mr. Hosoume is forced to handle domestic chores, though among issei "it is not conceivable for men to . . . adopt roles and styles of interaction perceived as female" (Yanagisako 102). As if that humiliation were not enough, another man now works beside his wife.

Mr. Hosoume's subsequent behavior suggests that his male pride is chafed by the change and by an unspeakable failure—his sexual impotence. Out of his sense of injured manhood he becomes increasingly irritable and despotic toward his household. He sees his children's disobedience as prompted by his indisposition: "Just because I'm ill just now is no reason for them to start being disrespectful" (53), he tells his wife. He also refuses to brook contradictions from Mrs. Hosoume. When she protests against his calling her "nama-iki" (saucy woman), he slaps her. The reader is told that it "was the first time he had ever laid hands on her" (53), an indication that his bad temper is not habitual but is linked to his disability. He then accuses Marpo, who has tried to calm him down, of being "increasingly impudent towards him since his illness" (54). His tendency to see other people's behavior toward him in terms of his own incapacity betrays an obsessive anxiety, and his unusually volatile temper can be diagnosed as stemming from his need to reassert male dominance.

Through double-telling Yamamoto reveals the immense psychological strain men too must bear in their efforts to maintain their masculine dignity under certain forms of patriarchy. If Mr. Hosoume thinks his family is turning against him out of scorn, his wife's love affair and ensuing pregnancy must be the ultimate affront to his manhood. His aggression on the way to the hospital can be better understood in the light of such mortification. Just as the Hiroshige both arouses Mr. Hayashi's jealousy and mocks his inadequacy, the fetus is a terrible reminder at once of cuckoldry and of Mr. Hosoume's impotence.

Mr. Hosoume softens noticeably after the abortion, for he is able to resume the role of "supporter and comforter" that Marpo took over during the earthquake (Yogi 1989, 175). He literally supports his now feeble wife as the couple walk from the hospital to the car, "she walking with very small, slow steps and he assisting her" (54). He even becomes "very gentle" (55) toward Mrs. Hosoume during her long bout of dejection after Seigo's death and encourages Yoneko to make her mother "laugh and forget about Seigo" (56). Sadly enough, these tender moments can take place only when the outspoken Mrs. Hosoume is falling apart, physically or emotionally, and when Mr. Hosoume is no longer threatened by her insubordination. He himself is not immune to bereavement, but as a man he refrains from displaying his grief. Seigo's death is no less a blow to the father than to the mother and is perhaps another ironic turn in the muted drama of masculine anxiety. Mrs. Hosoume's warning of divine retribution applies to her husband with withering vengeance: he has lost his only male heir and can never have another.

To mitigate the initial negative impressions of Mr. Hayashi and Mr. Hosoume is not to condone their actions. A sympathetic analysis of their behavior shows that Yamamoto eludes the simplistic dichotomy of male villains and female victims. While the oppressive silence of the two men must be distinguished from the submissive silence expected of their wives and children, they too suffer in their struggle to live up to the masculine image prescribed by their ancestral and adopted cultures. Had they been able to reveal their vulnerability, the tragic endings might have been averted; instead they practice *gaman* till their mounting fury erupts in violence. The two men's taciturnity most likely has widened the gaps between themselves and their spouses, who not surprisingly become drawn to the likes of Mr. Hayano, Mr. Kuroda, and Marpo; physical and intellectual attractions aside, these men communicate verbally with the women.

In her coded depiction of female and male conditions in these
two stories, Yamamoto exemplifies the open-endedness and multiplicity celebrated in women's writing. But we can better appreciate
the author's expansive vision by going beyond Eurocentric perspectives. Readers tend to react to the characters according to their
own cultural persuasions. Japanese-born readers of both sexes are
invariably more sympathetic than their American-born counterparts to the husbands, and more critical of the wives.[16] My own
perspectives proliferate with each reading. Denied direct access to
the spouses' thoughts and motives, the reader is all the freer to
reconstruct those buried lives from the nuances in the text.

Yamamoto herself seems ambivalent toward her cultural inheritance. Her naive narrators, embodying the free spirits of the young
nisei, highlight the rigid conventions that regulate the lives of issei
women and men. Patriarchy chokes both sexes, though to different
degrees and in different ways. The women in her stories are de-
terred from expressing themselves artistically or sexually; but their
male oppressors are even more inhibited, frozen in their masculine
roles. Seen through the startled or uncomprehending eyes of bicultural daughters who must soon come to grips with their maternal legacies, the mothers' private sorrow and the fathers' brooding
rage reverberate ominously. Even as Yamamoto renders the domestic drama, the feminist in her is beckoning her readers to enact
different scripts.[17]

At the same time, Yamamoto's stylistic restraint pays a tacit tribute to those cultural forerunners who can say more in less, who
can funnel vast meaning and feeling into seventeen syllables.[18]

[16] Japanese-born students have often found the behavior of Mrs. Hosoume toward her husband (during their squabble over nail polish) disrespectful and over-
bearing. Some believe that Mrs. Hosoume's contradiction of her husband in the
children's presence would be considered a serious offense even in contemporary
Japanese society.

[17] When asked about her writing, Yamamoto replies: "I guess I write (aside from
compulsion) to reaffirm certain basic truths which seem to get lost in the shuffle
from generation to generation, so that we seem destined to go on making the same
mistake over and over again. If the reader is entertained, wonderful. If he learns
something, that's a bonus" (Hsu & Palubinskas 113).

[18] Yamamoto reveals that although many details in "Seventeen Syllables" are
invented, it is basically the story of her own mother, who was a writer of senryo (a
form of satirical verse that contains seventeen syllables) (Koppelman 162). She has

Her strategy of double-telling is especially suited to evoking suppressed emotions, revealing the anxieties and hurts that lie beneath the surface of language. The hushed climax of each story is
captured in a verbal snapshot. By zooming in on the deliberate
destruction of the Hiroshige and on the unfeeling crushing of the
collie, she transmits and trans-mutes the characters' unspoken sentiments through her own rhetorical silence.

"The Legend of Miss Sasagawara"

The two stories discussed so far allow us to look closely into two
Japanese American families despite the use of naive narrators. The
structure of "The Legend" is more intricate, and distance between
the central characters and the reader is much greater. Here the
author uses unreliable points of view to communicate, in highly
veiled terms, the haunting story of a nisei woman driven "insane"
by the combined pressures exerted upon her as an "other"—in her
own family, in her ethnic community, and in American society at
large. To tease out the concatenate elements and to unfold the
Chinese-box structure of the story, let us look at domestic, communal, and political relations.[19] The formal structure of the story cannot be appreciated fully without knowledge of the underlying and
deliberately muted concrete historical situation.

Like "Seventeen Syllables" and "Yoneko's Earthquake," "The
Legend" is constructed on a suspended plot. But unlike the first
two stories, in which we are consistently given Rosie's and
Yoneko's points of view, assorted opinions literally make up "The
Legend." In this story we gain no intimate knowledge of any char-
acter, least of all the title character, about whom we find out only
bits and pieces. The point of view of the twenty-year-old narrator,
Kiku, is as limited as Rosie's or Yoneko's, though less by age than

---

also said of her father: "He wasn't much for women getting educated, he thought
they should get married, have children and help the husband—he was more of the
Japanese traditional male" (Blauvelt 19).

[19] I am much indebted to Stan Yogi, whose M.A. thesis heightened my awareness
of the political echoes in "The Legend." Unlike Yogi, however, I do not believe that
there is any one "true meaning of events" in this suggestive tale (1988, 117), which
insistently cautions against accepting subjective interpretations as certainties.

by distance. She is no close relative of the title character, but merely a fellow inmate at Poston, Arizona, one of the internment camps for Japanese Americans during World War II. Mari Sasagawara, a middle-aged ballerina, has transferred to Poston with her Buddhist minister father from another camp after the death there of her mother. At Poston her apparently aloof and eccentric behavior causes tongues to wag. She is a general spectacle—for Kiku too, initially. After being admitted to the camp hospital several times, Miss Sasagawara is sent to a sanatorium. She is found to be a friendlier person on her return to the camp, but she soon suffers a relapse and is committed to an asylum. When the war is over, Kiku comes across a published poem by Mari Sasagawara, which describes the agony of someone living in close proximity with a spiritual man oblivious of human emotions. Kiku's paraphrase of the poem—the center of the Chinese box containing the dancer's own voice—comes at the end of the story.[20]

The figure portrayed in the poem bears an unmistakable resemblance to Reverend Sasagawara:

This man was certainly noble, the poet wrote, this man was beyond censure. The world was doubtless enriched by his presence. But say that someone else, someone sensitive, someone admiring, someone who had not achieved this sublime condition and who did not wish to, were somehow called to companion such a man. Was it not likely that the saint, blissfully bent on cleansing from his already radiant soul the last imperceptible blemishes (for, being perfect, would he not humbly suspect his own flawlessness?) would be deaf and blind to the human passions rising, subsiding, and again rising, perhaps in anguished silence, within the selfsame room? The poet could not speak for others, of course; she could only speak for herself. But she would describe this man's devotion as a sort of madness, the monstrous sort which, pure of itself, might possibly bring troublous, scented scenes to recur in the other's sleep. (33)

Both "Seventeen Syllables" and "Yoneko's Earthquake" conclude with an impassioned mother confronting a daughter; in "The Leg-

---

[20] Yamamoto reveals that Mari Sasagawara is "based on a real woman" and that "she really was a writer," though Yamamoto didn't know that at the time she wrote the story (Crow 1987, 79–80).

end" Marie Sasagawara's poem—which Kiku finds "erratically brilliant and . . . tantalizingly obscure" (32)—is our only and final clue to the troubled relationship between a daughter and a dispassionate father. The saintly father with his devotional fanaticism, we infer, stifles the human yearning of "someone else"—his daughter. Who then is mad?

Through the story we have been given several suggestive glimpses of the Reverend. Kiku describes him as wearing "perpetually an air of bemusement, never talking directly to a person, as though, being what he was, he could not stop for an instant his meditation on the higher life" (22). We also learn that he was one of the three monks present at the funeral of Kiku's grandfather.

> There had been tears and tears and here and there a sudden sob.
> And all this while, three men in black robes had been on the platform . . . and the entire trio incessantly chanting a strange, mellifluous language in unison. From time to time there had reverberated through the enormous room, above the singsong, above the weeping, above the fragrance, the sharp, startling whang of the gong. (23)

The grief of the mourners puts in relief the detachment of the monks, whose immunity to worldly distress attests to their spiritual attainment, their ability to focus on a higher life. Set amid manifest human sorrow, it also comes across as insensateness.

The funeral scene prepares us for the anguished revelation in the autobiographical poem. Reverend Sasagawara is apparently blind to both the physical and the psychological suffering of his daughter. He is notably absent during her times at the hospital, even when she is visibly in pain. His absent presence may have compounded her sense of loss after her mother's death, which has freed the father for pursuit of holiness and enabled him to "extinguish within himself all unworthy desire" (32). The bereft daughter, as a result, is left alone by her surviving parent as well. In addition, the saintly asceticism jars with the sensibilities of the dancer, noted for her long "shining hair," "bright mouth," "glittering eyes," and "daily costume, brief and fitting closely to her trifling waist . . . and bringing together arrestingly rich colors" (20). The contrast in appearance between father and daughter must be striking. What Buddhist robe conceals ballet costume reveals. If Buddhism demands unflinching spiritual concentration, ballet dancing, while also requiring unremitting discipline, is very much an (em)bodied art. The artist's self-repression in her father's presence—an attempt that might have translated as her general unsociability—seems to heighten her latent sexuality. In the poem sexual overtones are insinuated in the close juxtaposition of the words "companion," "selfsame room," "human passions rising, subsiding, and again rising," and "scented scenes . . . in the other's sleep."

The private affair of a rejecting father and an admiring daughter is set against a communal tribunal. Both the Reverend and Miss Sasagawara maintain a certain distance from the nikkei community, which nevertheless judges the father's and the daughter's aloofness differently—evidently on account of gender. Traditionally man has been socialized to pursue individual goals, religious or otherwise; woman, only to socialize. It is not surprising, therefore, that the Reverend's blankness is deemed lofty and religious, while the daughter's similar expression is considered unfriendly and unhealthy. His attitude is respected, hers suspected.

Miss Sasagawara alternates between flamboyant display and reclusiveness. The latter mode is particularly remarkable in light of her profession. As a ballerina she must be accustomed to intense regard from an audience, directed both at her every movement and at her bodily contours. Even in camp her deportment attracts attention, literally at every step: "her measured walk said, 'Look, I'm *walking!*' as though walking were not a common but a rather special thing to be doing" (20). Yet she seems acutely self-conscious. Preferring not to eat in the mess hall, she has her meals in her room; she never willingly uses the shower room when anyone else is present.

To be sure, what is presented here as a curious contradiction may be quite natural. For someone who has to perform constantly in public, the wish for privacy may be particularly intense. But the story suggests that inquisitive scrutiny by fellow internees may be an additional source of Miss Sasagawara's anxiety. Communal curiosity peaks during one of the times she is "kept . . . for observation" at the hospital (26):

> The whole hospital staff appeared to have gathered in the room to get a look at Miss Sasagawara, and the other patients . . . were sitting up attentively in their high, white, and narrow beds. . . . she must be aware of that concentrated gaze . . . and of everyone else who tripped in and out abashedly on some pretext or other in order to pass by her bed. (26)

Miss Sasagawara had tried to escape and, when asked why, "said she didn't want any more of those doctors pawing her" (26). Her allegation of being "pawed" by the doctors can be construed in two ways. If one assumes (as everyone in the story does) that Miss Sasagawara overreacts, then she is guilty of "misinterpretation" (Yogi 1988, 118). Her misreading of the doctor's gestures fore-shadows several events in which her own behavior is possibly misread. Nevertheless, in view of her physical beauty, there is reason to suspect that excessive groping did occur during the med-ical examinations. But no one takes her allegation seriously; it is automatically dismissed as hysterics. The dismissal is quite under-standable. The predominantly male medical profession has tradi-tionally been sanctified as unquestionable authority. The female patient who dares to challenge and literally turns her back on such authority becomes the one conspicuously on trial.[21]

Like Janie in Zora Neale Hurston's *Their Eyes Were Watching God*, Toni Morrison's eponymous Sula, and the lesbian couple Lorraine and Theresa in Gloria Naylor's *Women of Brewster Place*, Miss Sasagawara runs afoul of the gender expectations of her communi-ty and is consequently encircled by its critical gaze. As Shoshana Felman points out, female defiance of gender roles is often in-terpreted as mental deviance: "From her initial family upbringing throughout her subsequent development, the social role assigned to the woman is that of *serving* an image . . . of man: a woman is first and foremost a daughter/a mother/a wife" (6–7). She cites Phyllis Chesler: "What we consider 'madness' . . . is either the acting out of the devalued female role or the total or partial rejec-tion of one's sex-role stereotype" (56, quoted in Felman 7). Miss

[21] My second interpretation may strike some readers as being overly influenced by increasing media coverage of sexual harassment. As far as I know, however, Yamamoto was the first writer who openly addressed that topic (in substance if not in name) in "The High-Heeled Shoes: A Memoir" (1948; 1988), 1–7.

Sasagawara is female, thirty-nine, evidently beautiful, and unmarried. Whether one gauges her by the traditional Japanese norm that views marriage as *giri* (obligation) or the romantic Western norm by which a woman defines herself in relation to a Prince Charming, her single status is sufficient to set her apart. (Kiku and her friend Elsie share the conventional feminine expectations—to find "two nice, clean young men, preferably handsome, preferably rich, who would cherish [them] forever and a day" [21].) In addition, she has spent most of her adult, prewar life away from her own ethnic group in a highly unusual career (for an Asian American at the time). The internees are likely to see her as an outsider from the start. Recalling what Mr. Hosoume has to say about Yoneko's flamingo nail polish—that it makes her "look like a Filipino" (52)—we may further assume that Miss Sasagawara's attire, though in line with her aesthetics, raises eyebrows among the inmates, especially at a time when nikkei least wanted to call attention to themselves. The community subtly distances itself from the dancer by addressing her as "Miss Sasagawara . . . although her first name, Mari, was simple enough and rather pretty" (22).

Her alienation is compounded by her popularity as an object of idle gossip: "If Miss Sasagawara was not one to speak to, she was certainly one to speak of, and she came up quite often as topic for the endless conversations which helped along the monotonous days" (22). The words bandied about make her out to be a stereotypical spinster with notorious idiosyncrasies. The first rumor is of an event that allegedly took place as soon as she and her father arrived in the camp. Mr. Sasaki, a fellow newcomer, apparently offers to help clean the barrack to which father and daughter are assigned, whereupon she shrieks: "What are you trying to do? Spy on me? Get out of here or I'll throw this water on you!" And, we are told, she duly carries out her threat. "Madwoman" is Mr. Sasaki's conclusion (21). But Elsie—who passes on his account to Kiku—has a different impression during her own direct encounter with Miss Sasagawara, finding her "quite amiable" (21).

Another rumor is told by Mrs. Sasaki, who apparently catches Miss Sasagawara ogling a group of neighboring teenage boys, the Yoshinagas, playing basketball in the backyard. Mrs. Sasaki claims that the dancer "wore a beatific expression as she watched the action. . . . [She] was so absorbed a spectator of this horseplay that her head was bent to one side and she actually had one finger in her mouth as she gazed, in the manner of a shy child confronted with a marvel" (31). "What's the matter with you, watching the boys like that?" Mrs. Sasaki scolded. "You're old enough to be their mother!" (31). The startled Miss Sasagawara then darts into her room and proceeds to bang on the walls. The sequel to this episode is told by one of those boys, Joe Yoshinaga. For several days Joe, who often reads before going to sleep, finds magazines he has carelessly thrown on top of a shelf at night to be stacked neatly the next day. He awakes one night to find Miss Sasagawara sitting beside him, "her long hair all undone and flowing about her. She was dressed in a white nightgown and her hands were clasped on her lap. And all she was doing was sitting there watching him, Joe Yoshinaga" (31). When Joe screams, she runs out the door. These oral reports paint a picture of a woman secretly obsessed with the opposite sex but who vehemently refuses to acknowledge the "fact." The disturbing "symptoms" lead to the patient's permanent confinement in an asylum: "Miss Sasagawara had gone away not long after" (32).

As several critics have noted, however, the narrator sedulously reminds us of the secondhand nature of these reports and questions their veracity (McDonald & Newman 27; Yogi 1988, 118). Kiku receives all the details from Elsie, who has in turn picked them up from other sources. Elsie herself is not exactly a reliable informant. After relating Mr. Sasaki's story she exclaims, "Oooh, that gal is really temperamental. I guess it's because she was a ballet dancer before she got stuck in camp, I hear people like that are temperamental" (20–21). As Yogi observes, Elsie is not above "resorting to a stereotype to explain Miss Sasagawara's behavior" (1988, 119). Even though she supposedly "knew all about Miss Sasagawara," her knowledge is wryly undercut by the narrator: "Where had she accumulated all her items? Probably a morsel here and a morsel there, and, anyway, I forgot to ask her sources" (20). And the ones the narrator is given to know turn out to be suspect:

> Elsie's sources were not what I would ordinarily pay much attention to, Mrs. Sasaki, that plump and giggling young woman who always felt called upon to explain that she was childless by choice, and Joe Yoshinaga, who had a knack of blowing up, in his drawling voice, any

incident in which he personally played even a small part (I could imagine the field day he had had with this one). (32)

The narrator's misgivings prompt us to reexamine the circumstantial evidence for Miss Sasagawara's alleged derangement. Mrs. Sasaki, as the wife of the man who has called the dancer a "madwoman," is likely to corroborate her husband's conclusion. For all we know, she may be projecting her own maternal frustration onto Miss Sasagawara, who, as a dancer, may be fascinated merely by the physical movements of those boys playing basketball. Whatever the reason, Mrs. Sasaki's shrill reprimand seems uncalled for, even downright rude. Faced with such rudeness, Miss Sasagawara has reason to express anger.

On the other hand, Mrs. Sasaki may have read real longing in the dancer's eyes. The narrator, "who had so newly had some contact with the recorded explorations into the virgin territory of the human mind," ventures an explanation: "Miss Sasagawara had no doubt looked upon Joe Yoshinaga as the image of either the lost lover or the lost son." However, no sooner has she hit this initial note of certainty than she qualifies her observation in an aside: "My words made me uneasy by their glibness" (32). Unlike the others, who all purport to know what is wrong with the dancer, Kiku at least allows that she could be mistaken. Yet partly for that reason her explanation remains tantalizing. Mrs. Sasaki has revealed earlier that Miss Sasagawara is old enough to be the boys' mother. The dual motif of lost lover and lost son has occurred before as a belated revelation in both "Seventeen Syllables" and "Yoneko's Earthquake."[22] In her youth Miss Sasagawara, too, may have had an affair that resulted in pregnancy; concern for her career as an aspiring dancer, or fear of paternal disapproval and communal censure, may have prompted an abortion. After all, her father—"whose lifelong aim had been to achieve Nirvana"—deeply regrets "his having acquired, when young and unaware, a family for which he must provide" (32). And her lost child would have been about Joe's age. Like Kiku, however, I cannot help feeling somewhat guilty in making these facile deductions. The progressive withdrawal of Miss Sasagawara—notwith-

[22] This motif also informs Wakako Yamauchi's "And the Soul Shall Dance" and "Songs My Mother Taught Me."

standing the "saner" interlude after her time out at the sanatorium—may precisely be her reaction against idle speculations, her
means of insulating herself from loose tongues and intrusive gazes.

The unnerving effect of public scrutiny is illustrated humorously
during the Christmas performance of a children's dancing class
under Miss Sasagawara's tutelage: "And the little girls, who might
have curtsied and stepped gracefully about under Miss Sasagawara's eyes alone, were all elbows and knees as they felt the
Block's one-hundred-fifty or more pairs of eyes on them" (29). The
comic description reminds us of Miss Sasagawara's daily trial, and
perhaps of what unremitting surveillance may do to mental balance.

Miss Sasagawara's role as a voluntary teacher suggests that she is
not naturally standoffish. Beneath her apparent distance lies a
longing for human connection, as is hinted when Kiku and Elsie
find the dancer peeling a grapefruit in front of her porch. The
dancer is at first unresponsive to Elsie's greeting; she merely
"looked up and stared, without recognition" (22). Kiku, however,
detects a further signal unnoticed by Elsie: "We were almost out of
earshot when I heard her call, 'Do I know you?' and I could have
almost sworn that she sounded hopeful, if not downright wistful,
but Elsie, already miffed at having expended friendliness so un-
profitably, seemed not to have heard, and that was that" (22).
Kiku's impression contradicts other reports concerning the strange
woman. Miss Sasagawara seems eager to know someone and to be
recognized as a person rather than viewed as a spectacle. But Elsie
is offended and her foreclosed opinion anticipates that of the many
people who remain distrustful of the dancer even after she returns
from the sanatorium a changed person: "She said hello and how
are you as often and easily as the next person, although many of
those she greeted were surprised and suspicious, remembering the
earlier rebuffs. There were some who never did get used to Miss
Sasagawara as a friendly being" (28).

Yamamoto succeeds, however, in unsettling any erstwhile con-
clusions. We have been led, for instance, to see camp life as quite
"normal." Life at Poston, as presented in the brisk tone of Kiku,
seems at first glance tolerable, even pleasant. That impression,
however, reflects more the evacuees' efforts to create some sem-
blance of normality under trying circumstances than it does the

actual conditions. Internees such as Elsie and Kiku have managed to take imprisonment in their stride, as though the detention camp were a summer camp. After regaining freedom the two even reminisce about "the good old days when we had worked in the mess hall together, the good old days when we had worked in the hospital together" (30). Granted that these statements may be somewhat sardonic, they no doubt also reveal the survival strategies of people who wish to paint over the humiliation of being incarcerated.

The internment was surely no laughing matter for Yamamoto herself, who turned twenty-one in camp and whose brother died in combat as an American soldier while most of his family were still in American custody. In an essay on literature about the internment written more than thirty years after the event she tells us:

> The camp experience . . . is an episode in our collective life which wounded us more painfully than we realize. I didn't know myself what a lump it was in my subconscious until a few years ago when I watched one of the earlier television documentaries on the subject, narrated by the mellow voice of Walter Cronkite. To my surprise, I found the tears trickling down my cheeks and my voice squeaking out of control, as I tried to explain to my amazed husband and children why I was weeping. (1976a, 11)[23]

We can also deduce from many a snippet throughout "The Legend" that the cheerful recollections of Kiku and Elsie hardly approximate grim reality. The very first sentence of the story places the dancer against an arid and barren environment: "Even in that unlikely place of wind, sand, and heat, it was easy to imagine Miss Sasagawara a decorative ingredient of some ballet" (20). The climate bodes ill for the physical and mental health of the internees. And one can hardly look to the camp hospital for ready cure. In fact, rather chilling information about its makeshift medical personnel can be gleaned from Kiku's offhand remarks. Introducing

[23] In the same essay Yamamoto points out that in real life there are Japanese Americans who remember the anguish of camp life and those who recall "its carefree joys." She compares the two types by way of an anecdote about a poet and a columnist: "I bring up this [example] to point up a possible clue to the creative personality. Hiroshi Kashiwagi, who remembers the pain, became the poet; and the other fellow, who lays claim to happy memories, has pursued a career centered around athletics" (1976a, 13).

us to "Dr." Moritomo, the first physician to examine Miss Sasagawara, the narrator notes parenthetically that "technically, the title was premature; evacuation had caught him with a few months to go on his degree" (25). The only other doctor who appears in the story is "trembling old Dr. Kawamoto," who, we are told again in a parenthesis, "had retired several years before the war, but he had been drafted here" (26). As for Elsie and Kiku, getting a job in the hospital is merely an alternative to working in the mess hall or with the garbage trucks.

By far the most unbearable feature of camp is the total lack of privacy, though this information is also presented casually, as a matter of fact. The narrator mentions passing in front of the Sasagawara "apartment," which was "really only a cubicle because the once-empty barracks had soon been partitioned off into six units for families of two" (22). We know the exact measurements from Michi Weglyn: "A degree of uniformity existed in the physical makeup of all the [relocation] centers. A bare room measuring 20 feet by 24 feet was . . . referred to as a 'family apartment'; each accommodated a family of five to eight members; barrack end-rooms measuring 16 feet by 20 feet were set aside for smaller families. A barrack was made up of four to six such family units" (84). Weglyn also deplores the absence of privacy in other areas: "Evacuees ate communally, showered communally, defecated communally. . . . No partitions had been built between toilets—a situation which everywhere gave rise to camp-wide cases of constipation. Protests from Caucasian church groups led, in time, to the building of partial dividing walls, but doors were never installed" (80). In this light, Miss Sasagawara's decision to dine and shower alone seems eminently sensible and far from antisocial.

Also implicit in the story is the stockade surrounding these tight private quarters and congested public places. Milton Eisenhower, former War Relocation Authority chief, said in his letter to President Roosevelt: "Life in a relocation center cannot possibly be pleasant. The evacuees are surrounded by barbed wire fences under the eyes of armed military police. . . . [I]t would be amazing if extreme bitterness did not develop" (22 April 1943; quoted in Weglyn 118). One begins to wonder whether the dancer—judged deviant by the community for not behaving "normally" under custody—is any more peculiar than Elsie and Kiku, who cherish their

"good old days" in camp; or than her father, who upon his imprisonment "felt free for the first time in his long life" because, since
"circumstances made it unnecessary for him to earn a competitive
living," he could "concentrate on that serene, eight-fold path of
highest understanding" (32, 33).

Such reconsideration brings us to the outermost layer of the
Chinese box—the political context. As Fredric Jameson has observed, Third World texts "necessarily project a political dimension
in the form of a national allegory" (1986, 69). The politics of the
time not only contributes directly to Miss Sasagawara's distress but
also figures indirectly at the allegorical level of the story. The congestion at camp intensifies the gaze on Miss Sasagawara and accel-
erates the spreading of gossip. As an allegory the scandal-loving
and finger-pointing community has a counterpart in the white majority, who allowed themselves to be swayed by prejudice and
hearsay into endorsing the imprisonment of an entire people. In
the essay on camp literature I quoted earlier, Yamamoto refers
briefly to "The Legend": "Anthologists of this story have com-
mented, 'The author is far less concerned with the social significance of the external environment than with the internal state of
the characters,' and asked, 'Is Miss Sasagawara insane or are those
who accept the life of the camps insane?'" (1976a, 15). That
Yamamoto has chosen to highlight those two points made by com-
mentators is instructive. Their first observation is, I believe, belied
by the answer(s) to their second question—a narrative crux that
connects the "internal state" to the "external environment" and
glues together the realistic and the allegorical dimensions of "The
Legend."

Just as the rumors about Miss Sasagawara accord well with the
stereotype of dancer or spinster, much of the incriminating "evidence" leading to persecution conformed to the ruling culture's
historical prejudice against people of Japanese descent.[24] Elsie's

---

[24] Yogi points out that the two major documents produced by the government to
justify the internment—*Final Report: Japanese Exclusion from the West Coast, 1942*, by
General John L. DeWitt, and the Justice Department's brief in *Hirabayashi v. United
States*—"are grounded in a series of misinterpretations." Japanese-language schools
were thought to be hotbeds of Japanese propaganda, for example, when in fact
most of these schools were conducted by Christian and Buddhist churches for
evangelical purposes. Kibei (nisei raised in Japan) were cited as a possible threat,
though many of these children were sent to Japan to free mothers for family labor.

questionable reading of Miss Sasagawara's vacant expression and Mrs. Sasaki's dubious inference have parallels in the many official misinterpretations of nikkei activities, misinterpretations that built up into what Ronald Takaki calls "the myth of 'military necessity' for Japanese-American internment" (379). J. Edgar Hoover, director of the FBI, noted at the time "that the claim of military necessity for mass evacuation was based 'primarily upon public and political pressure rather than on factual data'" (Takaki 387).

Tendentious information snowballed as rapidly as the gossip about Miss Sasagawara. Official statements to the press, based on assessments later proved inaccurate, "fueled rumors of sabotage committed by Japanese Americans in [Hawaii]—Japanese plantation laborers on Oahu had cut swaths in the sugar cane and pineapple fields to guide the Japanese bombers to the military installations, Japanese had parked cars across highways to block the traffic, and Japanese had given signals to enemy planes." The press, local and state politicians, patriotic organizations, and "voices from farming interests" joined the chorus clamoring for removal of the Japanese (Takaki 380, 389).

Rumors did not cease after Japanese Americans were put behind barbed wire. Weglyn reveals that "among some of the less educated members of the custodial staff . . . there was a pervasive tendency to look down on their charges as an untrustworthy, sinister, and morally inferior lot by the very fact that their incarceration had been deemed necessary" (116–17). She quotes the social analyst Alexander H. Leighton, who conducted a behavioral study of the camp population in Poston at the time:

> In spite of the fact that the FBI was doing a thorough job of security control there were government employees who thought vegetable cellars dug to conserve food because of the heat were caches for Japanese paratroops, who saw kitchen cooks as admirals in disguise and believed athletic teams were Japanese soldiers drilling. (Leighton 279, quoted in Weglyn 117)

DeWitt further implied that Japanese Americans settled in sensitive military areas with possible subversive intentions, though their settlement had been established long before the war. The Justice Department cited the dual citizenship of nisei as grounds to doubt their allegiance to the United States, but nisei were Japanese citizens by heredity rather than by choice (1988, 112–15). For detailed discussions and divergent opinions of the two official documents, see Ogawa 19–22; Sundquist; tenBroek et al. 268–82.

I am not arguing for any simple correspondence between the rumors enveloping the dancer and those hovering over nikkei at large, but I believe that "The Legend" goes well beyond an individual tragedy and that its many indirect political allusions press us to reinterpret the reports associated with Miss Sasagawara. Her hypersensitivity to being spied upon not only mirrors the wartime hysteria and paranoia of the white majority but also reflects back on the plight of her whole ethnic group. Her visibility and susceptibility to scrutiny bespeak the nikkei predicament during World War II, which drastically sharpened the external gaze on this Asian minority.[25] The community's assumption of Miss Sasagawara's pathology echoes the government's speculation that many nikkei on the West Coast could be devious spies. The isolation and eventual institutionalization of Miss Sasagawara correspond to the exclusion and ultimate detention of the race.

But the communal finger-pointing in camp must itself be seen in the context of the policing politics of the government. Historical circumstances turned nikkei into mutual informers. In an atmosphere of constant surveillance, informers issued inflammatory reports that led to false arrest and seclusion. Weglyn notes that as the drab conditions persisted despite protests, the "passive forbearance" of some internees shifted to "angry militancy" (116). Many of the so-called troublemakers—dissidents who used threats and violence against the informers or who simply publicized their disaffection with the government—were arrested without trial and imprisoned in highly guarded camps, notably Camp Moab (Utah) and Leupp Isolation Center (Arizona) (see Weglyn 121–28). "By a peculiar morality of the time in regard to the 'Japanese,'" Weglyn observes, "the traditional presumption of innocence was conveniently transformed into a presumption of guilt" (128). Judged by the patriarchal mores of the time, Miss Sasagawara, too, will always appear aberrant no matter what she does. The community's treatment of her echoes "the often capricious and arbitrary manner in which citizen dissidents were seized and isolated" by the government (Weglyn 126).

The arbitrariness was made abundantly clear by Paul G. Robertson, who was sent to administer the Leupp Isolation Center and

[25] Foucault uses the analogy of Panopticon, a model prison designed by Jeremy Bentham, to describe relentless surveillance, whereby "visibility is a trap" (1979, 200).

"saw no reason why eighty inmates had to be guarded by 150 armed troops," noting that most of the men "were not incorrigible at all." In time he "learned to like all of these fellows"; one became his gardener and "stayed with [his] children on numerous occasions. He wasn't in the least bit dangerous" (quoted in Weglyn 128–29).

Kiku similarly encourages second thoughts about the dancer's alleged lunacy. Estrangement by the internees has made Miss Sasagawara feel so much like a criminal that she tries to reassure young children: " 'Don't be afraid of me. I won't hurt you' " (28). During the most extensive meeting between Kiku and the dancer—"the only time [they] really exchanged words"—Miss Sasagawara, who "welcomed Kiku with a smile," seems most engaging and almost jovial. Upon hearing Kiku recount her sorry attempts with the violin, "Miss Sasagawara laughed aloud—a lovely sound" (28)—and told Kiku about her own experience with the Spanish guitar. In this firsthand encounter with the dancer, there is no hint of derangement at all.

Given the political circumstances, we may also modify our judgment of Reverend Sasagawara, whose insensitivity to his daughter parallels the government's callousness toward its citizens (who made up two-thirds of the internees). But the parallel here is far from clear-cut. The Reverend, silent almost throughout the text, is no less enigmatic than his daughter. If his Buddhism seems to align him with the masculine side of "Western" binary thinking, which places spirit (masculine) above body (feminine), as an "Eastern" religion it also constitutes a form of cultural resistance against the religious patronage of the dominant culture. During the "Block Christmas party," for instance, each child receives an "eleemosynary package" sent by "Church people outside," whom "every recipient must write and thank" (29).[26] While Christmas is openly observed in camp, the Reverend must confine his own worship to his tiny room. As a well-known priest in the Japanese American community, he would have been among the first arrested and interrogated after the bombing of Pearl Harbor. The government also

---

[26] Barbara Rodriguez points out in her dissertation (in progress, Harvard University) how humiliating such a requirement must be. I am indebted to her for the observation.

encouraged nisei to keep an eye on these "suspicious" characters in camp. (The dancer, as the Reverend's daughter, is therefore understandably wary of watchful eyes.)[27] Far from being a privileged patriarch, this father is himself subject to discriminatory legislation. His determination to achieve spiritual perfection may be a form of compensation for the travails he has encountered in the New World, where he is branded as a suspicious alien.[28] Unfortunately, in turning to religious absolutes, in blocking out the emotional needs of his daughter, he too becomes a virtual tyrant.

The father's obsessive spirituality is generally regarded as "beyond censure." Only Marie Sasagawara is aware of *his* madness, and even she frames her charge indirectly, through her poem, and most tentatively: "The poet . . . could only speak for herself" (33). The contrast with Mr. Hayashi's attitude toward his wife in "Seventeen Syllables" is striking: Mrs. Hayashi's engagement with poetry is perceived as an avoidance of domestic responsibilities and as an abnormal obsession ("Your mother's crazy"). In one story the father's spiritual pursuit is sanctified; in the other, the mother's artistic pursuit is vilified. One begins to see "madness" as defined largely by deviance from patriarchal norms.

In the face of the triple occlusion of Miss Sasagawara—as a daughter by her father, as a single woman by the community, and as a member of a persecuted people by the government—she exhibits perhaps the only appropriate response to the situation; her "madness" is also a flight from the crazy circumstances. Miss Sasagawara's poem, which challenges our earlier perceptions of madness and saintliness, aberration and innocence, should also make us wonder who was the guilty party during those "years of infamy" (Weglyn) when Japanese Americans became "the victims of gossip, their own and the nation's" (Chan et al. 1981, 29).

[27] I thank Brian Niiya for suggesting this point. For a biographical account of the travails of a Japanese American Buddhist priest during World War II, see Matsuura.

[28] The title character of Yamamoto's "Las Vegas Charley" is another father who ostensibly welcomes camp life, though it has left him handicapped: "He would be quite content to remain in this camp the rest of his life—free food, free housing. . . . It was true that he had partially lost his hearing in one ear, from standing by those hot stoves on days of unbearable heat, but that was a small complaint. The camp hospital had provided free treatment, free medicines, free cotton balls to stuff in his bad ear" ([1961] 1988, 80). The two fathers' attachment to camp provides a telling indictment of life "outside."

The use of naive narrators in "Seventeen Syllables" and "Yoneko's Earthquake" alerts us directly to the limited point of view in those two stories. "The Legend" replicates the gripping power of rumors well before it reveals their dubiousness. By constantly shifting our attitudes toward the title character and by giving her the last word via the poem, Yamamoto piques the conscience of any reader too ready to accept tendentious reports and pronounce judgment. The skepticism that she brings to "The Legend," particularly her interrogation of sources, finds insistent echoes in Kingston and Kogawa.

"The Legend" tells us much about the intricate relationship between poetics and politics and prods us to engage more critically with existing theories on women's writing. In terms of the palimpsest strategies discussed earlier, this tale is thrice muted: there is neither direct confrontation with the father nor explicit criticism of the nikkei community nor open protest against the American government. Its involuted presentation of gender and race bears comparison with Charlotte Perkins Gilman's "Yellow Wallpaper." Both stories treat female suppression and repression indirectly. In Gilman's tale a physician husband's implicit faith in science objectifies his wife and stifles her imagination till she loses touch with reality. Reverend Sasagawara's spiritual discipline similarly unhinges his daughter. The attic in which the doctor confines his wife, however, is commodious in comparison with the Sasagawaras' cubicle. The dancer must either remain in close proximity to her father—a situation that may have driven her insane in all senses of the word—or expose herself to the prying eyes of a community thirsty for sensationalism to relieve its boredom. Though both the physician husband and the Buddhist father mean well, in their single-minded pursuits they fail utterly to heed the needs of their female companions. Madness becomes the only release for both women—to unleash imagination in one instance and to escape the confinement of "Buddhist idealism" in the other (McDonald & Newman 28).

At the same time, both stories also conceal unsettling references to contemporary politics of color. Susan Lanser has called attention to the long-overlooked adjective in Gilman's title: "In California, where Gilman lived while writing 'The Yellow Wallpaper,' mass anxiety about the 'Yellow Peril' had already yielded such legislation as the Chinese Exclusion Act of 1882" (1989, 425). She then asks provocatively: "Is the wallpaper, then, the political unconscious of a culture in which an Aryan woman's madness . . . [is] projected onto the 'yellow' woman who is, however, also the feared alien?" (428–29). Lanser has cautioned earlier that hers may be an "over-reading" (424), insofar as the implications about race are completely subdued in the text. Yamamoto's allusions to white racist hysteria are so muffled that she is charged with ignoring the "external environment." My "overreading" suggests, on the contrary, that the dancer's psychological condition is precisely bound up with the spatial configuration of the story. The claustrophobic surroundings lend an ironical note to the reason given by Miss Sasagawara for remaining single: "she said she wasn't sorry she never got married, because . . . she got to go all over the country a couple of times, dancing in the ballet" (21). Artistic movement is here coupled with the freedom to travel; both are curtailed in the cubicle, the hospital, the camp, and, finally, the state institution.[29]

Why did Yamamoto camouflage the political allusions? Probing an author's intentions is perilous business and is at best speculative. I will merely venture that Yamamoto herself may have felt the pressure of personal, communal, and societal censorship. As I suggested earlier, Yamamoto—a talented writer drilled in nisei etiquette—may have projected her own "anxiety of authorship" (à la Gilbert and Gubar's *Madwoman in the Attic*) onto Mari Sasagawara, dancer and poet.[30] But we must also consider an even greater anxiety peculiar to the nisei writer. The odds against a Japanese American woman writer shortly after the war were long, especially against one who dared to treat the sensitive subject of internment,

[29] Mary Douglas's insight about the "two bodies" strikes a chord here: "The social body constrains the way the physical body is perceived" (93). As a medium of expression, Miss Sasagawara's body is restricted, literally, by the social body of the community and the state.

[30] Yamamoto has more than once diagnosed herself as "abnormal." As I mentioned earlier, for a while she adopted the pseudonym Napoleon avowedly "as an apology for [her] little madness." She also credits her hiring as a reporter by the *Los Angeles Tribune,* a black weekly, to her peculiar temperament: " I think personality-wise they saw I was just as neurotic as they were and Bean Takeda [a fellow applicant] was probably too normal" (Blauvelt 19). Here she seems to refer specifically to her anxiety as a member of a racial minority.

not to mention a treatment that impugned the community and the government. Reliving that experience through writing was in itself taxing. As Yamamoto has noted, "looking over the whole of Japanese American creative literature . . . we will find the Nisei writer choosing not to dwell on his camp experience. Perhaps this was all to the good, for his own health and well being" (1976a, 12). For over a decade after the war, Japanese Americans on the whole wished to present a positive image to the larger society that had found reason to incarcerate them. Out of concern for public opinion, they were likely to frown on writers who uncovered cracks in the ethnic circle or who challenged white racism. John Okada's *No-No Boy*, a novel that did both, was rejected by the Japanese American and the white community alike when it was first published, in 1957.[31] Before that time, nisei who wanted to vent their anger and bitterness openly would be hard pressed even to find a forum, since white publishers were generally reluctant to issue stories that explicitly challenged the dominant culture. Here Yamamoto's narrative elusiveness may have stood her in good stead. Like Miss Sasagawara's poem, "The Legend"—which weaves together a particular tale about human passion and saintly impassivity, a feminist critique of conventional gender expectations (defining who is normal and who is not), and a political allegory of racial prejudice and persecution—is "erratically brilliant and . . . tantalizingly obscure" (32) upon first reading. The external setting seems no more than an incidental backdrop to a personal memoir about an intriguing figure. Not once do the barbs of the author's covert social commentary puncture the smooth narrative surface. It is by orchestrating telltale details, eroding narrative authority, and encoding volatile political material in allegory that the author criticizes the ethnic community and the larger society for their intolerance of difference and for their mechanisms of exclusion. Meanwhile, the buoyant description of camp life may well have deflected the censorious gaze of white editors (cf. Solzhenitsyn's *Cancer Ward* and *One Day in the Life of Ivan Denisovich*).

Cultural and sociological considerations form an inalienable part

---

[31] "No-no boys" were nisei who refused induction into the armed forces. The phrase comes from answers put on the so-called loyalty questionnaire conducted among internees in conjunction with an army recruitment drive.

of aesthetic judgments. The interlocking of thematic and strategic silence in Yamamoto's fiction should make us rethink the debate on the distinction between literature and social history, between aesthetics and politics (see, for example, Kolodny 1975, Jehlen). Because the relationship between life and art is here as elsewhere indirect, these texts demand and deserve meticulous close reading. Only by anchoring them culturally and historically, however, can we fully disclose the author's formally complex design and the layers of emotions embedded in her ellipses.

3

Provocative Silence:
The Woman Warrior and *China Men*

> For Macherey, a work is tied to ideology not so much by what
> it says as by what it does not say. It is in the significant
> *silences* of a text, in its gaps and absences that the presence of
> ideology can be most positively felt.
>
> Terry Eagleton, *Marxism and Literary Criticism*

> Truth is undoubtedly the sort of error that cannot be refuted
> because it was hardened into an unalterable form in the long
> baking process of history.
>
> Michel Foucault, *Language, Counter-memory, Practice*

> Haunted by the voices and images that violated us, bearing
> the pains of the past, we are slowly acquiring the tools to
> change the disabling images and memories, to replace them
> with self-affirming ones, to recreate our pasts and alter
> them—for the past can be as malleable as the present.
>
> Gloria Anzaldúa, *Making Face, Making Soul*

Of the three authors analyzed in this book, Maxine Hong Kingston most openly reveals her feminist leanings. The feminist topos
of imposed silence, distrust of received knowledge, and multivocality find ardent expression in *The Woman Warrior* and *China
Men*. At the same time, the braiding of gender and ethnicity in
these texts produces an unusually resonant double-voiced discourse, one that upsets the opposition between women and men,
East and West, fable and fact, orality and chirography, talking and
listening, (re)vision and history.[1]

In Kingston's work, as in Yamamoto's and Kogawa's, silence

[1] Maxine Hong Kingston was born in Stockton, California, in 1940. She was
graduated from the University of California, Berkeley, in 1962, and currently teaches at Berkeley. Her publications include *The Woman Warrior* (1976), winner of the
National Book Critics Circle Award for nonfiction; *China Men* (1980), winner of the
National Book Award for nonfiction; *Hawai'i One Summer* (1987), a series of prose
sketches; and *Tripmaster Monkey* (1989), her first novel. Because the issues raised in
the novel are quite different from those that link Kingston's first two books of
(auto)biographical fiction, I've chosen not to treat *Tripmaster Monkey* in this chapter.

takes numerous forms. In *The Woman Warrior* we find it in the hushed disappointment attendant upon the birth of girls, in the expunging of the narrator's wayward aunt from family history, in the narrator's inability to speak a second language, in her choked-back anger at sexist maxims, in her impotent words against white bosses, and in her drawn-out illness incurred by self-hatred at being an inarticulate Chinese American. In *China Men* it extends beyond the exclusion of women to signify both the literal silencing of Chinese male laborers in Hawaii and the symbolic erasure of men of Chinese descent from mainstream American history.

Historical silences, for the most part, cannot be retrieved. For Kingston such intolerable absence provokes a telling that does not attempt to restore what is lost. Instead she amplifies the glaring omissions, provides what Fredric Jameson describes as "symbolic resolutions of real political and social contradictions" (1981, 80), and forges what Edouard Glissant calls "a prophetic vision of the past":

> The past, to which we were subjected, which has not yet emerged as history for us, is, however, obsessively present. The duty of the writer is to explore this obsession, *to show its relevance in a continuous fashion to the immediate present*. This exploration is therefore related neither to a schematic chronology nor to a nostalgic lament. (63–64; my emphasis)

The very silence that hobbles the chronicler enables the creative writer to dispense with time-honored authority and invent a braver world. Kingston's narrative strategies, which vary with the shades of silence in her texts, exemplify historical and revisionist impulses. Her "vision of the past" is, as it were, profoundly inlaid with the present.[2]

Unlike the elliptical style of Yamamoto, which answers to her theme of repression, Kingston's language seems anything but

[2] This double impulse accords well with Monique Wittig's feminist advice: "Make an effort to remember. Or, failing that, invent" (89). But such invention further questions our traditional notion of "history." According to Robert G. Lee, "Kingston's *Woman Warrior*, with its claim to autobiographical and thus historical status, at once demanded that new terrains of Chinese American history be explored and subverted the conventions of authenticity by which that history was to be framed" (52).

muffled. In fact, her works have all too often been read as factual testimony. As a result, the slippery and variable subject positions that underlie her polyphonic texts often escape the eyes of critics. Leslie W. Rabine and Stephen H. Sumida are notable exceptions. Rabine notes that *The Woman Warrior* is structured in a double and simultaneous movement, containing "the voice of a writer who in a certain sense has already returned to write about her people . . . but who writes as the girl who cannot return" (477–78). Sumida suggests that Kingston's autobiography is perhaps "a work of 'fiction' in which the author uses a 'naive' if not 'unreliable' narrator . . . whose very misunderstandings or misappropriations . . . of 'Chinese' history and culture are part of the author's critical characterization of her and of a narrow 'American' society which alienates her from seeing truly" (1989, 154). We shall see that there is more than one reason for what Sumida calls "misappropriations," and that the narrative strategies themselves contradict the narrator's explicit assertions.

Critics commonly approach *The Woman Warrior* as a "feminist" text and *China Men* as an "ethnic" text. What Malini Schueller calls the "conjuncture and relationship between female and ethnic identity" and Kingston's "dialogic subversions" (421) inform not only *The Woman Warrior*, as Schueller has demonstrated, but also *China Men*. While an explicitly antipatriarchal strain—directed most vocally against the Chinese immigrant community—constitutes the dominant chord in *The Woman Warrior*, a muted strain indicts the monocultural criteria of white America. The reverse strategy seems to be operating in *China Men*. This book, relatively ignored by feminist critics, is seen by several Asian American scholars as an attempt to reinstate Chinese partriarchy.[3] Kingston does quite the opposite. Much as she seeks to give voice to those male ancestors silenced by white history, she tacitly exposes patriarchal abuses by drawing parallels between the degradation of

---

[3] Linda Ching Sledge writes, "The ideal of family continuity gives these men strength to win at arduous 'epic' tests of manhood. The traditional authority ascribed to male family members gives them a core of selfhood allowing them to withstand danger and defeat" (5). Alfred S. Wang goes further when he compares the male characters in *China Men* to "the heroes in Chinese popular culture—Guan Goong, Liu Pei, and Chang Fei," and calls these characters "Maxine Hong Kingston's *Men Warriors par excellence*" (27).

Chinese men in white America and the suppression of women in traditional Chinese society. To read either text as espousing exclusively feminist or ethnic sensibility is to disregard Kingston's skillful orchestration of a compounded double-voiced discourse. This multivocality reflects her disaffection from both Chinese and white American patriarchy and her engagement as a minority woman with two "subcultures."

The tendency to read these texts as pure ethnography, rather than as self-conscious narratives that answer to provocative silences, has sparked protracted debate among Asian American critics concerning "authenticity."[4] Kingston has been accused of reinforcing racist stereotypes and of falsifying Chinese myths and history. The failure to discern her shifting point of view and deliberate fusion of fictive and empirical incidents not only eclipses the author's artistry but obscures the very "truths" her texts convey. The author emphatically resists the opposition of fact and imagination in the face of received falsehood and historical silence. She achieves feminist dialogic by integrating biography and poetics, and by re-visioning Chinese myths and mythologizing American history.

Two primary forms of double-voiced discourse infuse *The Woman Warrior* and *China Men*. Kingston renders the overlay of feminist and ethnic consciousness by sliding back and forth between a primary and secondary point of view, thereby unleashing internal contradictions. And by amalgamating fact and fable she is able to reproduce her struggle for cognition as well as to re-place the "history" of her people. "The blending of these narrative categories," Roberta Rubenstein observes, "not only results in the unique form of *The Woman Warrior* but also dramatically reflects the narrator's confusion of those realms in her actual experience" (169). Such blending, no less pervasive in *China Men*, further enables the narrator to expose the silences of history, unmask its distortions, and map out prospects for change. The two forms of double-voicing often work contiguously. In *The Woman Warrior*, for instance, the antifemale prejudice of the Chinese immigrant community and the narrator's internalization of the perspective of the dominant culture have produced a narrative that seems predominantly anti-

---

[4] On the vexing issue of ethnic authenticity, see Trinh 1989, 89–97, and Woo.

Chinese. Yet the structure of the book—reflecting the sensibility of an author older and wiser—undercuts the "truth" of the narrator's explicit statements by revealing her profound indebtedness to her Chinese American legacy. In both works, the narrator ultimately fractures Chinese and white American orthodoxies to make room for renewed gender and ethnic identities and for sexual, racial, and international politics grounded in reciprocity rather than in domination.

The Woman Warrior: Memoirs of a Girlhood among Ghosts

> At first she asked questions, being curious. But her father did not like questions. He said that one was not supposed to talk when one was either eating or thinking, and when one was not eating, one should be thinking. Only when in bed did one neither eat nor think.
> Jade Snow Wong, *Fifth Chinese Daughter*

> If you don't talk, you can't have a personality.
> Maxine Hong Kingston, *The Woman Warrior*

Asian American intellectuals have endlessly debated the "authenticity" of *The Woman Warrior*. Those who attack Kingston for blurring the line between reality and fantasy seem unmindful of the narrator's insistent admissions of her own penchant for fabrication and her inability to discern fact from fiction.[5] Even those on

[5] In a scathing parody of *The Woman Warrior* Frank Chin casts aspersions on its ethnographic status and places Kingston in the same company as the creators of Fu Manchu and Charlie Chan for confirming "the white fantasy that everything sick and sickening about the white self-image is really Chinese" (1984, 12). Jeffery Paul Chan castigates Knopf for publishing the book as "biography rather than fiction (which it obviously is)" (1977, 41). Benjamin R. Tong calls it a "fashionably feminist work written with white acceptance in mind" (1977, 20). Granted that much of the negative criticism has been generated by the classification of *The Woman Warrior* as autobiography, most scholars of the genre do recognize the constant traffic between self-representation and fiction. Diane Johnson writes, "Fiction and memoir have come to resemble each other more and more. Novelists make real historical figures speak to fictional characters. Memorialists dramatize the thoughts and speeches of their forefathers, as in a novel about them. The access of the autobiographer to dramatic techniques has allowed him to handle root meanings, the mysterious crises of spirit, even the intangibles of heritage, more essentially—that is, more truly—than he once could" (1982, 4). See also Eakin.

the author's side tend to defend her autobiography on the ethnographic ground that the narrator's experience accords well with
their own. Kingston, vexed by the anthropological approach to the
book, protests: "After all, I am not writing history or sociology but
a 'memoir' like Proust" (1982, 64). Subtitled *Memoirs of a Girlhood
among Ghosts*, *The Woman Warrior* is told mostly though not exclusively from the point of view of a confused female adolescent. I
believe that the work, insofar as it can be construed as mimetic,
mirrors not objective truth but the subjective experience of an
imaginative girl growing up as a member of a racial minority amid
conflicting imperatives. What Terry Eagleton says of writers in general is particularly true of the narrator of *The Woman Warrior*, who
"in trying to tell the truth in [her] own way . . . reveal[s] the limits
of the ideology within which [she] writes" (35). Maxine—a young
girl caught between an immigrant Cantonese culture that deni-
grates daughters and another culture that insists on a single given
(white) standard of femininity, beauty, and intelligence—is at
every turn blind to the ideological forces that shape her perceptions. The full-fledged author knows better.[6] By counterpoising the
partial and provisional perspectives of young Maxine with the author's adult insights, Kingston creates an "autobiography" that
chronicles the psychological development of an artist.

On the most obvious level, the development is from silence to
voice, a journey I have charted in detail elsewhere (1988). Here I
am more concerned with Maxine's cognitive struggle and the narrative strategies that replicate that struggle. Her epistemological
trajectory, which seems to eschew ethnicity in a move toward assimilation, is nevertheless punctuated by a series of oscillating
identifications with "abnormal" (ostracized, mute, demented) Chinese women and with celebrated Chinese heroines. These women,
placed as they are at opposite ends of the Chinese social scale, are
perhaps most like Maxine, who is on the margins of both Chinese
and American worlds. The narrator progresses eventually from
being buffeted by opposing cultural ideologies to blazing a syn-
cretic trail of her own.

The author's dialogic vision informs her chronicle of the phases
undergone by Maxine. Kingston combats patriarchal and mono-

---

[6] See n. 8 of my Introduction for the distinction between Maxine and Kingston.

cultural "truths" by introducing contradictory axioms and by undercutting Maxine's pronouncements with her own manner of telling. Her ploys are reminiscent of those tactics that feminist critics have associated with women's writing generally: the appropriation and subversion of dominant discourse (in Alice Jardine's words, the choice "to assume the symbolic armor, to name the law and attack it using the same laws" [231]) and the recourse to what Janis Stout calls "strategies of reticence." The first ploy is to declare open warfare: explicit protests, mythic revisioning, blatant defiance of traditional precepts. The second is to engage in guerrilla tactics—irony, indirection, and understatement—to vitiate the assertions in the text.

Kingston uses these feminist strategies against racism as well as sexism. She wages open warfare against Chinese patriarchy; her guerrilla tactics unveil oppressive monocultural practices in white America. The different maneuvers reflect the perceptual distance between young Maxine and the veteran writer. Maxine is much more aware of the antifemale prejudice of her family and community than of the cultural bias of the larger society. But the author who reproduces young Maxine's feelings calls attention to the shaping of those feelings by Anglo-American ideology. In this particular configuration of gender and race the double-voiced discourse noted in women's writing is transposed: the feminist voice—directed most vehemently against Chinese patriarchy—governs the dominant plot, while the critique of white norms is tucked into the margins of the text.[7]

Maxine finds herself baffled early on by her mother's China and by monocultural America. It is taxing to sort out what is traditionally Chinese and what is peculiar to her family: "Chinese-Americans, when you try to understand what things in you are Chinese, how do you separate what is peculiar to childhood, to poverty, insanities, one family, your mother who marked your growing with stories, from what is Chinese? What is Chinese tradi-

---

[7] Kingston may have muffled her criticism of the dominant culture for political as well as artistic reasons. Like Yamamoto, whose subtle telling of "The Legend" seems to reflect in part her sensitivity to the white gaze, Kingston, in writing *The Woman Warrior*—her first book—may be wary of the eyes of mainstream publishers. In *China Men* and *Tripmaster Monkey* she is much more open in denouncing overt and covert racism.

tion and what is the movies?" (5–6). Adding to her confusion is the habit of her mother, Brave Orchid, to dispense with the distinction between fact and fiction and select only what she considers to be the "useful parts" (6) in telling a story (so that the daughter must fill in the details with her imagination).

In kindergarten Maxine discovers the cost of becoming an American girl. ("American" is always synonymous with "non-Asian" or "un-Asian" in Maxine's usage.) The cost is silence:

> When I went to kindergarten and had to speak English for the first time, I became silent. . . . It was when I found out I had to talk that school became a misery, that the silence became a misery. . . . I read aloud in first grade, though, and heard the barest whisper with little squeaks come out of my throat. "Louder," said the teacher, who scared the voice away again. The other Chinese girls did not talk either, so I knew the silence had to do with being a Chinese girl. (165–66)

Even Maxine's loquacious mother fails to loosen her daughter's tongue. Brave Orchid claims that she cuts Maxine's frenum to enable her tongue "to move in any language" (164). Maxine instead imputes her inarticulateness to this act of mutilation.[8]

Kingston, however, suggests another reason for Maxine's problem: to be Chinese and a girl in American schools leaves one tonguetied. While Brave Orchid teaches her daughter by dosing her with dollops of fantastic detail, Maxine's American teacher calibrates her students with intelligence tests. Unable to speak English, Maxine is accorded a "zero IQ." She responds with a form of self-obliteration:

> My silence was thickest—total—during the three years that I covered my school paintings with black paint. I painted layers of black over houses and flowers and suns, and when I drew on the blackboard, I put a layer of chalk on top. I was making a stage curtain, and it was the moment before the curtain parted or rose. The teachers called my parents to school, and I saw they had been saving my pictures, curling and cracking, all alike and black. The teachers pointed to the pictures and looked serious, talked seriously too, but my parents did

[8] This episode, which cunningly ascribes verbal facility and difficulty to the same origins, forms a part of the larger artistic fabric spun out of crisscrossing strands.

not understand English. ("The parents and teachers of criminals were executed," said my father.) My parents took the pictures home. I spread them out (so black and full of possibilities) and pretended the curtains were swinging open, flying up, one after another, sunlight underneath, mighty operas. (165)

The passage juggles several contradictory speaking positions. First there is the bipolar consciousness of the child monitoring at once her own exuberant imagination and the negative judgment passed on her. The blackness of her pictures, vividly conceived by the child as "stage curtains," is seen by the teachers as the dark evidence of her total inability to communicate.

With parents unable to defend her against the cultural bias of intelligence tests, the child accepts the verdict and, in line with her histrionic disposition, seriously casts herself as "criminal." As she grows older she shifts the blame to her family and ethnic origin: "The only reason I flunked kindergarten was because you couldn't teach me English, and you gave me a zero IQ" (201). But the author subverts this denunciation by implying that the onus rests upon an American educational system that refuses to acknowledge bicultural identity.[9] Without any comment, she depicts the transformation of silenced bodies at the Chinese school:

> After American school, we . . . went to Chinese school. . . . There we chanted together, voices rising and falling, loud and soft, some boys shouting, everybody reading together . . . and not alone with one voice. When we had a memorization test, the teacher let each of us come to his desk and say the lesson to him privately. . . . The girls were not mute. They screamed and yelled during recess. (167)

The Chinese girls' rambunctiousness in Chinese school contradicts Maxine's inference that "silence had to do with being a Chinese girl." While Chinese culture admittedly does not generally encourage vocal behavior among the young, Maxine's confusion stems from *differences* in cultural evaluations of silence. The American schoolteachers perceive her silence as ineptitude, but the Chinese

[9] See Gould for a wholesale exposé of IQ tests. Richard Rodriguez tells us in his autobiography, *Hunger of Memory,* that he was similarly diagnosed as a problem student. Mike Rose, in *Lives on the Boundary,* shows that many monocultural educational standards persist to this day.

mentor in her fantasy cautions against speech: "The first thing you have to learn . . . is how to be quiet. . . . If you're noisy, you'll make the deer go without water" (23). Not that orthodox Chinese teaching is always obeyed in practice. Cantonese are, in fact, quite notorious for being noisy: "They turn the radio up full blast to hear the operas. . . . And they yell over the singers that wail over the drums, everybody talking at once, big arm gestures, spit flying" (171). Maxine describes her own mother as a "champion talker" (202).[10] Thus it is at least as much American as Chinese gender expectations that induce female inhibition. "Normal Chinese women's voices are strong and bossy," the narrator tells us. "We American-Chinese girls had to whisper to make ourselves American-feminine" (172).

Maxine's understanding of "American-feminine" decorum is echoed by Robin Lakoff, who argues that an American girl who "talks rough" will normally be scolded, and a girl who expresses herself tentatively will be greeted with social disdain: "So a girl is damned if she does, damned if she doesn't" (5–6). Surely not China alone but white America as well poses a double bind for the narrator. Lakoff goes on to describe a woman who learns to "switch from women's to neutral language under appropriate situations (in class, talking to professors, at job interviews)" and compares her with bilinguals: "Like many bilinguals, she may never really be master of either language, though her command of both is adequate enough for most purposes. . . . Shifting from one language to another requires special awareness to the nuances of social situations, special alertness to possible disapproval" (6–7).[11]

The implied challenge of being doubly bilingual—metaphori-

---

[10] As Sledge has noted, "Cantonese women were forced to assume total family governance after the emigration of male villagers to foreign lands. Thus, there arose a strong tradition of womanly self-sufficiency and aggressiveness among Cantonese. Kingston shows the persistence of that tradition among those few Chinese women, like the mother, who were allowed to enter the U.S. during the lengthy period of exclusion" (9–10).

[11] I disagree with Lakoff on two points, however. First, I object to her privileging of "neutral language," which smacks of monological scientific discourse. Second, I find her evaluation of bilinguals condescending. As we shall see, Kingston herself draws upon her bilingual heritage to forge a unique style and vision. See also Yaeger's discussion of "bilingualism" as one of the feminist "transgressive practices" (35–76).

cally as a woman and literally as a pupil grappling with two disparate languages—impedes Maxine's speech. The narrator recalls:

> Reading out loud was easier than speaking . . . but I stopped often, and the teacher would think I'd gone quiet again. I could not understand "I." The Chinese "I" has seven strokes, intricacies. How could the American "I," assuredly wearing a hat like the Chinese, have only three strokes, the middle so straight? Was it out of politeness that this writer left off strokes the way a Chinese has to write her own name small and crooked? No, it was not politeness; "I" is a capital and "you" is lower-case. I stared at that middle line and waited so long for its black center to resolve into tight strokes and dots that I forgot to pronounce it. (166–67)

The thoughtful child is punished for her repeated failures in pronunciation. To her mind the difference between the two words for the first-person pronoun goes beyond phonetics to self-definition; it is a choice between seeing oneself as singular and as relational.[12] Her confusions over cultural, linguistic, and gender identity leave her speaking from both "I's." Though her narrative insinuates an increasing alienation from her Chinese self, this is the self she reconstructs through fantasy.

The narrator declares open warfare against her Chinese female identity throughout the book, yet one can also detect, in the margins of the text, the author's resistance against the Americanizing imperatives that threaten to quash a ripe imagination. Behind the black curtains are Maxine's own yarns "twisted into designs" (163); she usurps her mother's methods to embellish her own "useful parts." As Sidonie Smith observes, she "reads herself into existence through the stories her culture tells about women" (151). The stories become her pre-texts for "self-invention" (Eakin).

This strategy is most evident in the opening chapter, about the nameless aunt in China who killed herself and her illegitimate baby after being humiliated by villagers. Since the narrator's father explicitly forbids any mention of the aunt and the mother furnishes only the bare facts, Maxine is free to construct variant versions of the aunt's story. Critics have credited Kingston with giving her

---

[12] See Kondo 26–33 for parallel differences between Japanese and American notions about selves.

aunt subjectivity through these versions. But in fact, her aunt—who could not possibly inhabit all these versions—remains inescapably silent. This haunting silence is precisely what gives wings to the niece's imagination, allowing Maxine to test her own power to talk story and to play with different identities. Not the aunt's but the narrator's subjectivity is unfurled.

Yet the narrator paradoxically casts her self-fashioning act as one of ancestor worship: "I alone devoted pages of paper to her, though not origamied into houses and clothes" (16). By recalling the Chinese custom she draws attention to her radical subversion of the traditional ceremony, one predicated upon filial piety. First, to mention the aunt at all is to violate the paternal edict. Second, to claim the aunt as her "forerunner" (8) is to supplant patrilineage with matrilineage (Rabine)—generated, moreover, by rebellion rather than obedience. Third, while one's ancestors are supposed to act beneficently, Maxine—as though to compensate for the No Name Woman's powerlessness during her life—imagines her aunt as a vengeful ghost: "She was a spite suicide, drowning herself in the drinking water. The Chinese are always very frightened of the drowned one, whose weeping ghost . . . waits silently by the water to pull down a substitute" (16). Finally, in place of origamied objects the narrator offers pages of her own writing, appropriating a textual privilege that has been predominantly male. Containing her own words rather than inherited scripts, these pages herald a new—Chinese American—tradition.

This conscious mutation of Chinese tradition is a hallmark of Kingston, who has declared her unwillingness to stick to the original and her desire to approximate a flexible oral tradition. Against charges that she has adulterated Chinese lore, Kingston replies: "We have to do more than record myth. . . . That's just more ancestor worship. The way I keep the old Chinese myths alive is by telling them in a new American way" (Pfaff 26). Instead of reading her text as ethnography, one must harken to her vested telling—one aimed precisely at dismantling traditional authority.

Such elastic telling, according to Kingston, has the further advantage of recovering orality: "The oral stories change from telling to telling. It changes according to the needs of the listener, according to the needs of the day, the interest of the time, so that the story can be different from day to day. . . . Writing is static. . . . What would be wonderful would be for the words to change on the page every time, but they can't. The way I tried to solve this problem was to keep ambiguity in the writing all the time" (Islas 18). Yet I believe the author does more than merely replicate the oral tradition: even as she claims its methodology she subverts it through writing. No matter how malleable the oral tradition, at any given time only one telling can occur. In the narrator's retelling of the aunt's story, contradictory versions exist side by side, undermining the oral version transmitted by Brave Orchid. Tapping both oral and literary traditions, Kingston's writing challenges the authority of both.

Traditional authority can retain its hold under a different guise, however. At times the scenarios presented by the narrator risk replicating or merely reversing the patriarchal order of binary opposition, and her deliberate subversion turns into what Julia Kristeva calls "counterinvestment" (1981, 24). Much as Maxine tries to break away from patriarchal strictures, she is repeatedly caught in the "law of the same" (to use Luce Irigaray's phrase in a different context), confusing sameness with equality. Her fantasy about the woman warrior, though a form of imaginary battle against patriarchy, also consigns her to the "master's tools." In envisioning herself as the traditional swordswoman Fa Mu Lan, Maxine assumes the male armor literally and symbolically: Maxine-as-warrior not only masquerades as a male soldier but derives power from the words carved on her back by her parents.

Both the thrills and the chills of appropriating patriarchal authority are attendant upon the warrior's adventure. On the one hand, the fantasy allows young Maxine to envisage herself as a self-made heroine and to escape from the unpleasant reality of growing up in a family that verbally devalues daughters with sayings such as "Girls are maggots in the rice" and "It is more profitable to raise geese than daughters" (43). More than simply invoking a traditional legend told her by her mother, Maxine projects her own desires onto the warrior. Whereas the original legend celebrates filial piety, Maxine's fantasy elaborates upon the warrior's military prowess, sexual exploits, and triumphant vengeance. Furthermore, unlike her prototype, Fa Mu Lan, who is not known to have been tattooed, Maxine-as-warrior has magical words etched onto her back. Since military, sexual, and verbal power are traditionally male prerogatives, the fantasy opens Maxine to unconventional ways of asserting herself.

On the other hand, the self-empowering fantasy is also self-defeating, attesting to the tenacity of patriarchal norms. Like the female writer who must adopt a male pseudonym to be taken seriously, the woman warrior can exercise her power only when she disguises herself as a man; on regaining her true identity she must once more be subservient, kowtowing to her parents-in-law and resuming her *son*-bearing function. "Now my public duties are finished," she says to them, "I will stay with you, doing farmwork and housework, and giving you more sons" (45). Her military distinction itself testifies to the sovereignty of patriarchal mores, which prize the ability to be ruthless and violent—to "fight like a man." Trying to conform to both the feminine and the masculine ideals of her imaginary Chinese society, Maxine-as-warrior grapples with a double bind.

A seemingly more radical move is taken by an alternative group of female warriors. After beheading the wicked barons, Maxine-as-warrior releases a group of "whimpering women" from a locked room.

> Later, it would be said, they turned into the band of swordswomen who were a mercenary army. They did not wear men's clothes like me, but rode as women in black and red dresses. They bought up girl babies so that many poor families welcomed their visitations. When slave girls and daughters-in-law ran away, people would say they joined these witch amazons. They killed men and boys. I myself never encountered such women and could not vouch for their reality. (44–45)

Sidonie Smith regards this telling as a "truly subversive 'story' of female empowerment" (in contrast to the original and revised tale of Fa Mu Lan): "Wielding unauthorized power, they do not avenge the wrongs of fathers and brothers; they lead daughters against fathers and sons, slaying the source of the phallic order itself. Moreover, they do so, not by masking, but by aggressively revealing their sexual difference" (159). Is the episode "truly subversive"? Granted that it may have expressed the unspoken anger of the young narrator, this tale within a tale is hardly more liberating than the central fantasy. Leading daughters against fathers and sons seems to be just the obverse of the phallic order (as presented in the chapter "No Name Woman"); such "sexual difference" merely enacts more instances of the same—the squelching of another sex by force. These episodes underscore the difficulty, even in the realm of the imagination, of transcending patriarchal thinking altogether. Ironically, it is in the narrator's "ordinary" life that she sees through the trappings of patriarchal fiction: "What fighting and killing I have seen have not been glorious but slum grubby. . . . Fights are confusing as to who has won. The corpses I've seen had been rolled and dumped, sad little dirty bodies covered with a police khaki blanket. . . . And martial arts are for unsure little boys kicking away under fluorescent lights" (51–52).[13]

Maxine-as-warrior turns tormentor herself in the everyday world. The magic words on her back revert to gibberish in the schoolroom. In a harrowing scene, she tries to force a quiet Chinese classmate—her alter ego—to speak by torturing her. She pulls her hair, twists her nose and ears, punches her cheeks, and needles her with words: "Do you want to be like this, dumb . . . your whole life? . . . You've got to let people know you have a personality and a brain" (180). The other girl cries but refuses to speak, inciting Maxine to even greater desperation and violence.

To read this incident simply as reflecting young Maxine's intense desire to explode the stock image of the quiet Oriental damsel obscures the extent of her indoctrination: silence equals a zero IQ. "If you don't talk," Maxine threatens the mute girl, "you can't have a personality" (180). This oft-quoted line has always been interpreted as the author's mature conviction. Undeniably, as a writer Kingston must believe in the importance of words, of self-expression, and The Woman Warrior does chronicle her progression from a silent child to a word warrior. A subtle but nevertheless important distinction must be drawn, however, between talk and

[13] Though merely a passing remark in The Woman Warrior, this expression of disillusionment with the traditional code of martial heroism will evolve into a full-blown pacifist commitment in Kingston's subsequent works, China Men and Tripmaster Monkey. For a discussion of the tension between feminism and martial heroism, see Cheung 1990b.

writing.[14] From the narrator's own eloquent written testimony about her inability to speak in school, it is clear that a quiet pupil can nevertheless be(come) an articulate writer. With the exception of the scene in which Maxine's "throat burst open" when she confronted her mother (201), the narrator's own feat of breaking silence is more evident in writing than in speech. She writes, as an adult, that "a dumbness—a shame—still cracks my voice in two" (165). She serves her apprenticeship as a storyteller largely through *listening* to her mother. A narrow feminist analysis may in fact perpetuate the ethnocentric correlation of speech with intellect and deepen the developmental block of nonnative speakers.

Young Maxine's valorization of speech tells more about the youngster's unquestioning acceptance of the American norm than about the author's hindsight. As I suggested earlier, speech in this tormenting context has a valence not unlike "the bluest eye" in Toni Morrison's novel of that name, another work that demonstrates how "the dominant culture exercises its hegemony through the educational system" (Gibson 20). Maxine's savagery toward the "mute" girl, which pointedly takes place in an "American" school, is reminiscent of the psychological violence suffered by Pecola because of the ubiquity of white standards. What Maxine so vehemently detests in the girl is not just her refusal to speak but "her China doll haircut" (173), her "straight hair turning with her head, not swinging side to side like the pretty girls" (176). Even more startling is the following disclosure: "If she had had little bound feet, the toes twisted under the balls, I would have jumped up and landed on them—crunch!—stomped on them with my iron shoes" (178). The gratuitous cruelty can be understood only in terms of Maxine's virulent self-contempt at being Chinese. The very words used to lure the girl to speech ("Don't you ever want to be a cheerleader? Or a pompon girl?" [180]) bespeak the narrator's aspiration to be a member of a white sorority.

[14] Many French feminists, building on Derrida's distinction between *parole* and *écriture*, associate writing with feminine dialogism and the spoken word with phallogocentrism. But as Leslie Rabine points out, such "symbolic gender" is not always coextensive with "social gender," for in Kingston "the social act of story telling belongs to the realm of women, and the social act of writing belongs to the realm of men. It is . . . the secret 'father places' that Kingston sets out to 'win by cunning'" (491).

In equating speechlessness in the Chinese girl with the absence of brain and of personality, Maxine has adopted the criteria of her schoolteachers. Her tyranny echoes the many imaginary and real bullies in her life: the Chinese man she imagines to have raped the no-name aunt, the racist white bosses, and the man who repudiates Moon Orchid, his former wife. Her threat to the other child clinches the parallel: "Don't you dare tell anyone I've been bad to you" (181). Her lingering illness after this incident, an illness that ironically deprives her of speech for an entire year, suggests that speaking under the aegis of the American school exacts a toll and that adopting a coercive tongue only exacerbates Maxine's speech impediment. Looking back, the adult writer comes to see her rough treatment of the Chinese girl as "the worst thing [she] had yet done to another person" (181). Just as the fantasy warrior can exercise her martial prowess only in male armor, young Maxine can become articulate in Western discourse only by parroting self-denigrating Western assumptions. Her tussle with her ethnic double represents a phase in the narrator's life when her racial self-hatred is most acute and her acceptance of white norms ostensibly complete.

Her alienation is aggravated, I believe, by political circumstances. The incident involving the mute girl, we are told, takes place "during the Korean War" (174). The basement where Maxine tortures the mute girl is also where the students hide during "air raid drills" (174). We can better understand Maxine's state of mind as an Asian at the time if we juxtapose the incident with a contemporaneous passage from *China Men:*

> For the Korean War, we wore dog tags and . . . had to fill out a form for what to engrave on the dog tags. . . . [O]ur dog tags had *O* for religion and *O* for race because neither black nor white. . . . Some kids said *O* was for "Oriental," but I knew it was for "Other." . . . Zero was also the name of the Japanese fighter plane, so we had better watch our step. (276)

The passage effectively illustrates what Louis Althusser calls "interpellation" or "hailing": the way dominant ideology " 'recruits' subjects among the individuals . . . or 'transforms' the individuals into subjects" (174). Because Korean, Japanese, and Chinese are collectively cast as "Other" and implicitly as cipher and as enemy, Maxine (who, naturally, does not wish to be perceived negatively) is "educated" to identify with the dominant culture and to dissociate herself from her kin and kind. She later sees an "American" education precisely as her ticket out of the Chinese community. When her throat does finally "burst open," she vocalizes her preference for American ideals and institutions: "I'm going away. . . . I'm going to college. And I'm not going to Chinese school anymore. I'm going to run for office at American school. . . . I'm going to get enough offices and clubs on my record to get into college. And I can't stand Chinese school anyway" (201–2). Implicit in her vocal assertions is an America that epitomizes enlightenment, freedom, and opportunity.

By contrast, Maxine looks at Chinese and Chinese customs from a critical distance. She depicts young male immigrants generically as "all funny-looking FOB's, Fresh-off-the-Boat's. . . . Their eyes do not focus correctly—shifty-eyed—and they hold their mouths slack, not tight-jawed masculine" (193–94). She also cringes at "the way Chinese sounds, chingchong ugly, to American ears" (171). Watching Brave Orchid and her sister Moon Orchid, both Maxine and her American-born siblings conclude that "Chinese people are very weird" (158). Describing what she considers to be the inscrutable rituals of worship followed by her parents, the narrator observes:

> Mother would pour Seagram's 7 into the cups and, after a while, pour it back into the bottle. Never explaining. . . . The adults get mad, evasive, and shut you up if you ask. You get no warning that you shouldn't wear a white ribbon in your hair until they hit you and give you the sideways glare for the rest of the day. (185)

The point of view presented in this passage brings out the slippery distinction between insider and outsider. Though putatively an insider, Maxine has taken the perspective of what Amy Ling, referring to other Chinese writers, calls an "alien observer" (15). While everything the narrator says is true in the sense that many Chinese and Chinese American children have witnessed similar rituals and taboos in their families, those who grew up in a predominantly Chinese society would find Brave Orchid's behavior perfectly explicable; it is Maxine's ignorance that seems glaring. The practice of recycling victuals (in this case Seagram's 7) after serving the gods is a common one. Many Chinese regularly observe religious holidays by setting dishes in front of the altars of dead ancestors or of gods. Once the symbolic worship is over, the food and drinks are either consumed by the worshipers or saved for use in another round of worship. As Kingston herself has noted, Chinese "have an amazing amalgam of practicality and imagination" (Talbot 10). A child who grows up as a member of a Chinese *majority* is unlikely to be nonplussed by a routine followed by many a family.

The taboo about the white ribbon is also easy to clarify, white being the color of mourning in Chinese culture. A white artificial (wool) flower in the hair signifies the recent death of a parent. Brave Orchid therefore has every reason to be upset when her daughter wears one. The mother withholds a *verbal* explanation about the exact nature of the daughter's misdeed because she believes in—and therefore is wary of—forms of "speech acts": "Be careful what you say. It comes true" (204). Words have a magic potency and no Cantonese equivalent of "Touch wood" can fully neutralize inauspicious remarks or gestures.[15]

Schooled in another set of values, Maxine can only judge her mother's behavior as "weird." Nor can she comprehend the Chinese custom of showing modesty (or fishing for compliments) by deprecating oneself or one's immediate kin in front of friends and strangers; a mother may say, for instance, that her daughter is ugly when she is in fact beautiful, or that she is stupid when she is a veritable genius. Maxine is infuriated by Brave Orchid's tendency to "say the opposite" (203). Above all, she resents the way Brave Orchid coalesces figments and facts: "I can't tell what's real and what you make up" (202).

More and more the narrator polarizes Chinese and American cultures, censuring the one and sanctifying the other. Sick of living among the "ghosts" of her mother's past, Maxine dismisses anything untoward as Chinese: "I push the deformed into my dreams, which are in Chinese, the language of impossible stories" (87). And

[15] Cf. the episode in which Brave Orchid flies into a temper when a druggist mistakenly delivers some medicine to her house.

she announces her preference for an "American-normal" (87)—
stereotypically white—lifestyle:

> I had to leave home in order to see the world logically, logic the new
> way of seeing. I learned to think that mysteries are for explanation. I
> enjoy the simplicity. Concrete pours out of my mouth to cover the
> forests with freeways and sidewalks. Give me plastics, periodical
> tables, t.v. dinners. (204)

This outright rejection of ethnic culture is not uncommon among
children of immigrants, and particularly among people of color in
the United States. In the words of Gloria Anzaldúa, "When we, the
objects, become the subjects, and look at and analyze our own
experiences, a danger arises that we may look through the master's
gaze, speak through his tongue, use his methodology" (1990, xxiii).

Much as the narrator tries to wrap her "American successes
around [her] like a private shawl" (52), however, she continues to
be reminded of being an "other" in the dominant culture. Meanwhile, she—"born among ghosts . . . [and] taught by ghosts"
(183)—has also become a ghost in the eyes of her own family.
"What's the matter with her?" someone asks when Maxine throws
a tantrum upon hearing misogynist sayings. "I don't know. Bad, I
guess," her mother answers (46). Like Yamamoto's Miss Sasagawara, Maxine is considered aberrant by both the white society and
the ethnic community because she departs from the norms of both.
Neither woman fulfills the gender expectations of her ethnic community; both are persecuted because of their race. (Maxine is fired
after refusing to type invitations for a boss who chooses to host a
company banquet in a restaurant picketed by CORE and the
NAACP.)

The parallel situations of Maxine and Marie Sasagawara, both
unusually creative women, further highlight the connection between social norms and the construction of insanity. Although
Maxine is not officially diagnosed as "mad," she suspects as much:
"I thought every house had to have its crazy woman or crazy girl,
every village its idiot. Who would be It at our house? Probably
me. . . . [T]here were adventurous people inside my head to
whom I talked. . . . I dropped dishes. . . . I picked my nose while I

was cooking and serving. . . . Indeed I was getting stranger every day" (189–90). Gifted with a vibrant imagination, she deliberately appears unattractive to avoid being married off by her family. She begins, in fact, to see herself as anomalous. Hence her interest in the stories of Chinese deviants.[16]

If the young narrator must constantly fight her way out of the constraints imposed by her Chinese family and by white American society, the adult author capitalizes on her bicultural upbringing. I have discussed at length Maxine's growing identification with the dominant culture at the expense of her Chinese roots. She tells her mother, "When I'm away from [home] . . . I don't get sick. I can breathe" (108). Yet the extensive use of Chinese legends—albeit in mutated forms—suggests that these stories have become very much a part of the narrator's (and the author's) self, thanks to her mother's influence. These stories, no less than the lessons she learns in American schools, inform her ways of knowing and becoming. The concluding legend of *The Woman Warrior* suggests that the narrator—now a writer—has finally learned to draw resourcefully upon both cultures without being constricted by either.

In "A Song for a Barbarian Reed Pipe," the last chapter of *The Woman Warrior*, Kingston reinterprets the Chinese legend of Ts'ai Yen—a poet amid barbarians—and, as she has done with the stories about the no-name aunt and the woman warrior, subverts its original moral. The legend describes a woman kidnapped by barbarians and forced to become a concubine and to raise her children on unfamiliar soil. The Chinese version highlights her eventual return to the Han people. Kingston's version, by contrast, dramatizes interethnic harmony through the integration of disparate art forms. Connections between fatherland and mother tongue, and between parents and children, are made not by spatial return to the ancestral land but through articulating and listening. *The Wom-*

---

[16] Incongruence between personal disposition and external construction can lead to actual insanity, however, as in the case of Moon Orchid, Brave Orchid's sister. Although Moon Orchid has played the role of a dutiful Chinese wife, she too becomes a victim of externally imposed identity. She is caught between a bossy sister who casts her in the role of "the Empress of the East" (143) and a Westernized husband who views her as a character "in a book [he] had read long ago" (154). Neither Brave Orchid nor the husband pays any attention to Moon Orchid's own feelings. Unable to inhabit the fictional roles others have created for her, Moon Orchid gradually loses touch with reality.

an Warrior begins with the narrator listening to her mother's talk-story; it ends with Ts'ai Yen's children listening to their mother's song. Yet the story of Ts'ai Yen is also Maxine's continuation of Brave Orchid's narrative, rounding out the passing of a maternal legacy: "Here is a story my mother told me, not when I was young, but recently, when I told her I also talk story. The beginning is hers, the ending, mine" (206).

Ts'ai Yen resembles but transcends the other influential female figures in Maxine's life. Like Fa Mu Lan, Ts'ai Yen has fought in battle, but as a captive soldier. She engages in another art hitherto dominated by men—writing—yet she does not disguise her sex, thus implicitly denying that authorship is a male prerogative. Like the no-name aunt, Ts'ai Yen is ravished and impregnated; both give birth on sand. But instead of being nameless and ostracized, Ts'ai Yen achieves immortal fame by singing about her exile. Like Brave Orchid, she talks in Chinese to her uncomprehending children, who speak a barbarian tongue, but she learns to appreciate the barbarian music.

It is by analogy to Maxine—alienated alike from the Chinese world of her parents and the world of white Americans—that Ts'ai Yen's full significance emerges. The barbarians attach primitive pipes to their arrows, so that they whistle in flight. Ts'ai Yen has thought that this terrifying noise is her nomadic captors' only music. But now, night after night, she hears from those very flutes "music tremble and rise like desert wind" (208):

> Then, out of Ts'ai Yen's tent . . . the barbarians heard a woman's voice singing, as if to her babies, a song so high and clear, it matched the flutes. . . . Her words seemed to be Chinese, but the barbarians understood their sadness and anger. . . . She brought her songs back from the savage lands, and one of the three that has been passed down to us is "Eighteen Stanzas for a Barbarian Reed Pipe," a song that Chinese sing to their own instruments. It translated well. (209)

Maxine does not (and does not want to) return to China, but she reconnects with her ancestral culture through her writing. Instead of struggling against her Asian past and her American present, she now seeks to emulate the poet who sings to foreign music. The sadness and anger are not dissipated, but the lyrical ending intimates that the narrator, merged with the author by this point, has worked the discords of her life into a song.

Faced with this harmonious ending, the reader may yet puzzle over the deliciously ambiguous sentence that concludes "A Song for Barbarian Reed Pipe" and the book: "It translated well."[17] Although the sentence refers explicitly to Ts'ai Yen's stanzas, it obviously alludes to Kingston's own echoing "song." It suggests that different worlds can be bridged, by the narrator/author as by Ts'ai Yen. Still one wonders what is being translated by Kingston (Chinese into English? Chinese culture into Chinese American culture?) and whether she translates well. If we stick to a conservative meaning of "translation," so that merit consists in close adherence to the original, then *The Woman Warrior* offers a poor—inaccurate—rendering of Chinese material. To translate, then, is also to traduce, to speak falsely, to betray—a charge that has been leveled repeatedly against *The Woman Warrior*. The betrayal is perpetrated on a more personal level against Brave Orchid, whose voice can never be reproduced fully in what to her is a ghostly tongue. "Part of the pain of *The Woman Warrior* is the daughter's betrayal of her mother," write Colleen Kennedy and Deborah Morse. "Her daughter's narrative . . . reveals the secrets of her language and culture to a hostile audience—one that will call her knowledge 'primitive,' her power over ghosts 'superstition' " (128).

Ironically, Chinese translations of *The Woman Warrior* are no more faithful to the original. Kingston describes her mother's response to these translations:

> She reads the translations that have been pirated in Taiwan, Hong Kong, and China. Since pirates work fast, they use ready-made literary forms. They do not take the care to experiment with language or to try new shapes—to find the new shapes that I'm working in. The easiest given form is soap opera, which fakes passion and revelation. . . . She takes the world's praise of my work at face value and assumes that she and our family come off well. (1991, 23)

Kingston implies that she herself has been fashioning "new shapes." If we judge her book as a personal and creative transposing of Chinese culture from a distinctively Chinese American per-

[17] I thank Nancy K. Miller for calling my attention to the word "translation."

spective and in a hybrid idiom, then the author has improvised boldly, poetically, and magnificently. The notion of translating thus keeps alive the tension and the double vision sustained throughout the macaronic text.

Like Yamamoto, who is at once critical and appreciative of her nikkei heritage, Kingston evinces deep ambivalence toward her cultural legacy. Although the narrator of *The Woman Warrior* does not overcome her adolescent rancor against her mother and the culture she represents till the end of the novel, the author—possessing the wisdom of hindsight—allows her dialogic vision to pervade the entire work. As Rabine notes, she "simultaneously relives the young girl's negative feelings for her mother, her family, the community, and its myths and also measures the distance that bestows on them their positive and irreplaceable value" (477). Occasionally this "double voice" of the narrator is sounded in succession: "From afar I can believe my family loves me fundamentally. They only say. 'When fishing for treasures in the flood, be careful not to pull in girls.' . . . But I watched such words come out of my own mother's and father's mouths. . . . And I had to get out of hating range" (52). The narrator has come to realize that her family's apparent disparagement of girls (often by the folk sayings they mouth) does not reflect the feelings they do have for their own daughters.

Most of the time, this colloquy of anger and retrospection is detectable only in the mismatch between the narrator's assertions and the author's strategies. The narrator criticizes Brave Orchid bitterly for befuddling her:

> I don't want to listen to any more of your stories; they have no logic. They scramble me up. You lie with stories. You won't tell me a story and then say, "This is a true story," or, "This is just a story." I can't tell the difference. . . . I can't tell what's real and what you make up. (202)

Perhaps there is no greater index of the disparity between the narrator's pronouncements and the author's strategies than the ironic fact that the very criticism Maxine levels against her mother anticipates the criticism many Asian American intellectuals have leveled against *The Woman Warrior*. Kingston undercuts Maxine's open statements by her own mode of narration, which, by drawing freely on her maternal bequest, provides a subtext of appreciation beneath the stated rebellion. Maxine declares her refusal to listen to her mother, but the author has been listening carefully all along. Much as the child Maxine resents her mother's jumble of fact and fancy, Kingston does not scruple to conflate myth and reality and to admit contradictory voices into her narrative. By thus qualifying Maxine's plaintive juvenile perspective with the tacit yet affirmative perspective of the adult writer, whose innovative ways of telling defy logic and rationalism, Kingston implicitly questions the Western values that the young narrator loudly endorses.

Through the deployment of thematics and poetics, surfaces and depths, *The Woman Warrior* evokes what Rachel Blau DuPlessis calls a "both/and vision," one "born of shifts, contraries, negations, contradictions" and "linked to personal vulnerability and need" (1985a, 276). DuPlessis also notes that such a vision, while characteristic of "female aesthetic," is shared by "all social practices which wish to criticize, to differentiate from, to overturn the dominant forms of knowledge and understanding with which they are saturated" (285).

Kingston seems to be well equipped to dismantle these dominant forms. Aside from being able to see the world from the vantage point of someone doubly marginalized by gender and race, she has access to an exceptional maternal and bilingual heritage, which redounds to her critique of monologic discourse and to her construction of alternative poetics. The author inherits the craft of storytelling from Brave Orchid, "champion talker" (202). With Brave orchid as a model, she can write simultaneously out of a male literary tradition and a female oral tradition.

Women authors such as Virginia Woolf, Adrienne Rich, and Luce Irigaray trace their early attempts to write to the primary influence of their fathers or of male writers and deplore the silence of their biological or literary mothers. It has been pointed out, however, that many ethnic women writers view their maternal heritage differently. The difference between Virginia Woolf and Alice Walker is noted by Joan Radner and Susan Lanser: whereas Woolf sees her maternal legacy strictly in terms of *literary* heritage and therefore concludes that there was none, Walker discovers that though her mothers did not write, they were "creating . . . gardens, songs, and quilts" (414). Kingston differs from both writers in that she inherits from her mother a distinctly verbal art—"talk-story"—through which a literary tradition is transmitted orally.[18]

One grants that the oral transmission is far from smooth: the dissonance between the lip service Brave Orchid pays to the Chinese precepts regarding female silence and her own oral pyrotechnics perplexes her impressionable daughter. But as Trinh T. Minh-ha rightly notes, "What Hong Kingston does *not* tell us about her mother but allows us to read between the lines and in the gaps of her stories reveals as much about her mother as what she *does* tell us about her" (1989, 135). Though the influence is not openly acknowledged, the consistently inconsistent mother nurtures the narrator's ability to entertain contradictions, to doubt absolutes, to see truth as multidimensional, and to escape from the scientific authority that sets empirical truth and the voice of reason above the promptings of the imagination.

Maxine not only draws strengths from her mother but also mobilizes her own bicultural resources—resources that Brave Orchid, set in Chinese ways, does not possess. The daughter is able, for instance, to allow the play of dominations to take its course. To know that there is both a Chinese and an American way to be "feminine" is to deprive each of absolute claim, thereby deessentializing femininity. By pitting Chinese patriarchal rules against Euro-American ones, Kingston splinters the force of both Chinese and white cultural authority.

Alternatively, an eclectic solution may supervene. Young Maxine has had difficulty reconciling the intricate, communal Chinese "I" with the singularly exposed American "I," all too capitalized in the American ideal of individualism. Yet these disparate signifiers come to signify different ways of composing a self. The adult writer's choice of autobiography—an American genre par excellence—suggests that she has chosen to amplify her American "I" in defiance of the Chinese precept of self-effacement and concern for "guarding family secrets" (1989, 275). Yet, for all her assertion of individualism, the narrator has introduced a community of women

[18] The distinction between literary and oral tradition is itself dubious in the light of Chinese literature, much of which ("the chant of Fa Mu Lan" included) is written with recitation in mind.

into her "autobiography." By giving voice to various female ancestors in this work of putative self-representation, she acknowledges (much in the way Hélène Cixous proclaims herself to be a
"feminine plural") the familial and cultural influence on her formation as an intertextual artist. She even expresses a longing to be
welcomed back to the fold of the community via her art: "The
swordswoman and I are not so dissimilar. May my people understand the resemblance soon so that I can return to them. What we
have in common are the words at our backs" (53).[19] Her writing
("the words") constitutes the symbolic return. Far from suggesting
a split personality, her tale inscribes a composite self whose mind is
"large, as the universe is large, so that there is room for para-
doxes" (29).

China Men

We return to those empty spaces that have been masked by
omission or concealed in a false and misleading plenitude.
          Michel Foucault, *Language, Counter-memory, Practice*

Ah Goong does not appear in railroad photographs.
          Maxine Hong Kingston, *China Men*

China Men is devoted almost exclusively to historical and communal portraits of men, yet the feminist in Kingston is not mute.
As noted earlier, I differ with critics who view *The Woman Warrior*
and *China Men* distinctly as "feminist" and "ethnic" or as "female"
and "male." Suzanne Juhasz, for instance, argues that Kingston
develops a "female" mode of narration in the first book and a
"male" mode in the second: "because a daughter's relation to her
mother is psychologically and linguistically different from her relation to her father, so is the telling of these stories different" (173).
While the two books admittedly have different orientations—the

[19] This double longing—to leave and to return to her ethnic community—is also
expressed by Esperanza, the narrator in Sandra Cisneros's *House on Mango Street:*
"One day I will pack my bags of books and paper. One day I will say goodbye to
Mango. I am too strong for her to keep me here forever. One day I will go away.
Friends and neighbors . . . will not know I have gone away to come back" (101–2).
In both instances the return is enacted symbolically through writing. See also Auer-
bach on the recurrent motif of female communities in women's fiction.

one invoking female ancestors and the other reclaiming male ancestors—classifying Kingston's narrative techniques according to the gender of her subject is misleading. The most prominent legend in each book pivots on gender reversal. Maxine as woman warrior impersonates a male soldier and enters the masculine world of martial adventures; Tang Ao, the central figure in the opening legend of *China Men*, falls captive in the Land of Women, where he is transformed into an Oriental courtesan. Femininity—a negative quality in the scheme of patriarchal binary oppositions— is imposed on the racial "other" in *China Men*. Through these "men's stories" Kingston draws connections between sexual and racial subjugation, and defamiliarizes patriarchal practices by reversing sex roles.[20]

Whereas *The Woman Warrior* is related primarily by an adolescent girl groping for a viable female identity, *China Men* is presented by a woman capable of grasping the tangle of race and gender in Chinese America and of extending her feminist sympathy to men. Kingston herself has noted:

> To best appreciate *The Woman Warrior*, you do need to read *China Men*. You'll see that "I" achieve an adult narrator's voice. . . . "I" am nothing but who "I" am in relation to other people. In *The Woman Warrior* "I" begin the quest for self by understanding the archetypal mother. In *China Men*, "I" become more whole because of the ability to appreciate the other gender. (1991, 23)

The distance between author and narrator narrows considerably in the latter book. Unlike the narrator in *The Woman Warrior*, who is not fully conscious of the social forces that shape her perceptions,

[20] The connotations of "Chinamen" have changed over time: "In the early days of Chinese American history, men called themselves 'Chinamen' just as other newcomers called themselves 'Englishmen' or 'Frenchmen': the term distinguished them from the 'Chinese' who remained citizens of China, and also showed that they were not recognized as Americans. Later, of course, it became an insult. Young Chinese Americans today are reclaiming the word because of its political and historical precision, and are demanding that it be said with dignity and not for namecalling" (Kingston 1978, 37). In a television interview with Bill Moyers in 1990 Kingston said that she separates the term into two words—China Men—to replicate the spondaic quality in the Cantonese language and to differentiate her term from the traditional slur. See also David Li (483–84) on the evolution of Kingston's title.

the one in *China Men* speaks from a clearly developed critical consciousness.

China Men, which portrays the silencing of Chinese American men, at once employs feminist strategies and inverts certain feminist preconceptions. The author is skeptical here about the representation of her male ancestors, and she deploys polyphony against male and white authority together. The two forms of double-voicing noted in *The Woman Warrior*—her overlapping awareness of gender and race and her mediation between facts and fiction—do have parallels in *China Men*. Even at the moment she portrays the emasculation of her Chinese fathers, she hints at patriarchal abuses within Chinese culture. She shuttles between facts and fantasies in both books, but whereas the strategy is used in *The Woman Warrior* to forge a matrilineage through the female tradition of talk story, here it is used to challenge the authority of "facts" and to reclaim through imagination a buried cultural biography. By interweaving personal and national events, memory and countermemory, she reconstructs not only a family saga but also a Chinese American epic, as Linda Ching Sledge has noted—one that gives voice to the many China Men whose presence was for decades unacknowledged in American history.

The two modes of double-voicing converge in the opening fable, which collapses racist and sexist oppression as it mythologizes Chinese American history. The legend is adapted from an eighteenth-century Chinese classic, *Flowers in the Mirror*, by Li Ju-chen (c. 1763–1830), a political allegory and probably one of the first "feminist" novels written by a man.[21] In Kingston's version, Tang Ao, the male protagonist, is captured in the Land of Women and forced to have his feet bound, his ears pierced, his facial hair plucked, his cheeks and lips painted red—in short, to be transformed into an Oriental courtesan. The transformation extends to etiquette. We hear Tang Ao speak only once in the course of his

---

[21] Lin Tai-yi, the translator of *Flowers in the Mirror*, calls it "a social commentary and a human satire. . . . [It] has the combined nature of *Grimm's Fairy Tales*, *Gulliver's Travels*, *Aesop's Fables* and the *Odyssey*, with *Alice in Wonderland* thrown in for good measure" (6). The section on the Land of Women also resonates with Virginia Woolf's *Orlando*, Djuna Barnes's *Nightwood*, and Monique Wittig's *Guérillères*. In the Chinese work it is not Tang Ao but his brother-in-law Lin Chih-yang who is captured by women; to avoid sexual relations with the queen on the nuptial night, Lin pretends to be impotent.

painful ordeal, whereupon an old woman, with needle in hand, jokingly threatens to sew his lips together. Instead she pierces his ears. This episode foreshadows two of the causes of silence explored throughout the book: the inability to speak and the inability to hear. The book is rife with China Men who cannot, or are not allowed to, talk as well as those whose voices are shut out of history.

The story of Tang Ao can be read from several feminist angles. As with Maxine's fantasy about Fa Mu Lan and the witch amazons, a first glance yields yet another instance of women's "counterinvestment," their strategy of reversing oppression by aping the oppressors. But the depiction of Tang Ao's excruciating pain—felt, I believe, by male and female readers alike—suggests not so much vindictiveness on the author's part as her attempt to foreground the asymmetrical construction of gender. Whereas Fa Mu Lan ventures into the male arena voluntarily, Tang Ao's crossover, as Donald C. Goellnicht observes, represents a "demotion": "no one, it seems, wants to fill the 'feminine' gender role" (1992, 192). In making women the captors of Tang Ao and in inverting masculine and feminine roles, Kingston defamiliarizes patriarchal practices. Like the author of *Flowers in the Mirror*, Kingston contravenes the commonplace acceptance of Chinese women as sex objects by subjecting a man to the tortures suffered for centuries by Chinese women.

To read this fable in a feminist register alone is to obscure its significance as "metahistory." The story concludes as follows: "Some scholars say that that country [the Land of Women] was discovered during the reign of Empress Wu (A.D. 694–705), and some say earlier than that, A.D. 441, and it was in North America" (5). Although others have speculated about a Chinese discovery of America around the fifth century (see Chen 5, Tsai 1), the association of the Land of Women with North America is to my knowledge purely Kingston's invention. Kingston's reference to invented sources—a ploy she shares with George Eliot, who provides many of the epigraphs that open the chapters of her later novels (Radner & Lanser 416)—is at once a parody of the patriarchal tradition of authorities and a form of self-authorization. In presenting obvious fiction as though it were history, Kingston lays bare the method she is to use throughout the book. She not only challenges the "historical" construction of China Men but presents alternative accounts as "counter-memory."

Since Kingston associates the Land of Women with North America, critics familiar with Chinese American history will readily see that the ignominy suffered by Tang Ao in a foreign land symbolizes the emasculation of China Men in the United States, where the peculiar racial discrimination suffered by them is often tied to an affront to their manhood.[22]

The book refers repeatedly to the forms of emasculation suffered by men of Chinese ancestry. The first and probably the most painful is sexual deprivation: 90 percent of early Chinese immigrants were male; antimiscegenation laws and laws prohibiting Chinese laborers' wives from entering the United States forced these immigrants to congregate in the "bachelor society" of various Chinatowns, unable to father a subsequent generation. The pain of such denial is most vividly dramatized in the episodes concerning Ah Goong, "grandfather of the Sierra Nevada Mountains." Watching the stars one night, Ah Goong "felt his heart breaking of loneliness" at the thought that "the railroad he was building would not lead him to his family" (129). His sexual longing intensifies with time; he becomes obsessed with his genitals and often wonders "what a man was for, what he had to have a penis for" (144). On one occasion when he is lowered into a valley in a wicker basket to drive supports for a bridge, his desire spills over:

> One beautiful day, dangling in the sun above a new valley, not the desire to urinate but sexual desire clutched him so hard he bent over in the basket. He curled up, overcome by beauty and fear, which shot to his penis. He tried to rub himself calm. Suddenly he stood up tall and squirted out into space. "I am fucking the world," he said. The world's vagina was big, big as the sky, big as a valley. He grew a habit: whenever he was lowered in the basket, his blood rushed to his penis, and he fucked the world. (133)

Pathos and humor come together in this ejaculatory act. Ah Goong's defiant act of impregnating the world underscores both the insufferable deprivation of China Men and their strategies of survival through grandiose imagination. The literal debasement of

---

[22] Alfred S. Wang discerns in *China Men* "three distinctive patterns of emasculation: 1. personal degradation espoused by society; 2. collective slavery instigated by collective interest group; 3. sexual deprivation sanctioned by law" (18).

being lowered in a wicker basket is countered by an uplifting sense of cosmic potency. Contradicting the stereotype of Chinese as serious and earthbound, the author presents Ah Goong as a ludic figure with a resilient and indomitable spirit, not unlike the famed title character in Lu Xun's *Ah Q* or the many tricksters in Native American writing (see Lincoln, 1993). A subversive imagination and a sense of play enable both the dispossessed natives and the exploited Chinese immigrants to survive despite the odds. The author's own transformation of tragedy into comedy exemplifies the characteristics she attributes to China Men and engages the reader in a way no straight-faced account of peonage could.[23]

Another tragicomic treatment of the theme of single husbands appears toward the end of "The Father from China," which depicts the youthful days of four Chinese "bachelors" in America. Ed, the narrator's father, and his three male friends operate a laundry in New York. Ed at first enjoys his freedom as a single man: "The Gold Mountain was indeed free: no manners, no traditions, no wives" (61). To allay sexual loneliness, they seek the expensive company of white dancing girls on weekends. In a reverse construction of the exotic Oriental, these China Men idolize blondes, changing the wording of passionate lyrics from "dark as her hair" to "yellow as her hair" (62). The description of Ed's erotic encounters is humorous enough. The chapter, however, is immediately followed by a brief section titled "The Ghostmate," a Chinese fable in which a young man pampered by a gorgeous widow eventually discovers this lover to be a succubus.

The placement of Ed's adventure next to the "gothic" romance yields covert authorial commentary. As an "intertext" for the chapter on Ed, "The Ghostmate" operates on several levels, now sympathetic to China Men, now critical of them.[24] At its simplest, the romance bespeaks a collective fantasy of men away from home who yearn for unexpected fortune. "I can give you your wishes,"

[23] Kingston discloses in an interview that she consciously writes against the stereotype of Asian Americans as being too serious, as lacking a sense of humor: "I think I might overemphasize showing how Chinese and Chinese Americans are the most raucous people. . . . And so in *China Men* and in *Tripmaster Monkey* I really go overboard to emphasize that part of the character" (Fishkin 788).

[24] On the coding technique of juxtaposition, see my discussion of "Seventeen Syllables" in chap. 2. I am indebted to my student Shu-mei Shih for her insights on "The Ghostmate" and "On Immortality" and for her use of the term "intertext."

says the widow in the allegory, who offers the nameless youth sumptuous meals, comfortable lodging, love, the promise of wealth, and, above all, singular raw materials for his craft, whatever it is: "She brings glazes in textures, blues, and greens the potter has not been able to mix, mounds of white lamb's wool to the weaver, paper with deer and willow and mountain watermarks to the poet, rolls of leather and cloth, threads like skeins of rainbows to the cobbler and tailor" (77, 78). His adventure contrasts sharply with the Spartan existence of the four Chinese bachelors in New York, who gulp their dinners in "four-and-a-half-minute[s]" before returning to work (60), make "the ironing tables into beds" (63), and live for a long while without women. Unlike the young man in "The Ghostmate," who can fulfill his artistic and sexual desires, Ed is frustrated on both counts. Instead of practicing calligraphy, he does bookkeeping for the laundry; this scholar, so eloquent in China, turns inarticulate in America. "You like come home with me?" he asks a blonde in his halting English, only to be politely yet firmly rejected: " 'No, honey,' she said. 'No' " (66).

But the young man's adventure also intersects with Ed's sojourn in New York at various points. The young traveler who is "far from home . . . feels his freedom" (74); Ed similarly enjoys his freedom in America. The traveler considers the "ghostmate" to be "the most beautiful woman he has ever seen" (75); the infatuated Ed moons away in the arms of a blonde dancer. More significant, just as Ed and his male friends push the memory of their wives and children behind as they philander ("Not one of the four [men] told any blonde that they were married and were fathers" [66]), the young man in "The Ghostmate" succumbs to the temptation of the widow because she seems so much more seductive than his "toilsome" spouse: "His wife is waiting at home, cooking roots and bark for the children. . . . She is a brave cooking wife. She has never had a romantic dinner for two. He'll have to ask her if she can manage without sweating so, and he doesn't like the calluses on her hands and feet either" (77).

The author thus indirectly arraigns the Chinese double standard. While dandies such as Ed spend money on one $200 suit after another to impress blondes, their wives are expected to remain faithful and to work hard to take care of their husbands' relatives. Ed's wife tells her husband: "I had to build roads. . . . Since your father is too crazy to work, and you were away, I had to pay the labor tax for two men" (69). (Once she is in New York she also takes over the "feminine" tasks of cooking and doing the dishes.) These hardworking women are often shunned for their work-worn appearance. Those waiting wives who dare to contact other men risk the fate of the No Name Woman in *The Woman Warrior*. Ed, on the other hand, has no qualms about telling his wife that he has danced with blondes. "You danced with demonesses?" she asks incredulously (71), providing the reader with a direct verbal link between the ghostmate and the white belles. The juxtaposition of the Chinese and American romances exposes Ed's carefree interlude in New York for what it is: a fool's paradise. The blonde women are interested only in fleecing the China Men. As though speaking on behalf of Ed's wife, the narrator concludes "The Ghostmate" with a moral: "Fancy lovers never last" (81).

The meeting between China Men and the pointedly blonde women also harks back to the legend of Tang Ao. Discernible in the description of both the Chinese legend and the American event is the constant slippage between a feminist and an ethnic consciousness. The purely fantastical Land of Women, where females hold sway over males, takes on realistic dimensions in North America, where white women could indeed wield dangerous power over men of color historically.[25] In stark contrast to the unknown man who impregnates the No Name Woman by merely ordering her to yield (1976/1989, 7), the China Men in North America must take no for an answer, a no that is also written into (antimiscegenation) law.

Emasculation also comes in the form of menial occupation and enforced invisibility. The contributions of the many early Chinese immigrants who built railroads, mined gold, and cultivated plantations long went unrecognized.[26] Furthermore, because white workers would not brook Chinese competitors, China Men such as Baba (father) and China Joe were forced to take on traditional

[25] I thank Cederic Robinson for alerting me to this parallel. See Angela Davis, for instance, on white women's complicity in promulgating the "myth of the black rapist," which led to the lynching of black men.

[26] Things have changed in recent decades, thanks to the development of Asian American studies. For detailed accounts of early Chinese immigrant history, see Sucheng Chan (1986, 1991), Chen, Lai et al., Nee & Nee, and Tsai.

"women's work" by becoming cooks, laundry operators, and wait-ers. Edged into such occupations, these men were then ridiculed or exploited for their involuntary "femininity."

Kingston uses the motif of silence—on both literal and figurative levels—to underscore the parallels between the plight of China Men and that of women generally. The opening of the narrative proper contains a lengthy description of the father's unnerving gloom. Since Baba was a poet-scholar-teacher in China, his present uncommunicative behavior must be attributed in large part to his American experience. As a laundryman who could hardly speak English, he was once cheated by a gypsy and then harassed by a policeman:

> When the gypsy baggage and the police pig left, we were careful not to be bad or noisy so that you [Baba] would not turn on us. We knew that it was to feed us you had to endure demons and physical labor.
> You screamed wordless male screams that jolted the house up-right. . . . Worse than the swearing and the nightly screams were your silences when you punished us by not talking. You rendered us invisible, gone. (13–14)

Even as the narrator deplores the father's "male screams" and gloomy silences, she ascribes his bad temper to his sense of mor-tification in a white society. As in the analogous situations of Cholly Breedlove in Toni Morrison's *Bluest Eye* and Grange Copeland in Alice Walker's *Third Life of Grange Copeland*, male tyranny is here viewed in the context of racial inequality. Men of color who have been abused in a white society are often tempted to restore their sense of masculinity by venting their anger and self-hatred at those who are even more powerless—the women and children in their families. They combat their invisibility by rendering others invisi-ble.

Silence—a mask for Baba's humiliation—is inflicted literally on the narrator's great-grandfather, Bak Goong, a temporary worker in Hawaii. The white bosses there order the Chinese laborers to observe a "rule of silence" while hacking up the jungle. Bak Goong, who has been "fined for talking" (100), devises ingenious ways to express his anger, such as coughing out Cantonese invec-tives against his foremen even though he would prefer to sing like a farmer in an opera: "The deep, long, loud coughs, barking and wheezing, were almost as satisfying as shouting. He let out scolds disguised as coughs" (104).[27] Bak Goong, whose musical disposition is stifled, complains: "If I knew I had to take a vow of silence . . . I would have shaved off my hair and become a monk. Apparently we've taken a vow of chastity too. Nothing but roosters in this flock" (100). The connection between silence and virtual castration is openly drawn. To relieve himself and his sickly countrymen of guttural congestion, Bak Goong tells a story that sparks an insurgence. The men dig a gaping hole through which they shout their longings and frustrations to China. Frightened by the racket, their white bosses leave the China Men alone. The hole—literally a receptacle for the hitherto muffled voices of China Men and figuratively an orifice for their pent-up sexual desire (Goellnicht 1992, 204)—is filled in as soon as the "shout party" is over: "Talked out, they buried their words, planted them. 'Like cats covering shit,' they laughed" (118).

Although both Ah Goong's insemination of the world's vagina and Bak Goong's oral penetration—he literally pounds away at the earth—are depicted as acts of heroic survival and potent imagination, the coupling of genital imagery and the rhetoric of conquest may leave the feminist reader uneasy.[28] Kingston may be consciously provoking the discomfort, but these scenes, along with those revolving around Fa Mu Lan in *The Woman Warrior*, also suggest the difficulty, even for a feminist writer, of imagining heroics independent of force. Not until the last chapter of the book, "The Brother in Vietnam," does Kingston meet this challenge head on.

Suffice it to note for now that the China Men's lust for physical and verbal conquests are presented as reactions to severe repression. The episode of the shout party instances the stubborn though contained resistance of early China Men and the mass "burial" of their voices. To survive in a hostile environment, the early settlers had to appear quiet and submissive, and their reticence was naturalized as an Oriental trait (Tong 1971, 1–31).

---

[27] Bak Goong's chicanery is an example of the coding strategy of distraction (Radner & Lanser 417–18) and may be compared with African American slaves' banging on pots to cover up a bold song such as "Oh Freedom" (Pratt 183).

[28] I thank my student Rachel Lee for pointing out how Kingston uses sexual imagery to cast territorial conquest as a form of rape.

Asian American silence is perpetuated on a more symbolic level by the white historians who are deaf to the contributions of China Men. No matter how loudly they speak through their labor, their exploits remain untold, uncredited. The narrator is determined to rectify these glaring omissions. The chapter on Bak Goong ends on an incantatory note: over the spot inseminated with words "the new green shoots would rise, and when in two years the cane grew gold tassels, what stories the wind would tell" (118). If the stories are to be heard, however, a willing listener is required. Not two years but generations pass before a great-granddaughter comes seeking ancestral voices in the Sandalwood Mountains: "I have gone . . . as far as Hawai'i, where I have stood alongside the highway at the edge of the sugarcane and listened for the voices of the great grandfathers. . . . I have heard the land sing" (88, 90). With this interpolation the speaker makes it quite clear that what she presents vividly as the story of her great-grandfather is indistinguishable from informed inspiration. (Most of the details for Bak Goong's story and the insurrection are drawn from Ovid's account of King Midas.)[29]

Just as "The Ghostmate" and "The Father from China" act as mutual glosses, two brief sections—titled respectively "On Mortality" and "On Mortality Again"—furnish intertextual responses to the chapter on Bak Goong, "The Great Grandfather of the Sandalwood Mountains." Both sections impute the loss of human immortality to the inability to keep quiet. In "On Mortality," Tu Tzuchun is asked by a Taoist monk to observe the rule of silence no matter what he sees in his hallucinatory state so that the monk can prepare an elixir. Tu succeeds in refraining from speech as he watches his wife and himself being tortured; after he sees himself reincarnated as a mute woman, however, Tu screams at the crucial moment when her husband, tired of her muteness, tries to wound their son. Because Tu breaks the rule, humankind is forever subject

[29] Ovid's Apollo punishes King Midas by giving him the ears of an ass. The king's shame is known only to his barber, who, unable to contain the secret, shouts it into a hole in the ground. Though he fills up the hole afterward, the weeds that grow from the spot whisper the secret to the wind (*Metamorphoses*, 11.174–93). In the Wife of Bath's version of the story, it is Midas's wife who, in defiance of the rule of female silence, discloses the secret about her husband's ears (*Canterbury Tales*, 951–82).

to mortality.[30] The theme recurs in "On Mortality Again." Maui the Trickster has almost succeeded in stealing from Hina of the Night the heart that would bestow immortality on men and women "when a bird, at the sight of his legs wiggling out of [her] vagina, laughed" (122). The laughter wakes Hina, who kills Maui by shutting herself.

Whereas the rule of silence causes a "sickness unto death" among the plantation workers, it is speech that ushers in mortality in the two folktales. By putting the three segments side by side, Kingston debunks the patriarchal fables that dictate oral abstinence or that ensure female subordination in the name of religion. As usual, her sympathy for China Men carries a feminist edge. Bak Goong's story, in particular, brings out the sexual asymmetry in Tu's story, which, like the myth of Tang Ao, defamiliarizes patriarchal mores by causing a man to feel what many women have felt. When Tu is transmigrating, the gods and goddesses decide that he will be born a woman because he is "too wicked to be reborn a man" (120). The reincarnated (female) Tu is at first complimented by her prospective husband for being literally dumb: "Why does she need to talk . . . to be a good wife? Let her set an example for women" (121).[31] Men such as Tang Ao, Tu, and Bak Goong, all of whom have been put in women's shoes, know that silence is no less painful and talk no less essential for women than it is for the great-grandfather of the Sandalwood Mountains (though they never acknowledge this revelation).

In this gendered context, the violation of the Taoist rule of silence by Tu-as-woman prompts further ironic reflections. As Goellnicht observes, the story harks back to the biblical account of the Fall, in which Eve's disobedience—also perpetrated orally—brings mortality to the world. While Tu-as-man is able to withstand the temptation to speak despite intense provocation, Tu-as-woman readily

[30] This story is based on a Chinese fairy tale, "Tu Tzu-chun," in *T'ai P'ing Kuang Chi*, ed. Li Fang et al. (109–12). In the original it is not the wife's muteness but the son's silence that eventually infuriates the father.

[31] Both of the husband's sexist remarks are based on the Chinese original. The literal translation of the second one reads: "What need does a virtuous wife have for speech? Let her [Tu] set an example for long-tongued [i.e., shrewish] women" (Li Fang 111; my translation).

fails the test. The Chinese fable thus ostensibly confirms women to be weaker than men. For a mother to scream at the wounding of her child is hardly a weakness, however. On the contrary, "maternal love . . . is an emotion even men (Tu-as-woman) must learn" (Goellnicht 1992, 196). "Wicked" Tu has become regenerated by his sex change into a woman; the maternal anxiety he experiences attests to the superiority of human love over the abnegation of emotion advocated by divers patriarchal religions as essential to salvation. The Taoist priest's demand is not unlike Reverend Sasagawara's extreme asceticism—a religious zeal that manifests itself as indifference to other human beings, including his own child. Both Yamamoto's and Kingston's "legends" belie the conventional hierarchy of masculine spirituality and feminine emotionalism.

China Men inverts the biblical genealogy: "In the beginning was the word."[32] In the beginning of *China Men* was (male) silence. The text—fabricated mostly out of women's talk-story—is, along with *The Woman Warrior,* a rebellion against the externally imposed and self-imposed silences of men and a covert tribute to the talkative women who have been instrumental in Kingston's reconstruction of the past. The women's words, reproduced and refashioned by the author, are what ensure the immortality of the Chinese American ancestors. Reworking the analogies in the two myths that equate silence with eternal life and speech with death, the narrator uses her words to "kill" the silences, including those of her father. As Carol Neubauer notes, the task of writing *China Men* is considerably more difficult than the one taken up in the earlier book:

> In *The Woman Warrior,* it is clear that although Kingston relied heavily on Chinese folklore and legends, she possessed a nearly limitless wealth of background material in the person of her mother, Brave Orchid, who mastered the art of "talk-story." For *China Men,* however, the most obvious source of family history was her father, but he was a man of silence. . . . With the most immediate and potentially valuable witness silenced, Kingston was forced to rely on her own memory in spite of its apparent limitations. (18)

[32] I thank Norma Alarcón for alerting me to Kingston's play on the biblical opening.

Baba—the avatar of silence—uses it as a carapace around himself in America. Venting his own self-contempt at being emasculated in his adopted country, he hardly speaks except to utter obscenities about women. His temperament differs markedly from that of the other male ancestors. Bak Goong and Ah Goong, though no less harassed and subdued by "white demons," continue to assert themselves through talk-story and imaginative subterfuge. Baba, by contrast, loses not only his voice but also his humor. The difference may have roots in the varying investments of these male ancestors in the new country. Whereas the other two grandfathers are sojourners who know that they will one day return to China, Baba is here to stay; and staying, as it turns out, entails a brutal self-transformation.

Baba's disillusionment with America seems to have shrunk his mental horizon. Here is a man who imagined himself to be Fred Astaire dancing on the steps in front of the New York Public Library. The narrator remembers a time when her father was "lighthearted," affectionately creating an "airplane" out of a dragonfly for each of his children (11). But the world does not treat him with good humor. He is cheated by people of all colors, including his fellow China Men. And he loses his job in a gambling house. Gradually he sinks into a long depression. China becomes either too painful or too perilous for memory:

> You say with the few words and the silences: No stories. No past. No China.
> You only look and talk Chinese. There are no photographs of you in Chinese clothes nor against Chinese landscapes. . . . Do you mean to give us a chance at being real Americans by forgetting the Chinese past? (14)

The narrator's concluding question—a somber reflection on a Chinaman's chance of being acknowledged as American—explodes the myth of a presumably pluralist country. Having severed his ties to his Chinese past, Baba is resigned to a brooding present. His self-flagellation parallels that of his daughter at her American school. Father and daughter alike pay a high price to become "real Americans."

Unlike the father, however, the daughter does regain her ethnic pride and her voice. Now an adult, she longs to uncover her ancestral past and challenges her father to tell his story:

> What I want from you is for you to tell me that those [misogynist] curses are only common Chinese sayings. That you did not mean to make me sicken at being female. . . . I want to know what makes you scream and curse, and what you're thinking when you say nothing. . . . I'll tell you what I suppose from your silences and few words, and you can tell me that I'm mistaken. You'll just have to speak up with the real stories if I've got you wrong. (14–15)

Interwoven are anguished pleading and empathetic understanding, feminist anger and a (now articulate) daughter's sympathy for a tight-lipped father.

The narrator's apostrophe to her father recalls the double-voicing registering dual allegiance; it also forecasts that other discourse which enmeshes factual and fabricated details. Just as Brave Orchid's injunction against telling in *The Woman Warrior* provokes Maxine to imagine the story of her no-name aunt, just as the father's taciturnity here provokes the daughter to invent his life, so the exclusion of China Men from white American history goads the narrator to create an alternative history by extrapolating from the meager resources available. Conversely, art could provoke some "real" telling. Kingston has disclosed that the challenge put out by the narrator successfully goaded her father to words: "The . . . pirated [Chinese] edition of *China Men* has nice wide margins, in which my father wrote commentary in his beautiful calligraphic hand." Kingston finds her father's reactions "more satisfying" than her mother's (1991, 23).

Meanwhile, the narrator's task of retracing the past is complicated by her strong distrust of received information and by her determination to avoid furnishing the one-dimensional lore of traditional historians. The skepticism she has learned as a child as a result of her mother's refusal to distinguish between "a true story" and "just a story" is now applied to putative "history" and to received knowledge generally. The child's erstwhile difficulty develops into an adult vigilance, which will not allow "facts" to be taken for granted.

This characteristic of the narrator is clearly seen in the section called "The Wild Man of the Green Swamp." The narrator reads in a newspaper that in 1975 a Chinese man was arrested in Florida after hiding for months in a mosquito-infested swamp. The police, with the help of a Chinese translator, learned that the wild man had worked on a Liberian freighter to support his seven children in Taiwan. He resisted his shipmates' attempt to confine him to an asylum in Tampa by escaping into the green swamp. When the U.S. Border Patrol decided to send him back to Taiwan, he hanged himself in jail.

The narrator does not, however, allow the seeming "truth" of reported facts to diminish her habitual inquisitiveness. Instead she inserts clues in her retelling of the story to make the reader wonder whether the man was indeed deranged. Before his capture, the residents reported, "he made strange noises as in a foreign language" when other human beings approached him (222). But the need for a translator implies that the man *was* speaking a foreign language. The story he told the Chinese translator was largely confirmed by his former employer. Other details further call into question the official assessments. At first the police doubted the residents' report because "man-eating animals lived in the swamp, and a human being could hardly find a place to rest without sinking" (221). Another group of officers also concluded that "no one could live in the swamp. The mosquitoes alone would drive him out" (221). The eventual discovery of the man attests to his exceptional resourcefulness.

Finally, the photograph of the wild man also renders the official appraisal suspect. As Neubauer observes, the narrator's "careful eye spots the important details—the shirt tucked in, the white undershirt, the short hair, which strongly suggest to her that the man may be temporarily disoriented by his interrupted seclusion in Green Swamp but is far from 'wild'" (30). The narrator concludes the episode with a parallel case closer to home: "There was a Wild Man in our slough too, only he was a black man. . . . The newspaper said he was crazy; it said the police had been on the lookout for him for a long time, but we had seen him every day" (223). The juxtaposition of these two men of color, both of whom appear rather harmless to the narrator, suggests that insanity may be a matter of interpretation and that skin color may well play a

和平幸福　小鬍何足介懷
三緘其口　避免許多麻煩

你被吉普賽女人害過兩次。有個把洗的衣服就解開放在櫃臺上。她抖出紫色和紅色的衣服彎起來說，『你把我最好的衣服弄破了。哦，看。還有裙子，都成了破布了。還有襯衫，都撕破了。一塌糊塗。你要賠我。哦，我的新桌布。賠錢來，我好買新衣服。這麼多衣服都破了。賠，快賠，賠。』她用手指穿過小洞。當然，這些衣服本來就是破的。

『不，』你說，『你的衣服本來就是舊的。』

來。兩個女人話說個不停，兩個耳環隨着下巴的動作搖動。房中電扇和空氣調節器吹動了她們頭髮的油脂味道。警察藍身制服的尷尬體軀似乎塞滿在房間中，他一直在說，『民事法庭。』騙逐出境。於是你賠了，按下收銀機『非出售』的按鈕賠了。兩次。

吉普賽把那些乾淨燙過的破衣服一扔便跑出門去，她帶了另一個吉普賽女人和一個警察進門

『我知道她有鬼，』媽媽大聲叫。『記得我整理她的破衣服，我說，「吉普賽人怎麼洗得起破衣服？」我知道那些女鬼沒有好事。她叫那個替她去警察局作證。你又不會用英語和他爭辯。已經兩次了，上了兩次當。』

『操你女鬼媽的屁，』你咬着牙根說，『操死你女鬼的媽的屁。』廣東話中的『婆』是指祖母，但也是指個老女鬼。在後面儲藏室中有個黑袋和一個白袋，我們從沒打開過它們。你也叫那些吉普賽人作『老鬼婆』，你呐呐地把它當做山爬上去，我們稱它為白袋婆和黑袋婆，你也叫那些吉普賽人作『老鬼婆』，你呐呐地

• 17 •

Annotations by the father of Maxine Hong Kingston in the right margin of a page of a Chinese translation of *China Men*. The printed page begins: "You are tricked twice by gypsies" (p. 12 in the Vintage International edition). The annotations read: "When peace and happiness reign, allow for small losses; when lips are sealed, much trouble is avoided."

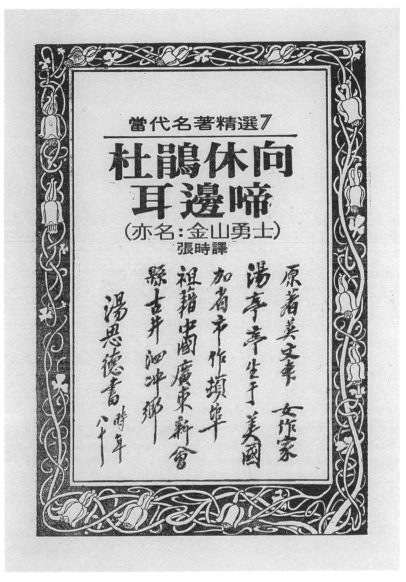

The title page of a Chinese translation of *China Men,* bearing annotations (lower section) by Kingston's father. The characters describe Kingston's American place of birth and place of ancestral origin.

part in official judgment. These men certainly have reasons to seek invisibility.[33]

By far the most distorted "representation" of China Men is its absence from American chronicles. Ah Goong, the narrator's paternal grandfather, worked on the transcontinental railroad in the nineteenth century. Although he was captured in several snapshots collected in the family album, not a single Chinese laborer appeared in the historic photos taken at the completion of the railroad: "While the demons posed for photographs, the China Men dispersed. It was dangerous to stay. The Driving Out had begun. Ah Goong does not appear in railroad photographs" (145). The last sentence captures in succinct understatement the enormous erasure of China Men. These "binding and building ancestors" (146), who risked their lives to blast holes through mountains, were expelled with no visual record for recall. Kingston's imaginative rendering of the lives of various male ancestors must be read in the context of such misrepresentation and underrepresentation.

A sample of the domineering voice of official history—which Kingston's talk-story seeks to confound—is reproduced in a section of *China Men* titled "The Laws" (152–59). This midway section enumerates, with little comment, the various U.S. statutes concerned with the Chinese, from the Burlingame Treaty of 1868 to the immigration law of 1978. Most of these laws openly discriminated against the Chinese: "1878: . . . No 'Chinese or Mongolian or Indian' could testify in court 'either for or against a white man.' . . . 1924: Any American who married a Chinese woman lost his citizenship; any Chinese man who married an American woman caused her to lose her citizenship" (153, 156). With their stamp of legality, these statutes had the effect of reducing China Men to a subspecies. Kingston's sketches of China Men in the Hawaiian fields and on the railroads may not be "factual," but they are surely truer than the reductive images inscribed in the merciless canons.

---

[33] Americans are not alone in holding such prejudice. The narrator relates the harrowing experience of a black woman brought back to China as the third wife of the narrator's maternal grandfather: "When she came to China she 'jabbered like a monkey,' but no one answered her. 'Who knows what she was saying anyway?' She fell mute" (86). Both this incident and that of the Wild Man suggest that the beastly perception imposed on the Other has to do with racial and linguistic difference.

Bak Goong's opium trip similarly provides a counterpoint to the laws of the white ruling fathers. On the rough voyage from China to Hawaii, Bak Goong takes opium to relieve his boredom, nausea, and nostalgia. In his ensuing vision, he feels affiliated with everyone and everything: "Men build bridges and streets when there is already an amazing gold electric ring connecting every living being as surely as if we held hands, flippers and paws, feelers and wings. . . . Even the demons abovedeck let out a glow" (95). This pipe dream is thrice removed from reality and triply illusory. First, the profound alliance is only a hallucination. More poignantly, it contrasts sharply with the reality Bak Goong will find at the Hawaiian plantation, where he is not only exploited by "white demons" but cheated by his own people. Finally, the dream is the narrator's reconstruction. Yet the episode effectively presents a utopian vision that decries brute reality and that jibes with the author's own pacifist world view.

An antiwar motif—countering also the policy lines of contemporary American governments—recurs throughout the book, most notably in the last full-length chapter, "The Brother in Vietnam." Being Chinese American, the narrator's brother is especially confused by the Vietnam War. The distance, in the American popular imagination, between Chinese American and other American military men is pointed out by the narrator, who recalls the portrayal of a Chinese character in *Blackhawk* (a wartime series of comic books about a squadron of allied pilots): "Chop Chop was the only Blackhawk who did not wear a blue-black pilot's uniform. . . . He wore slippers instead of boots, pajamas with his undershirt showing at the tails, white socks, an apron; he carried a cleaver and wore a pigtail, which Chinese stopped wearing in 1911" (274). Whereas the other Blackhawks are drawn "like regular human beings," Chop Chop "looked like a cartoon." Such offensive images of China Men, propagated by print and visual media alike, could not possibly induce in the brother any strong sense of pride in belonging to the U.S. Army.[34]

---

[34] Japanese fared no better in white representation during World War II. Joy Kogawa notes in *Obasan* that in war comics "the Japs have mustard-coloured faces and buck teeth" (101). But at least these were portrayals of the "enemy." For a detailed discussion of the "emasculation" of Asian men in American popular culture, see Chin 1972; Chin & Chan.

To worsen matters, the brother is visually almost indistinguishable from the enemy. "They'd send a gook to fight the gook war," he muses (283). Nevertheless, his experience in the Far East, for all its horror, complements the vision of Bak Goong, who feels a bond with everyone and everything. The soldier is haunted instead by a series of nightmares, in which the distinction between kin and foe collapses:

> He takes up his sword and hacks into the enemy, slicing them; they come apart in rings and rolls. He grits his teeth and goes into a frenzy, cutting whatever human meat comes within range. When he stops, he finds that he has cut up the victims too, who are his own relatives. The faces of the strung-up people are also those of his own family, Chinese faces, Chinese eyes, noses, and cheekbones. He woke terrified. (291)

This nightmare indirectly affirms Bak Goong's epiphany. To recognize a deep bond between the people of the world is to undo the binary opposition between friends and enemies, to acknowledge the ultimately self-defeating outcome of any war. The brother's nightmare is a far cry from Maxine's thrilling fantasy of the woman warrior. The narrator obsessed with revenge in the first book has become a pacifist in the second.

Because Kingston's ethnopoetics has so often been misconstrued as inaccuracy or even as false testimony, it is worth discussing at some length. Aware of the limitations of history, memory, and language, the author offers only her own revision of the past. In *China Men* she fills the silences *symbolically*—in the fullest sense of the word—even as she divulges and decries them. The narrator concedes early on that much of the story of her father and grandfathers is based on fallible recollection and unverifiable evidence. China itself, she tells us, is purely her own construction.

> I'd like to go to China if I can get a visa. . . . I want to talk to Cantonese, who have always been revolutionaries, nonconformists, people with fabulous imaginations, people who invented the Gold Mountain. I want to discern what it is that makes people go West and turn into Americans. I want to compare China, a country I made up, with what country is really out there. (87)

Her recourse to talk-story—which blurs the distinction between straight facts and pure fiction—accomplishes two key objectives: to reclaim a past and, more decisively, to envision a different future.

The first method by which Kingston recreates her ancestors is analogous to typology. Having been a witness to the birth of her brother in America, she can paint a picture of her father's birth in China; cognizant of her brother's (and perhaps also her own) exasperating experience as a teacher, she fabricates parallel situations for her father, a former teacher in a Chinese village. Though Kingston incorporates details from Chinese folklore in recreating her father's early life, there are striking parallels between the scenes set in China and those set in America.[35]

A second method by which Kingston talks story is through the retelling of both Eastern and Western fables, a method that has aroused considerable furor among some Chinese American critics. Although the use of literary allusions and the remolding of ancient material is a well-established practice, Kingston has come under fire for tampering with her sources. The charges range from bastardization of Chinese folktales to downright plagiarism. Evidently such writers as Milton, Joyce, Woolf, and Christa Wolf are free to refashion ancient material because most readers are familiar with the classics and the Bible. Since many American readers are unfamiliar with Chinese legends, in surreptitiously transforming them Kingston is allegedly guilty of misleading those readers who, in all innocent ignorance, will mistake the retelling for the original. The double standard unwittingly privileges Euro-American writers and readers. A writer's imagination should not be circumscribed by potential readers' backgrounds, and it is not the writer's fault if a reader cannot pick up the plethora of allusions that enrich Kingston's texts. Scholars and critics must assume the responsibility of identifying the more esoteric references (see, for example, Chua 1991, S. Wong 1991).

[35] Frederic Wakeman, Jr., in his review of *China Men*, first noted this method (42), used repeatedly in the book to recreate the lives of ancestors of whom the author has no direct knowledge. At the end of *China Men* she relates that she learns from an old man in Hawaii that his greatest joy is "to work in a cane field when the young green plants are just growing up" (306). Kingston presumably recreates from this detail the scene in which Bak Goong marvels at the new canes.

Reverence for ancient authority, generic purity, and East-West dichotomy is especially alien to Kingston, who consciously defies conventional boundaries in both of her texts. To require her to be faithful to the original story is not only to counter her refractive purpose but also to occlude one of her most innovative—and uniquely Chinese American—narrative strategies: Americanizing Chinese tales and Sinicizing Euro-American ones. Contrary to the beliefs of those who argue that Kingston dares to remold only Chinese legends, not Western ones, she in fact takes ample liberties with both. Just as she grafts the story of a male general (whose mother engraves words on his back) to the story of Fa Mu Lan and transplants the myth of Tang Ao to North America, she turns the stories of King Midas and Robinson Crusoe into Chinese yarns.[36] In altering and embroidering historical sources she finds precedents in both American and Chinese literary traditions, in William Carlos Williams's *In the American Grain*—to which *China Men* is an acknowledged sequel (Pfaff 25)—as well as in Luo Guan-Zhong's *Romance of the Three Kingdoms.* (The colorful Chinese epic is based on a rather dry chronicle.) Such mixing of codes—cultural interplay at its friskiest—requires considerable knowledge and ingenuity. If Milton has been venerated for his erudite allusions and admired for his seamless adaptation of classical and biblical source material, an author who can manipulate two even more disparate literary traditions should not be discredited in the name of "cultural authenticity."

A third way by which the narrator recreates the past is by presenting multiple, often mutually exclusive versions of ancestral stories. Given Baba's implacable reserve and the editorial forces of society that bury minority history, invention is the narrator's obvious recourse. But the author also uses these silences as a pre-text for turning a family history into a collective Chinese American epic and for invoking a plurality of possibilities rather than relying on any one authority. For instance, she offers two entirely different versions of her father's arrival in America. In the illegal version, her father smuggles himself into New York Harbor inside a wood-

---

[36] In *China Men* Robinson (Crusoe) becomes Lo Bun Sun, who "grew beans and made tofu and bean sauce" (227); he rescues a cannibal and names him Sing Kay Ng ("Friday" in Cantonese).

en crate. The vivid account ends, however, with a refutation: "Of course, my father could not have come that way" (53). In the legal version, the father is detained indefinitely in the immigration station on Angel Island, where he inscribes a poem on the wall urging his compatriots to hold on to their "Gold Mountain dreams." (Many such poems were indeed inscribed on the walls in the Angel Island detention camp.) By imagining the various ways a man like her father sought entry into the United States, Kingston extends the parameters of family history to encompass the experiences of diverse China Men. Using honorific titles such as "father," "grandfather," and "great-grandfather" instead of individual names, the narrator transforms individual family members into archetypes. Together the two versions of the father's entry to America signify the inhuman treatment accorded to China Men, once the need for navvies was past, to undermine their determination to trespass or outstay their unwelcome. Trinh writes that "truth is both a construct and beyond it; the balance is played out as the narrator interrogates the truthfulness of the tale and provides multiple answers" (1991, 12). Kingston's "multiple answers" allow for a fuller, and therefore truer, picture of the historical situation than any single factual account can provide.

Finally, talk-story allows a shift into pure fantasy (as in Bak Goong's pipe dream). Kingston's impulse to retrieve China Men from historical oblivion is offset by an equally strong desire to project an alternative world untrammeled by the oppressive rules of society. This is a point often overlooked by critics who have stressed her role as a historian in *China Men*.[37] If her genealogical compulsion propels her toward accurate representation, the revisionist impulse leads her to project her own dreams onto her "forerunners." Kingston uses fantasy the way other women writers (Charlotte Perkins Gilman, Doris Lessing, Joanna Russ, for example) use science fiction, historical romance, or utopian novels, for a "visualization of the world as it could be" (DuPlessis 1985b, 179).

Just as the stories of various China Women and China Men must be "heard" by the acquisitive narrator before they are retold, talk-

---

[37] The historicist critics include Neubauer, Sledge, and Wang. By contrast, David Li, San Juan, Lee, and Goellnicht (1992) have called attention to Kingston's subversive use of historical and literary sources.

story—both as a strategy and as a tradition—is predicated upon the attention of listeners. *China Men* thus concludes appropriately with the section "On Listening," in which the narrator, obsessed with (feminist) self-expression in the first book, here stresses the equal importance of listening to the voices of others/Others. At a party she is told diverse stories about her Chinese ancestors' quests for the Gold Mountain, set variously in the Philippines, Mexico, and Spain. When the narrator raises questions about a particular legend, the teller promises to send the answers to her. "Good," she thinks to herself, and ends with a possibly hortative comment to her own audience: "Now I could watch the young men who listen" (308).

The idea of listening presented here is no less rich in interpretive possibilities than the notion of translating at the conclusion of *The Woman Warrior*. Both translating and listening presupposes that there is more than one language, more than one story. In thus ending her two books, Kingston has figured out a strategy that has implications, I believe, for one of the most pressing tasks facing feminists today: how to forge alliances among heterogeneous women, let alone among women and men.

Brave Orchid, teaching her children about sanity and insanity, remarks: "Sane people have variety when they talk-story. Mad people have only one story that they talk over and over" (1989, 159). The mother's lesson is played out in both of Kingston's books, particularly at the end of *China Men*, where the author cunningly displaces one Gold Mountain story with multiple versions. As E. San Juan, Jr., has pointed out, "none of these versions is privileged so that the questions posed by the 'I' who seeks an authoritative, official version never receive a definitive answer. Hence, the only recourse is to appreciate the virtue of listening, of being open to the possibilities created by our persevering struggles to subvert a monologic political economy" (560).

But subverting monologism is only one use of listening. While the endings of both *The Woman Warrior* and *China Men* recapitulate Kingston's feminist preference for open-endedness and multiplicity, no less implicit in her espousal of translating and listening is the hope for connection across differences. To translate from different languages, to listen without insisting on a single story line is also to reach out beyond one's workaday horizon, to see with other eyes, to open oneself to a variety of experiences, and to spin an intersubjective network. The wish to affiliate through talk-story can be heard throughout both texts. In *The Woman Warrior* the narrator writes concerning the No Name Woman: "Unless I see her life branching into mine, she gives me no ancestral help" (8). In *China Men*, kinship goes beyond consanguinity: "Even the demons abovedeck let out a glow."

My reading of Kingston suggests that her feminist and ethnic sensibilities reinforce each other and that she uses feminist strategies to divulge the historical oppression of China Men. I further suggest that these strategies disrupt the dichotomy of vocal males and voiceless females. Her feminism extends to men but not to Chinese or American patriarchy. Though bilingual and bicultural, Kingston does not set out to replicate traditional sources and master-narratives. Much as the narrator of *The Woman Warrior* vindicates her intertextual "I," the narrator of *China Men* (de)claims an open-ended Chinese American tradition. She does so neither by choosing one heritage over the other nor by simply mixing the two. She reinstates herself in both traditions by recasting both Asian and Western myths, thereby exorcising ancient authorities and freeing herself from their patriarchal or colonial grip. She redeploys fable, dream, and fantasy to evoke a world independent of time-worn rules, monocultural imperatives, and binary oppositions.

4
Attentive Silence: *Obasan*

To the *issei,* honor and dignity is expressed through silence,
the twig bending with the wind. . . . The *sansei* view silence
as a dangerous kind of cooperation with the enemy.
Joy Kogawa, in an interview with Susan Yim

On the one hand, each society has its own politics of truth;
on the other hand, being truthful is being in the in-between
of all regimes of truth.
Trinh T. Minh-ha, *Woman, Native, Other*

There is a silence that cannot speak.
There is a silence that will not speak.
Beneath the grass the speaking dreams and beneath the
dreams is a sensate sea. The speech that frees comes forth
from that amniotic deep. To attend its voice, I can hear it say,
is to embrace its absence. . . .
Unless the stone bursts with telling, unless the seed
flowers with speech, there is in my life no living word. The
sound I hear is only sound. White sound. Words, when they
fall, are pock marks on the earth. They are hailstones seeking
an underground stream.
Joy Kogawa, *Obasan*

Most reviewers of Joy Kogawa's *Obasan* have applied the hierarchical opposition of language and silence to the very novel that
disturbs the hierarchy. Those who note the pervasiveness of silence in the novel frequently describe this theme in purely negative
terms. To Edith Milton the book is "a study in painful silence, in
unquestioning but troubled obedience to the inevitable" (8); to
David Low it is "clearly a novel about the importance of communication and the danger of keeping silent" (22); to Joyce Wayne it is "a
tale of the submissive silence of the oppressed" (23). Language, by
contrast, has been all too readily embraced as the medium of truth
and the solution to the "tragedy of silence" (Low). Behind the
wholesale endorsement of verbal expression lies the assumption
that words are transparent and that *Obasan* itself is a simple historical novel. J. R. Morita writes, "While not entirely factual, the novel
is based on historical truth, from which it draws strength" (516). B.

A. St. Andrews concurs: "The history of one extended family . . . reflects the history of the Japanese-Canadian experience during and after the Second World War" (30).

The limits of such mimetic readings have been pointed out by Donald C. Goellnicht, who argues that the text "problematizes the very act of reconstructing history by comparing it to the process of writing fiction" (1989, 287–88). Both Goellnicht (288) and Manina Jones (214) rightly view *Obasan* as "historiographic metafiction," a genre that, according to Linda Hutcheon, "inscribes and then subverts its mimetic engagement with the world. It does not reject [mimesis] . . . but it does irrevocably change any simple notions of realism or reference, by confronting the discourse of art with the discourse of history" (1987, 25).

One may also trace the reviewers' widespread condemnation of silence to the bias of language itself, which, as Paula Gunn Allen notes, "embodies the unspoken assumptions and orientations of the culture it belongs to" (225). Whereas in English "silence" is often the opposite of "speech," the most common Chinese and Japanese ideogram for "silence," 静 is synonymous with "serenity" and antonymous with "sound," "noise," "motion," and "commotion." In the United States silence is generally looked upon as passive; in China and Japan it traditionally signals pensiveness, vigilance, or grace.[1]

These differences are all too often eclipsed by a Eurocentric perspective; even revisionist critics may succumb to it. As Chandra Talpade Mohanty has argued, much of Western feminist representation of oppressed "third world" women is pitted against the implicit self-representation of Western women as educated and liberated (and, I would add, verbally assertive): "These distinc-

[1] The ideogram is pronounced *jing* in Chinese and *jo* or *sei* in Japanese. See *Cihai* 3:4555 and Nelson 174 for various "conjugations" of the character. According to Tsukasa Nishida, "the primary concern of the Japanese is an interpersonal communication situation is to 'catch' the other's feelings or emotion, not only through verbal expression but, also, from various cues, such as nonverbal expressions, eye movement, and facial expression. The emphasis on action rather than words is expressed in many sayings in Japan, such as, 'Express in deed not in words' . . . 'To say nothing is a flower.' . . . Verbalization is considered a means of covering one's timidity, ill will, or weakness" (45–46). On the distinction as well as continuity between Japanese and Japanese American culture, see chap. 2. See also Fujita on the "sensibility of silence" in *Obasan;* Magnusson and Goellnicht 1989 on Kogawa's ambivalence toward language.

tions are made on the basis of the privileging of a particular group as the norm or referent" (337; see also Spivak 134–53). A similar norm frequently governs the assessment of racial minorities. Marilyn Russell Rose, a sophisticated critic keenly aware of the danger of Orientalist discourse, nevertheless places inordinate blame on the victims in *Obasan:* " 'Orientalism' has been so internalized by this Oriental minority, that their silence is an inadvertent bow to the occidental hegemony which legitimizes their abuse" (1987, 293). To counter Orientalism is to challenge Western reduction or homogenization of Asian traits, but not necessarily to deny or denounce the traits themselves. Undeniably, nikkei have been subject to political exploitation, but to view their reticence as no more than the internalization of Western stereotypes is to tune out the "other" perceptions of silence in the novel.

Situated on the crossroads of cultures, Kogawa in *Obasan* shows a mixed attitude toward both language and silence and reevaluates both in ways that undermine logocentrism. She reveals the strengths and limits of discursive power and quiet forbearance alike; in doing so, she maintains the complementary functions of verbal and nonverbal expression. Certainly, words can liberate, but they can also distort and wound;[2] and while silence may obliterate, it can also minister, soothe, and communicate. The verbal restraint that informs Kogawa's theme and style manifests not only the particular anguish of voicelessness but also what Gayle K. Fujita describes as the narrator's specific nikkei legacy—"a nonverbal mode of apprehension summarized by the term 'attendance'" (34). Whereas Fujita subsumes several forms of reticence under the rubric "attendance," I believe Kogawa distinguishes among (and regards with varying attitudes) protective, stoic, and attentive silence. She also deplores silencing through censorship and enforced invisibility. Like Kogawa, I do not endorse silence per se, though I may stress the positive use of nonverbal behavior as a corrective to the prevailing critical trend that privileges speech.

The thematics and poetics of silence and speech are tightly woven in the novel. On the thematic level, the protagonist negotiates between voicelessness and vociferousness, embodied by her

---

[2] Both Delgado and Matsuda have discussed from the legal point of view the severe harm wrought by hate speech on the victims of racism.

two aunts. The style of the novel likewise evinces a "two-toned" heritage (Gates 1984, 4). The biblical injunction to "write the vision and make it plain" which is reiterated in the novel, is soft-pedaled by what Stanford Lyman would characterize as nisei indirection (cited in Chapter 2).[3] Kogawa confronts the outrages committed against the nikkei during World War II without raising her voice. Instead, she resorts to elliptical devices such as juvenile perspective, fragmented memories and reveries, Western fairy tales and Japanese fables—devices that at once accentuate fictionality and proffer a "truth" that runs deeper than the official records of the war years spliced into the novel. The gaps in the narrative demand from the reader a heedfulness that corresponds to the narrator's attentiveness.

Sound and Stone

Kogawa bases *Obasan* on her own experiences during World War II and on letters, journals, and documents of the time.[4] After the

---

[3] It would, of course, be ill advised to use cultural upbringing as the sole explanation for an author's style. Narrative indirection, as I have argued in the case of Yamamoto, has many causes—the particular disposition of the author, the influence of other writers, and the constraints resulting from gender, class, and race. Yet Kogawa herself consistently associates verbal indirection with the more traditional nikkei, particularly those born or raised in Japan. Obasan, the title character and an issei, is the epitome of indirection: "Her answers are always oblique and the full story never emerges in a direct line" (18). One may use the same words to describe Kogawa's own narrative style. Christianity and Buddhism, both of which are evoked in the novel, also hold contradictory attitudes toward word (logos) and silence. Whereas the Christian prophetic tradition stresses the importance of voice, Buddhist meditation evinces reverence for silence. For an explication of Zen meditation, see Watts 154–73.

[4] Joy Nozomi Kogawa was born to issei parents in Vancouver, British Columbia, in 1935. During World War II her family was evacuated to Slocan, a ghost town in the old silver-mining region of eastern British Columbia. Kogawa was six—one year older than the novel's narrator, Naomi—when her family was relocated. Her family, unlike Naomi's, was not separated: "Her minister father, mother and brother survived the relocation together and then moved to a small town in Alberta" (Yim D1). Kogawa attended the University of Alberta in 1954, the Anglican Women's Training College and Conservatory of Music in 1956, and the University of Saskatchewan in 1968. She has worked as a schoolteacher and as a staff writer for the office of the prime minister in Ottawa. Since 1979 she has lived in Toronto. *Obasan*, her first novel, won her the Books in Canada First Novel Award in 1981, the Canadian

Japanese attack on Pearl Harbor in December 1941, over 21,000 Canadians of Japanese ancestry (17,000 of whom were Canadian-born) were divested of their rights and possessions and were forced to leave their homes on the coast of British Columbia. They were sent first to Hastings Park in Vancouver and then to various ghost towns (hastily reconstituted by the wartime authorities) in the interior of British Columbia. Those who resisted the evacuation were imprisoned in a camp at Angler, Ontario. The novel lays bare the racism that prompted the evacuation: "Why in time of war with Germany and Japan would our government seize the property and homes of Canadian-born [Japanese] Canadians but not the homes of German-born Germans?" asks a character (38). By 1944 Japanese Canadians who still remained in the interior of British Columbia were required to choose between resettlement east of the Rockies and deportation to Japan—a country most of them had never seen. Unlike Japanese Americans, who could return to the West Coast after the war, Japanese Canadians were not allowed to return to British Columbia until 1949.[5]

The novel is presented from the point of view of Naomi Nakane, a thirty-six-year-old schoolteacher. The narrator in *Obasan*, similar to the one in *The Woman Warrior*, shuttles between past and present and between juvenile and adult perspectives. The story begins in 1972, when Naomi's uncle Isamu is still alive in Granton, Alberta. A month later, Isamu dies and Naomi goes to comfort his widow, Aunt Aya, the title character. *Obasan* is "aunt" in Japanese, but it can also mean "woman." The title thus implicitly "acknowledges the connectedness of all women's lives—Naomi, her mother, her two aunts" (Fujita 41). At Obasan's house Naomi finds a parcel from her aunt Emily which contains wartime documents, letters, and Emily's own journal, written between December 1941 and May

---

Authors Association Book of the Year Award in 1982, and the Before Columbus Foundation American Book Award in 1982. Among her other publications are *Naomi's Road* (1986), a juvenile version of the novel, and four volumes of poetry: *The Splintered Moon* (1967), *A Choice of Dreams* (1974), *Jericho Road* (1977), and *Woman in the Woods* (1985). *Itsuka*, her second novel and a sequel to *Obasan*, was published in Canada in 1992—unfortunately too late to be included in my discussion.

[5] For detailed discussions of the treatment of Japanese Canadians during the war see Adachi, Broadfoot, Sunahara, and Peter W. Ward. See Takaki and Weglyn for the contemporaneous treatment of Japanese Americans. Daniels discusses the nikkei experience in both the United States and Canada.

1942; the journal was addressed to Naomi's mother but was never sent.[6] As Naomi sifts through the contents of this package, she reluctantly sinks into her own past, particularly the uprooting and dissolution of her family during and after the war. The extended family was an unusually close-knit one: "the Nakanes and Katos were intimate to the point of stickiness, like mochi. . . . My parents, like two needles, knit the families carefully into one blanket" (20). But as the family was banished, first to Slocan and then to southern Alberta, it disintegrated: her father died of tuberculosis; two of her grandparents died of physical and mental stress. Naomi and her older brother, Stephen, were raised by Uncle Isamu and Aya Obasan. Hovering over the tale is the mysterious absence of Naomi's mother, who had accompanied her own mother to Japan on a visit shortly before the war, when Naomi was five. Only at the end of the book do Naomi and Stephen (and the reader) discover that their mother had been totally disfigured during the nuclear blast in Nagasaki and died a few years later. Before her death she had asked Obasan and Uncle to spare her children the truth. *Kodomo no tame ni* (for the sake of the children) is a refrain throughout the novel. The adults succeed all too well; Naomi does not find out about her mother's fate for over thirty years.

The novel depicts the plight of a child who does not know and cannot tell. Naomi has been withdrawn throughout childhood and adolescence; her quiet disposition seems tied to her mother's unexplained absence. As a girl she questions but receives no answer; as an adult she desists because she, like Rosie at the end of Yamamoto's "Seventeen Syllables," dreads knowing. As A. Lynne Magnusson has observed, "Naomi's individual drama is closely caught up in her linguistic anxiety, which comes to serve as a synecdoche for her estrangement—from others, from her cultural origins, from the absent mother who preoccupies her thoughts, from her past" (58). For Naomi, as for Maxine, bicultural upbringing against the backdrop of a hostile dominant culture is first experienced as a source of linguistic and personal pain and confusion. Both narrators must struggle to translate their pain into a resource.

---

[6] Emily's letters of protest to the Canadian government are based on the real letters of Muriel Kitagawa, a Japanese Canadian activist. Kogawa said that the impulse to explore Kitagawa's writing came to her in a dream (Wayne 23).

In her quest for resolution Naomi is influenced by her two aunts' contrary responses to their harrowing experiences during the war. Obasan, the reticent aunt who raises Naomi, counsels her to forget and to forgive. Aunt Emily, the political activist, represents the impulse to speak out roundly against the injustices done to Japanese Canadians. As she presses her niece to "write the vision and make it plain" (31), she challenges Naomi to confront her past. Emily brings to mind the Old Testament prophets who cry for justice; Obasan, the New Testament preaching of humility, forgiveness, and charity. Both sets of behavior also have roots in Japanese culture. As Michiko Lambertson points out, "There are two poles in the Japanese way of thinking. One is a fatalistic attitude of acceptance, endurance, and stoicism and the other is a sense of justice, honour, and fair play" (94). Obasan's behavior is as much Buddhist as Christian. She moves with equal ease in Christian and Buddhist burial ceremonies, always ready with her serving hands. Emily's activism is ascribed to her Canadian schooling. But it is also reflected in Kogawa's rendition of the Japanese tale of Momotaro, the boy who defends his people valiantly against cruel bandits (Fujita 40–41). Naomi remarks:

> How different my two aunts are. One lives in sound, the other in stone. Obasan's language remains deeply underground but Aunt Emily, BA, MA is a word warrior. She's a crusader, a little old grey-haired Mighty Mouse, a Bachelor of Advanced Activists and General Practitioner of Just Causes. (32)

The two aunts call to mind the helpless Moon Orchid and the veritable Brave Orchid—another word warrior—in *The Woman Warrior*, though Obasan is far more hardy than Moon Orchid.[7] Just as Maxine resents her mother's dominance and ridicules Moon Orchid's timidity, Naomi resists Emily's words and puzzles over Obasan's wordlessness. She undercuts Emily's polemics with irony and strains to hear Obasan's inner speech.

---

[7] The difference in the characterizations of Moon Orchid and Obasan may be due in part to the different perspectives of the narrators. As young Maxine is more Westernized than Naomi, she would be likely to view quiet Obasan as weak and self-demeaning.

White Sound and Living Word

Kogawa articulates her misgivings about documentation and history primarily through Naomi. When Naomi receives Emily's package, bulging with words, she at first resists reading its contents and reopening old wounds: "What is past recall is past pain" (45). Much as she tries to forget the past, however, it continues to haunt her, as in dreams: "I would like to drop the lid of the trunk, go downstairs and back to bed. But we're trapped, Obasan and I, by our memories of the dead—all our dead—those who refuse to bury themselves" (26). Past grievances lurk ominously in the psyche, like the leftovers in Obasan's refrigerator, "too old for mould and past putrefaction" (45). The dream also echoes an argument that took place years before between Naomi and Emily:

"Why not leave the dead to bury the dead?"
  "Dead?" she asked. "I'm not dead. You're not dead. Who's dead?"
  "But you can't fight the whole country," I said.
  "We are the country," she answered. (42)

Most reviewers of the book agree with Emily and view Obasan and Naomi as passive and ineffectual. But the author's allegiance is much more complex. Although her novel acknowledges the importance of expression in retracing the past, it also exposes the many pitfalls of language (Goellnicht 1989, 291–94). To begin with, language is insidiously gendered so that synonymous words, such as "spinster" and "bachelor," take on vastly different connotations. As Robin Lakoff has noted, "bachelor" is often used as a compliment, but "spinster" is normally pejorative: "The metaphorical connotations of 'bachelor' generally suggest sexual freedom; of 'spinster,' puritanism or celibacy" (33). When Naomi is called a "spinster" by one of her students, she recalls Emily's objection to the epithet: "She says if we laundered the term properly she'd put it on, but it's too covered with cultural accretions for comfort" (8). Saddled with time-honored prejudice, words have a way of perpetuating patriarchal ideology.

The perversion of language has been painfully etched in the mind of Naomi, who as a child was sexually abused by a neighbor,

Old Man Gower: "He lifts me up saying that my knee has a scratch on it and he will fix it for me. I know this is a lie. The scratch is hardly visible and does not hurt" (63). The child Naomi was jolted into simultaneous awareness of sexuality and of linguistic duplicity.

The description of the incident and its aftermath is dense with psychoanalytic overtones. Before Naomi's encounter with Gower, she has felt at one with Mother: "I am clinging to my mother's leg, a flesh shaft that grows from the ground, a tree trunk of which I am an offshoot. . . . The shaft of her leg is the shaft of my body and I am her thoughts" (64). After the molestation Naomi feels truncated: "The secret has already separated us. . . . My legs are being sawn in half" (64–65). We are told in the next chapter that Mother disappears "around this time" (66). Magnusson notes:

> Kogawa's representation of the myth of separation from the mother perhaps approximates most closely to Jacques Lacan's reinterpretation of Freud via Saussure and structural linguistics. . . . In this version the crisis of separation from the mother's body coincides with entry into the symbolic order of language [which] presupposes the absence of the object it signifies. Hence to enter into a world of relationships mediated by language is to enter into a world of endless yearning. (61)

Naomi's entry into the symbolic order is, however, doubly removed from reality: the deliberate deception in Gower's words compounds the sign's inherent elusiveness.

No less insidious is the language of the social and political realm, though it carries all too real consequences. As Goellnicht points out, "Language shapes, rather than merely reflects, reality for both the victimizers and the victims, its manipulation resulting in empirical, concrete actions" (1989, 291). It becomes especially treacherous when abusive slurs pass for news and oppressive edicts for laws.[8] Emily writes, "There's this horrible feeling whenever I turn on the radio, or see a headline with the word 'Japs' screaming at us" (83). The newspapers, she goes on to say, are printing "out-

---

[8] This theme has numerous analogues in Kingston's *China Men;* see also Palumbo-Liu on equivocation in American legal discourse. Several examples of linguistic manipulation cited in this section were first noted in Goellnicht 1989.

right lies": "There was a picture of a young Nisei boy with a metal lunch box and it said he was a spy with a radio transmitter" (85). Similarly, the government justified evacuation of Japanese residents by claiming they were a security risk; but not a single charge of treason was laid.

More subtle are the racist lies embedded in institutional rhetoric. During the war the Canadian bureaucracy used words to camouflage the most offensive actions against people of Japanese ancestry. Nisei—Canadian-born citizens—were dubbed "enemy aliens" (92); prison camps were dressed up as "Interior Housing Projects." Emily fumes, "With language like that you can disguise any crime" (34). As Goellnicht (1989, 292) has noted, members of Naomi's family are confined in places with names such as "Sick Bay" and "Pool," yet water—a life-giving image in the novel—is notably absent.

> Sick Bay, I learned eventually, was not a beach at all. And the place they called the Pool was not a pool of water, but a prison at the exhibition grounds called Hastings Park in Vancouver. Men, women, and children outside Vancouver, from the "protected area"—a hundred-mile strip along the coast—were herded into the grounds and kept there like animals until they were shipped off to road-work camps and concentration camps in the interior of the province. (77)

Places that sound like convalescent and recreational areas turn out to be corrals where Japanese Canadians are treated like animals and kept "at bay." (Grandpa Nakane literally becomes sick in Sick Bay.) One further wonders who is protected in the "protected area." Surely not the dispossessed Japanese Canadians, whose homes are looted and later impounded.

Not only do white Canadian officials and nikkei citizens hold opposite views about the evacuation; opinions among members of Naomi's family also diverge. Aunt Emily wants to fight "fascist" Canada, but Uncle and Obasan feel only gratitude to their adopted country: "This country is the best. There is food. There is medicine. There is pension money" (42).[9] Their memories also vary:

[9] Kogawa disclosed in an interview that Obasan and Uncle are like other issei: "There's a feeling of gratitude that they weren't murdered. . . . It's a feeling that the more vocal third generation . . . don't understand. It has created a generation gap

"Aunt Emily's Christmas 1941 is not the Christmas I remember,"
Naomi remarks (79). And the perspective of one person shifts with
time. Emily, who once "worshipped the Mounties" to the extent of
brandishing their motto—*Maintiens le droit*—is appalled by how
rudely her erstwhile heroes treat her people at the Pool. Her former
motto is translated literally into a sour question: "Maintain the
right?" (100).

Even so-called facts are the prey of interpretation. Language,
whether or not it is used to deceive, can convey only partial and
subjective realities. The narrator observes her distance from her
vociferous aunt: "For [Emily], the vision is the truth as she lives it.
When she is called like Habakkuk to the witness stand, her testimony is to the light that shines in the lives of the Nisei, in their
desperation to prove themselves Canadian, in their tough and gentle spirit. The truth for me is more murky, shadowy and grey" (32).

Naomi's sense of truth is shared by Yamamoto, Kingston, and
Kogawa; all of them question the notion of a transparent language,
a transparent history. Yet their questions and their multiple answers are themselves ploys to get at truth. Trinh T. Minh-ha says of
effective storytelling in general: "Truth . . . is not attained here
through logocentric certainties. . . . The boundaries of lie and
truth are . . . multiplied, reversed, and displaced without rendering meaningless either the notion of lie or that of truth. Directly
questioned, the story is also indirectly unquestionable in its truthfulness" (1991, 13–14). The observation applies equally to the
works of our three authors, who recoil at "logocentric certainties."
These writers share Trinh's skepticism that

> without a certain work of displacement, "speaking about" only par-
> takes in the conservation of systems of binary opposition (sub-
> ject/object; I/It; We/They) on which territorialized knowledge de-
> pends. It places a semantic distance between oneself and the
> work. . . . It secures for the speaker a position of mastery. . . . Truth
> is the instrument of a mastery which I [speaker] exert over areas of
> the unknown as I gather them within the fold of the known. (12)

---

among the Japanese Canadians lobbying for an official apology and reparations
from the Canadian government" (Yim D8). Kogawa wishes to close the gap.

As we saw in Chapter 3, verbalization may not in itself touch the root of a speakers inhibition; Maxine's attempt at command only exacerbates her linguistic anxiety. Naomi, no stranger to coercive speech, is all too wary of parroting authorities. Her insistence on the murkiness of truth is her way of abdicating mastery. She cannot make her vision "plain" because she refuses to place a "semantic distance" between herself and the story she is telling.

One of Naomi's gray areas concerns her memory of Slocan. In her young mind even a deserted ghost town takes on Edenic qualities after Uncle joins them: "Uncle makes a rock garden in the front yard with a tiny stream and waterfall winding around the base to a small pool" (138). Life becomes a "quiet and pleasant holiday" (138) until they undergo a second "exile from [the] place of exile" (197):

> The fact is that, in 1945, the gardens in Slocan were spectacular. . . . The fact is that families already fractured and separated were perma nently destroyed. The choice to go east of the Rockies or to Japan was presented without time for consultation with separated parents and children. Failure to choose was labelled non-cooperation. (183)

The word "labelled" suggests that "fact" is manufactured discursively, and the rest of the passage discloses its subjective nature. Naomi's nostalgic evocation of Slocan—where she lives in a dilapidated wooden hut—may well be an impressionist painting. But she succeeds in conveying the fact that the industry of her kin has transformed a wasteland into an idyllic environment and that in comparison with the beet fields in Alberta, Slocan is indeed a paradise lost. And precisely because its beauty is hard won, the second uprooting hurts all the more.

Then there are those experiences painful or horrifying beyond words. Nettled by Emily's imperative to tell all, Naomi recalls the ordeal of stoop labor in the "oven" of Alberta and stalls: "I cannot tell about this time. . . . The body will not tell" (196). But even these ineffable hardships are dwarfed by the holocaust in Nagasaki. The grandmother's attempt to describe its ravages is "chaotic," "the details interspersed without chronological consistency" (236). The unspeakable event strains enunciation.

Ultimately the narrator doubts the very effectiveness of language. She wonders whether anything tangible can come out of Emily's polemics:

> All of Aunt Emily's words, all her papers, the telegrams and petitions, are like scratchings in the barnyard, the evidence of much activity, scaly claws hard at work. But what good they do, I do not know—those little black typewritten words—rain words, cloud droppings. They do not touch us where we are planted here in Alberta. . . . The words are not made flesh. . . . All my prayers disappear into space. (189)

To Naomi, Emily's collections of facts and didactic analysis are but so much sound; they hardly alleviate actual suffering or inspire redeeming vision, let alone "bring contentment" (42). Speaking of her own writing, Kogawa remarked: "Documents and facts are intended to direct our prejudiced hearts but rarely provide direction by themselves. I have boxes and boxes of documents but what I need is vision and vision comes from relationship. Facts bereft of love direct us nowhere" (Redekop 15).

These instances address the contradictory dimensions of language. On the one hand, language is often equivocal, owing to its shifting signifiers and the partial nature of "truth." On the other hand, the effect of language varies with the speaker. Words spoken by the powerless have no impact; they only tantalize as "prayers disappear into space" (189). Language issued by the powerful, however, can constitute a form of speech act, commanding performance. Emily writes:

> They're making (they say) accommodation for 1,200–1,300 women and children in that little Park! Bureaucrats find it so simple on paper and it's translated willy-nilly into action—and the pure hell that results is kept "hush hush" from the public, who are already kicking about the "luxury" given to Japs. (92)

Thinking back on the internment, she remarks, "It was an evacuation all right. . . . Flushed out of Vancouver. Like dung drops. Maggot bait. . . . None of us . . .escaped the naming. We were defined and identified by the way we were seen." Japanese Canadians were portrayed by a newspaper in British Columbia as "a stench in the nostrils of the people of Canada" and "were therefore relegated to the cesspools" (118). Semantics forms and deforms politics.

Precisely because language, no matter how inaccurate and distorted, carries material consequences, lies must not stand uncontradicted. Discourse, though tied to power, may also unveil the abuse of power. In Foucault's words, "Discourse transmits and produces power; it reinforces it, but also undermines and exposes it, renders it fragile and makes it possible to thwart it" (1976/1980, 101). Edward Said, however, sees a certain limit in Foucault's emphasis on the ubiquity of power: "If power oppresses and controls and manipulates, then everything that resists it is not morally equal to power, is not neutrally and simply a weapon against that power. Resistance cannot equally be an adversarial alternative to power and a dependent function of it" (1983, 246).

Emily tries (as does Maxine) "to assume the symbolic armor, to name the law and attack it using the same laws" (Jardine 231). Naomi, however wants to find a different verbal medium altogether, one that is "not morally equal to power," one that can hold a listener without coming across as coercive or dogmatic, that can transform "white sound" into "living word."

Attentive Silence

If skepticism about language and interrogation of consensus align Kogawa with many a woman writer and postmodernist thinker, her ability to project a spectrum of silence is, as Fujita suggests, traceable to her bicultural heritage. To monitor this peculiar sensibility, one must avoid gliding over the tonalities of silence in the novel. The protagonist, to be sure, struggles against oppressive silencing. She also feels divided about the protective and stoic restraint of the issei, which has sheltered her as a child but paralyzes her as an adult. She continues nevertheless to cherish the quiet attentiveness of her female forerunners. These forms of silence must be addressed separately.

Oppressive silence in the novel takes both individual and collective forms, inflicted on women and men alike. After molesting Naomi, Old Man Gower forbids her to divulge the violation:

" 'Don't tell your mother,' he whispers into my ear" (64).[10] Later, when the Canadian government suppresses the Japanese Canadians, Emily notes: "All cards and letters are censored. . . . Not a word from the camps makes the papers. Everything is hushed up" (101).

Benedict Anderson has convincingly argued that print media have a way of cohering people by creating an "imagined community" of readers (47, 49). The reverse, Kogawa suggests, also holds. When a people are deprived of a voice in the general press, they are ex-communicated from the larger community. And to demolish their ethnic press and other ethnic forums is forcibly to shatter a cohesive community and expunge its cultural identity. Naomi laments: "We are the despised rendered voiceless, stripped of car, radio, camera and every means of communication" (111). Such silencing accords well with the intent, announced in one newspaper, "to prevent further propagation of the species" (98). Naomi insinuates as much: "Some families grow on and on through the centuries, hardy and visible and procreative. Others disappear from the earth without a whimper" (21).

By tracing the decline of Naomi's family, Kogawa, like Yamamoto and Kingston, furnishes insights into the matrix of gender and race that go beyond the obvious double jeopardy of minority women and the general equation of men with powerful patriarchs. Japanese Canadian men, too, are emphatically not immune to persecution in *Obasan*. Naomi's grandfather, father, and surrogate father are subject not only to the "Laws of the [white] Ruling Fathers" (Goellnicht 1989, 298) but also to the "ill-will" of the Canadian Imperial Order of Daughters of the Empire, who, Emily reports, "said we were all spies and saboteurs" (82). The three nikkei fathers are singled out for "special" treatment: they are abruptly separated from their families and put to work in road camps or imprisoned. Stephen, a child at the time of the war, sustains permanent, if invisible, damage: he turns his back on Japanese culture completely.

The silencing inflicted upon each of the male characters constitutes a muted yet distinctive strain in a novel concerned largely with female interaction. Uncle (Isamu Nakane), a boat designer

[10] Similar silencing after sexual molestation by a father figure occurs in Maya Angelou's *I Know Why the Caged Bird Sings* and Alice Walker's *Color Purple*.

and builder in Vancouver, is removed from the coast that he loves to Alberta. To assuage his longing, he looks on the undulating prairie grass as a sea. His enforced separation from the ocean gains in poignancy if we recall that his own father (by adoption) had found abiding solace in the sea on leaving Japan: "When he left his familiar island, he became a stranger, sailing towards an island of strangers. But the sea was his constant companion. He understood its angers, its whisperings, its generosity" (18). Uncle is thus twice exiled—from his home and from the sea—to a rasping wasteland.

Now the "craft" most often associated with him is "stone bread." The change from boat to stone-bread signals the loss of his vocation and his enforced domestication, a hardening experience that accounts in part for his deep withdrawal. But the stone-bread also betokens his own hardiness. In Naomi's eyes, Uncle, no less than Obasan, is an icon of rugged endurance unto his last days: "Uncle could be Chief Sitting Bull. . . . He has the same prairie-baked skin, the deep brown furrows like dry river beds creasing his cheeks" (2).

Unlike Uncle and Obasan, Father (Mark Nakane) does not survive the war. Unable to protect his family, he probably experiences a greater degree of mortification than Uncle. His gradual loss of voice bespeaks his sense of impotence and foreshadows his end. Father, the accomplished singer and versatile musician who "plays every instrument by ear" (51), contracts tuberculosis during the war. Aggravated by the condition of the road camps, the illness leads eventually to death. His physical deterioration is auditorily conveyed: "his rich baritone voice is weak and thin as if his throat is in pain" (177). But his ailment does not dampen his musical zeal. We get a telling glimpse of Father from Emily, who comments on a letter he sent from a road camp: "Crazy man. All he thinks about are Stephen's music lessons" (105). Father evidently wants, against all odds, to protect his son's inherited talent.

Notwithstanding the paternal concern, Stephen also undergoes a silencing at once literal and figurative. After the bombing of Pearl Harbor he is attacked by white boys who break his violin; in Alberta his flute cracks from the parching heat. Stephen eventually receives widespread recognition as a Western classical musician, touring Europe frequently. But only at the cost of renouncing his Japanese heritage. Deviating from the considerate behavior that so characterizes everyone else in his family, he adopts the prejudice and rough ways of his oppressors.[11] More and more he spurns his own people and culture. He tells Obasan to "talk properly" (81) and repeatedly brushes Naomi off. On hearing his uncle recite a Japanese poem, he inquires curtly, "Whazzat?" (217). His younger sister, by contrast, has no difficulty supplying an appreciative answer: "It's a haiku, a seventeen-syllable word picture" (217). The limp that Stephen develops just before the internment (a period when he begins to remove himself gradually from his relatives' Japanese ways) seems to be a physical sign of the social handicap he feels as a nikkei.[12] The "white cast up to his thigh," likened to a "cocoon" (112), embodies the defensive shell he builds around himself. As though to vent his anger at being punished for no reason, he exercises reckless violence as soon as he arrives at Slocan, lashing out at butterflies with his crutch: "Within moments, the ground and grasses are quivering with maimed and dismembered butterflies" (123). As an adult he escapes his family. On one rare occasion he visits Granton for a brief afternoon with a French divorcée. Obasan prepares a meal "that was as non-Japanese as she could manage but they left without eating" (223). Eight years pass before he reappears again, at Uncle's funeral.

The experiences of Uncle, Father, and Stephen undermine the popular feminist opposition of powerful males and powerless females. In *Obasan*, as in "The Legend" and *China Men*, racial abuse is as stifling as sexual molestation. The similarity of these two forms of oppression is made explicit by Naomi. When Stephen is beaten up by white boys, he refuses to tell Naomi what has caused his injury. Naomi intuits, "Is he ashamed, as I was in Old Man Gower's bathroom?" (70). Rape, Erika Gottlieb points out, is used here as a "metaphor for any kind of violation" (45). Like Stephen,

[11] Though Emily may strike some readers as aggressive, she is a most caring relative. After Uncle's death she anxiously inquires after Obasan in a long-distance call to Naomi, who thinks to herself. "It's such a relief to feel her sharing my concern" (78). The subtext of Naomi's remark is that Stephen, the only other remaining relative, has become coldly apathetic toward his kin. See Kogawa 1988 for further examples of Stephen's callousness.

[12] Such an inward wound, inflicted or aggravated by the war, is also felt by the narrator of Monica Sone's *Nisei Daughter:* "An old wound opened up again, and I found myself shrinking inwardly from my Japanese blood, the blood of an enemy" (145–46). For a detailed comparison of *Nisei Daughter* and *Obasan*, see Lim 1990.

many Japanese Canadians refuse to describe what Rose calls their "political and spiritual rape" by the Canadian government (1988, 224).

The metaphor effectively secures the connection between oppression and repression. Instead of voicing anger at the subjugators, most victims of rape seal their lips in shame. The child Naomi, whose relationship with her mother has been one of mutual trust, begins to nurse a secret that separates her from her mother after her molestation. Dispossessed and dispersed all over the country after the war, many nikkei tried to assimilate quickly into the dominant culture so as not to be noticed. "None of my friends today are Japanese Canadians," Naomi discloses (38).[13] All she wants at first is to forget the past: "Crimes of history . . . can stay in history. . . . Questions from all these papers, questions referring to turbulence in the past, are an unnecessary upheaval" (41, 45). Her resignation is ultimately complicit with social amnesia: her self-imposed silence feeds the one imposed externally.

Naomi's evasions, which fall readily into a pattern explored in psychology as "posttraumatic stress disorder," are shared by many actual victims of sexual and political abuse. "The conflict between the will to deny horrible events and the will to proclaim them aloud is the central dialectic of psychological trauma," the psychiatrist Judith Lewis Herman observes. "The ordinary response . . . is to banish them from consciousness. Certain violations of the social compact are too terrible to utter aloud: this is the meaning of the word *unspeakable*." But these experiences, Herman emphasizes, "refuse to be buried. . . . Remembering and telling the truth about terrible events are prerequisites both for the restoration of the social order and for the healing of individual victims" (1). Similarly, Naomi learns that it is both impossible to bracket the past and self-destructive to do so. Emily warns her: "You have to remember. . . . You are your history. If you cut any of it off you're an amputee. Don't deny the past. Remember everything. If you're bitter, be bitter. Cry it out! Scream! Denial is gangrene" (49–50).

[13] Kogawa is apparently writing from her own experience: "There are still a great many Japanese Canadians who fled into the woods as I did, to try to hide from our ethnicity. We learned to shun one another and to view any Japanese-Canadian gathering as a gaggle of ghettoized geese. One of my points of rediscovery came when I found that I could actually have Japanese-Canadian friends" (1985, 60).

Yet Naomi's ability to scream has been curbed by her schooling in the protective and stoic silence of the issei and nisei. During a childhood crisis when she watches a big white hen peck a batch of infant yellow chicks to death (an incident that clearly adumbrates the pending interracial dynamics), Mother comes immediately to the rescue: "With swift deft fingers, Mother removes the live chicks first, placing them in her apron. All the while that she acts, there is calm efficiency in her face and she does not speak" (59). Obasan also exhibits serenity in the face of commotion: even on the eve of the evacuation "Aya is being very calm and she doesn't want any discussion in front of the kids. All she's told them is that they're going for a train ride" (108). An involuntary exodus is recast as a pleasant excursion—"for the sake of the children."

A point comes when such silence, as a form of enforced inno-cence, infantilizes. An older Naomi regards this protection with ambivalence. As she presses for more information about her moth-er, she is constantly frustrated by tight-lipped Obasan: "The great-er my urgency to know, the thicker her silences have always been. No prodding will elicit clues" (45). When Naomi asks her about the letters written in Japanese—letters describing the bombing in Nagasaki—Obasan produces instead a photograph of Naomi taken with her mother before she left for Japan. In substituting sweet memory for harsh facts, Obasan submits to the wishes of Naomi's mother. But this complicit silence has caused the greater anguish. As Michael Fischer has pointed out in discussing Michael Arlen's *Passage to Ararat*, "by attempting to spare children knowledge of painful past experiences, parents often create an obsessive void in the child that must be explored and filled in" (204). Although such exploration can give wing to creativity, as I have argued for *The Woman Warrior* and *China Men*, such is not the case (as least not in any immediate sense) with Naomi, who holds herself responsible in some way for her mother's disappearance. In contrast to Max-ine, who vehemently reports sexist and racist abuse, Naomi is weighed down by guilt and "drowned in a whirlpool of protective silence" (21). She tries to escape the marauding memories of her own abuse, but the "obsessive void" in her is filled by one night-mare after another. In retrospect, the narrator blames her mother (and by implication Obasan) for seeking to "protect [Stephen and her] with lies" (242).

The stoic silence of the issei is presented with a similar mixture of appreciation and criticism. The issei, as we saw in Chapter 2, believe in *gaman*, in quiet forbearance, in dignified silence. During the war they mustered enormous strength to swallow white prejudice, weather the ravages of the internment, and, above all, shelter the young as much as possible from physical and psychological harm. Wakako Yamauchi eloquently tells of this quiet strength, which the nisei have also inherited:

> The sansei accuse us [nisei] of not wanting to talk about the evacuation experience. And it's true. . . . And when we do see those old photographs of the mass evacuation . . . few of us can hold back the tears that most often smack of self-pity, but maybe somewhere behind those tears we know that this is the event that changed the course of our lives, and though there were those among us who had more insight, more courage, whatever path we chose, we have survived—whole. Maybe that's why so many of us remain silent about our camp experience. Maybe in our silence we ask you to honor us for that—survival. . . . The fact of our survival is proof of our valor. And that is enough. (1979, lxxi)

The issei grandfather in Janice Mirikitani's *Shedding Silence* goes further: "Silence is a form of strength. / More is said / with wordless defiance" (137–38). In the eyes of the dominant culture, however, such silence suggested passivity and hence open season. Kogawa capsulates these opposite perceptions of silence in two successive images: "We are the silences that speak from stone. . . . We disappear into the future undemanding as dew" (111–12). Stone connotes sturdiness, endurance, and impregnability; dew, by contrast, suggests fragility, evanescence, and vulnerability. Placed side by side, the two figures embody the "tough and gentle spirit" of the nikkei. The images also reveal the complex attitude of the Japanese Canadian author. Kogawa acknowledges the physical and inner strength of the issei: steeling or petrifying oneself is a requisite to survival in taxing environments such as the ghost town of Slocan and the beet farm of Alberta. The silence exemplified by Uncle and Obasan attests at once to their strength to endure and their power to forgive. At the same time, their magnanimity—redoubled by their Christian belief in turning the other cheek—

lends itself to exploitation by the dominant culture. Like dew, they can be easily "wiped out."

Yet Kogawa does not allow the negative implications of silence to engulf its positive manifestations, of which the most disarming is attentive silence. This form of silence seems related to the Japanese notions of *sassi*, a "mental function of catching a sign from a speaker" (Nishida 47) and *ishin-denshin*, "telepathy" or "sympathy, quiet understanding" (Nelson 126). As a noun *sassi* can be translated as "conjecture, surmise, guess, judgment and understanding what a person means and what a sign means"; in its verb form, *sassuru*, "its usage is expanded to mean "imagine, suppose, and even sympathize with, feel for, and make allowances for" (Nishida 47). The phrase *ishin-denshin*—literally "by means of heart to heart"—has Chinese roots (Kunihiro 57); it describes an "immediate communication (of truth) from one mind to another," or a "tacit understanding" (Masuda 556).[14]

Attentive silence in *Obasan* incorporates the visual sensitivity and the anticipatory responsiveness implied in *sassi*, the intuitive understanding implied in *ishin-denshin*, and the empathy implied in both. As Fujita observes, "attendance" is instilled in Naomi since infancy, through the very decor of her prewar home in Vancouver (38): "Above my bed with the powdery blue patchwork quilt is a picture of a little girl with a book in her lap, looking up into a tree where a bird sits. One of the child's hands is half raised as she watches and listens, attending the bird" (52–53). This "looking" and "watching" are the very antitheses of the kind of staring directed toward Miss Sasagawara in Yamamoto's "Legend." A stare turns an "other" into an object; attentive watching tries to get inside the other and to anticipate the other's need. The narrator in *Obasan* differentiates a discrete look, a stare, and a protective look:

[14] I thank my student Barbara Jung for pointing out the relevance to *Obasan* of *sassi* and *ishin-denshin*. Kunihiro observes that in Japan, which is by and large an endogamous society, "explanations through the medium of language often become unnecessary, and the intuitive, nonverbal communication of the sort that develops among family members living under the same roof spreads throughout the society" (58). But Kunihiro also notes that "the traditions which developed this subtle communication by means of wordless expressions" have been eroded to some extent by "modern civilization with its overemphasis on logic" (58). Such erosion probably occurs at an even faster rate in nikkei societies, constantly exposed to and judged according to Western norms.

"My mother's eyes look obliquely to the floor, declaring that . . . in all public places, even a glance can be indiscreet. But a stare? Such lack of decorum . . . is as unthinkable as nudity on the street" (47–48). She later describes her mother's ability to sense and minister to her need: "Her eyes are steady and matter of fact—the eyes of Japanese motherhood. They do not invade and betray. They are eyes that protect, shielding what is hidden most deeply in the heart of the child" (59). But visual attendance does more than shield; it also monitors feeling. On the day Naomi learns that her family is to be dislocated again, this time from Slocan to Alberta, she senses trouble from her father's averted gaze: "I can see it in Father's eyes . . . the eyes searching elsewhere" (172). Years later, when she asks Aunt Emily about Mother and Grandma, she again grasps what is communicated without words: "I could feel that somewhere, beneath her eyes, a shutter had clicked open and shut at my mentioning Mother and Grandma. It was as if my unexpected question was a sudden beam of pain that had to be extinguished immediately" (186). The telltale signs halt further questions.[15]

Visual attendance, as depicted in the bedroom picture, is inseparable from the little girl's thoughtfulness and poised hand. Far from suggesting passivity, this form of silence entails both mental vigilance and physical readiness. The picture's message is enacted by Grandma, Mother, and Obasan, who also supply positive reinforcement for Naomi:

> When I am hungry, and before I can ask, there is food. If I am weary, every place is a bed. . . . A sweater covers me before there is any chill and if there is pain there is care simultaneously. If Grandma shifts uncomfortably, I bring her a cushion.
> "Yoku ki ga tsuku ne," Grandma responds. It is a statement in appreciation of sensitivity and appropriate gestures. (56)[16]

---

[15] Kogawa's emphasis on communication through the eyes resonates with "forms of unspoken communication such as *haragei* [the art of subtle communication] and *me wa kuchi hodo ni mono o ii* [the eyes say as much as the mouth], forms that are in constant use in Japan "to keep interpersonal relations harmonious through nondialectic means" (Kunihiro 58).

[16] Fujita, who translates the Japanese words as "You really notice/are aware/are attentive, aren't you?" also notes that the phrase "looks back to the painting of the girl 'attending' the bird" (39). See also Magnusson 61.

The "alert and accurate knowing" of Mother and Grandma involves neither explicit request nor open inquiry. At the point when
Naomi's grandparents have been taken to the hospital, Obasan
similarly offers unspoken consolation. Naomi reflects:

> We must always honour the wishes of others before our own. We will
> make the way smooth by restraining emotion. Though we might
> wish Grandma and Grandpa to stay, we must watch them go. To try
> to meet one's own needs in spite of the wishes of others is to be
> "wagamama"—selfish and inconsiderate. Obasan teaches me not to
> be wagamama by always heeding everyone's needs. That is why she
> is waiting patiently beside me at this bridge. (128)

These instances trace attentive silence to a maternal tradition in
Japanese culture. Naomi has learned it from Grandma, Mother,
and her surrogate mother, Obasan, all of whom have been raised
in Japan.[17] Yet it is also to be directed beyond one's kin, as is
evident from what occurs on the train from Vancouver to Slocan. A
young woman who has given birth just before boarding does not
have a single baby item with her. Obasan, who discerns "hurt and
a need for tenderness" (113), quietly places a bundle containing a
towel and some fruit in front of the mother. Her kindness inspires
another old woman to follow suit. Little Naomi, taking stock of
these acts, is herself moved to munificence: she notices her brother's unhappiness and "in a fit of generosity" slips a present (her
favorite ball) into his pocket (116).

These acts contrast sharply with the church people's charity in
"The Legend." In *Obasan* the anticipatory acts are performed without speaking so that the receiving party need not feel embarrass-
ment. In Yamamoto's story the interned recipients of "eleemosynary" Christmas presents are specifically *required* to "write and
thank" their benefactors "outside" (29), thereby experiencing a
heightened sense of humiliation and alterity. In comparison, the
Japanese Canadians on the train, where "even strangers are addressed as 'ojisan' [uncle] or 'obasan'" (112), foster intimacy. The
scene has a utopian quality that reminds one of Bak Goong's pipe
dream in *China Men*. Given sufficient caring and empathy, both
Kingston and Kogawa imply, strangers could turn kin indeed.

---

[17] Caudill & Weinstein 1969 observe that the mother-infant relationship is much
less verbal in Japan than in America.

Grandma and Mother disappear early in Naomi's life. The person who influences Naomi into adulthood is Obasan.[18] In this aunt the woe and wonder of silence converge. Kogawa chooses her name as the title of the book because, as she said in an interview, Obasan "is totally silent." "If we never really see Obasan," she noted, "she will always be oppressed" (Wayne 23). Obasan's quiet fortitude makes her an easy target of subjugation, and Kogawa appeals openly to the reader to hear in Obasan "the silence that cannot speak." But she does not enjoin Obasan to emulate Emily. As readers, we must be wary of adopting the attitude of Stephen, who scorns Obasan's Japanese ways; or that of Mrs. Barker, whose "glance at Obasan is one of condescension" (224).

The "'world'-travelling" advocated by María Lugones points to a better way:

Through travelling to other people's "worlds" we discover that there are "worlds" in which those who are the victims of arrogant perception are really subjects, lively beings, resistors, constructors of visions even though in the mainstream construction they are animated only by the arrogant perceiver and are pliable, foldable, file-away-able, classifiable. (402)

The narrator herself never regards Obasan arrogantly. Her difference from Stephen, and also from Maxine in *The Woman Warrior* (both of whom have been "educated" to look upon their own people as aliens), may ironically be attributed to her delayed North American schooling. She was still at preschool age when she was removed to Slocan, where, for a while, life was a "quiet and pleasant holiday" (138). Not until May 1943, when she was seven, did she "first attend school" (138). Inculcated instead in Obasan's ways, she can still travel to that "silent territory" as an adult.

Because of this close contact, Naomi has a notable respect for Obasan's silence. She divines unspoken meanings beneath Obasan's reticence and wishes to enter "the vault of her thoughts" (26). She textualizes the inaudible: "The language of her grief is silence. She has learned it well, its idioms, its nuances. Over the years, silence within her small body has grown large and powerful" (14). The quietest character in the novel, Obasan is also the

[18] See also Gottlieb 52, Fujita 40, and Lim 1990, 203, on Obasan's mixed impact on Naomi.

most attentive. Like the old woman in Toshio Mori's "Woman who Makes Swell Donuts," she is remarkable for being unremarkable. (She performs what Wordsworth in "Tintern Abbey" eulogizes as those "little, nameless, unremembered acts of kindness and of love.") One marked achievement of this novel is the finesse with which the author renders a wordless figure into an unforgettable character. But Kogawa cautions us against viewing this character solely through Eurocentric or even revisionist eyes: "Obasan . . . does not come from this clamorous climate. She does not dance to the multi-cultural piper's tune or respond to the racist's slur. She remains in a silent territory, defined by her serving hands" (226).[19]

The passage may be read in the light of Kogawa's preface to *Issei*, by Gordon Nakayama, her father: "I do not wish to romanticize the Issei but to humbly and gratefully acknowledge what it was that shone with such deep energy through their lives—in their hands, in their silences" (1984, 7). Naomi's ability to harken to Obasan's body language, to esteem her "serving hands," evinces her Japanese inheritance. Acculturated in attendance, Naomi continues to exemplify it as an adult. Watching Obasan ascend to an attic, she follows her with a posture similar to that of the little girl in the bedroom picture—"holding the railing with my left hand, my right arm poised to catch her if she stumbles" (23). During the wake for Uncle, Naomi has a strong urge to burrow into Emily's journal, yet she desists: the journal "feels heavy with voices from the past . . . but right now it is Uncle's absent voice that speaks even more urgently and that I must attend." The voice bids her to "care for Obasan" and "to keep her safe" (46). Since Uncle is no longer physically present, his communication with Naomi is an instance of *ishin-denshin*, which can occur in the absence of speech and gestures. Naomi, accordingly, watches quietly beside her aunt: "My arms are suffused with an urge to hold, but a hug would startle her. I can only sit quietly beside her and wait for small signs of her return" (27).

[19] Houston notes that Japanese Americans and white Americans frequently have different attitudes toward serving: "In my family, to serve another could be uplifting, a gracious gesture that elevated oneself. For many white Americans it seems that serving another is degrading, an indication of dependency or weakness in character, or a low place in the social ladder. To be ardently considerate is to be 'self-effacing' or apologetic" (20). The dominance of such an attitude perhaps explains why so many reviewers have found Obasan unappealing.

Even attentive silence has its slippery side. Unqualified endorsement of attentiveness can reinforce traditional mores (such as those also associated with motherhood) that, precisely because of their positive valences, are especially binding for women. Constant heed to the needs of others—as is normally required of mothers—is often achieved at great expense. Obasan, serving others all the time, has obviously taken insufficient care of herself. For all her inner strength, she has become extremely weak in sight and speech and hearing in her old age. On one level, her handicaps play out the classic paradox (the blind sees, etc.); on another, it bespeaks sociopolitical constraint as well as self-censorship (she was an accomplished koto player before she married). The narrator, being culturally and "visually bilingual," like Aunt Emily and Father (47), can both credit Obasan's attentiveness and take account of the toll it has exacted from her aunt.

The climax of the novel recapitulates the destructive as well as the enabling aspects of silence. Naomi finally learns (from her grandma's letters) about her mother's disfigurement. Bewildered, she at first can only bewail her mother's excessive protection: "Gentle Mother, we were lost together in our silences. Our wordlessness was our mutual destruction" (234). The mother's precaution has inflicted a "double wound" on the daughter: "The child is forever unable to speak. The child forever fears to tell" (243). These utterances, when heard against the child Naomi's association of silence with Mother's immediate presence, with anchorage and safety, measure the distance the narrator has since traveled. As Magnusson observes, "the mother's silence after Nagasaki alters the quality of her silence in Naomi's childhood" (66).

Yet I disagree with Magnusson's conclusion: "This revision of the past privileges speech over silence, language—with all its inadequacy—over a delusory wordless security" (66). First, the binary opposition of language and silence (an opposition that I myself have not been able to circumvent entirely owing to the common usage of the terms) often breaks down in Kogawa's novel, where silence becomes, as it were, a figure of speech ("The language of [Obasan's] grief is silence"; "Aunt Emily and father . . . are visually bilingual"; "wordless word"). Second, silence in *Obasan*, as I have demonstrated, connotes much more than "a delusory wordless security." Most important, Kogawa never "privileges" speech over silence in all its manifestations.

Almost in the same breath that the narrator remonstrates against protective silence, she invokes "attendance," which, as Fujita observes, "supports Naomi in her moment of greatest need" (39). The act ushers in the process of healing: "Gradually the room grows still and it is as if I am back with Uncle again, listening and listening to the silent earth and the silent sky as I have done all my life. . . . Mother. I am listening. Assist me to hear you" (240). In this receptive state she hears "the sigh of . . . remembered breath, a wordless word" (241). She is able to conjure up her mother's presence, and empathy restores the original bond: "Young Mother at Nagasaki, am I not also there?" (242). The communion continues:

> I am thinking that for a child there is no presence without flesh. But perhaps it is because I am no longer a child I can know your presence though you are not here. The letters tonight are skeletons. Bones only. But the earth still stirs with dormant blooms. Love flows through the roots of the trees by our graves. (243)

Naomi breathes life into the "bones only" letters by means of *ishindenshin*, "from heart to heart." Her grasp of an absent presence through imaginative empathy grows out of her sedulous heedfulness. She finally discovers the key to the cryptic epigraph: "The speech that frees comes forth from that amniotic deep. To attend its voice, I can hear it say, is to embrace its absence."[20]

Speaking Dreams

Attuned to the contradictory potential of both words and silence, Kogawa uses multivocal discourses to articulate the manifold nature of reality and employs a number of elliptical devices to harness the power of the unspoken. The polyglossia of *Obasan* has often been noted. Manina Jones describes it as "a simultaneously literary, historical, and theoretical work" (214; see also Merivale 68;

---

[20] Kogawa said in an interview that she connects the mother's absence with divine abandonment: "Love's presence is only understood when stripped of its potency and paradoxically its power to heal us comes when we embrace its impotence" (Redekop 17).

Goellnicht 1989, 294; Lim 1990, 291). Like Kingston, Kogawa mingles the journalistic with the poetic and admits contesting voices into her novel. As the preface points out, much of the novel is "based on historical events, and many of the persons named are real." A number of quotations in Emily's journal are drawn from files in the Public Archives of Canada, and much of her private journal is reconstructed from the real letters of Muriel Kitagawa, a public figure. The juxtaposition of official and personal letters erodes the boundary between public and private discourse. These interconnected voices make for multiple layers of perception in her novel.

Less obviously, the voice of the narrator is undercut by her act of narration. As in *The Woman Warrior*, the explicit narrative voice and the implicit narrative action frequently clash. Although Naomi expresses misgivings about all kinds of political maneuvers, *Obasan*— published at a time when Japanese Canadians were seeking reparations for the internment and when the antinuclear movement was gathering strength in Europe and North America—resonates with political implications. It is perhaps no coincidence that the book emerged when it did. According to Herman, "In the absence of strong political movements for human rights, the active process of bearing witness inevitably gives way to the active process of forgetting. Repression, dissociation, and denial are phenomena of social as well as individual consciousness" (9).[21] The kind of political activism that Emily/Kitagawa participates in provides the necessary condition for Naomi/Kogawa to break her personal silence. *Obasan* ends not with the narrative proper but with an "excerpt from the memorandum sent by the Co-operative Committee on Japanese Canadians to the House and the Senate of Canada, April 1946" (248). Through this inset document, which protests against the deportation of Japanese Canadians, the author tacitly acknowledges the many political activists who have fought for the cause of justice.

---

[21] Herman shows that the systematic investigation of psychological trauma also "depends on the support of a political movement": the study of hysteria grew out of the anticlerical political movement of the late nineteenth century in France, the study of combat neurosis took place during an antiwar movement that peaked after the Vietnam war, and the study of sexual and domestic violence emerged during the feminist movement (9).

Another disjunction between the narrative voice and the narrative act occurs in the evaluation of history. Throughout the novel
Naomi denies the possibility of knowing history, for "ordinary
stories are changed in time, altered as much by the present as the
present is shaped by the past" (25). Yet "history has begun to
emerge . . . as early as the novel's first chapter" (Rose 1987, 292). A
specific example of such duality occurs when Naomi casts doubt on
Emily's conviction that one can "get the facts straight" (183). As we
saw earlier, she finds in Emily's package a newspaper clipping and
an index card with the words "Facts about evacuees in Alberta."
The clipping has a photograph of one family, all smiles, standing
around a pile of beets; the caption reads: "Grinning and Happy"
(193). Naomi, for her part, remembers Alberta differently:

> It's so hard and so hot that my tear glands burn out. . . . The lumps
> of clay mud stick on my gumboots and weight my legs and the skin
> under the boots beneath the knees at the level of the calves grows red
> and hard and itchy . . . and the fine hairs on my legs grow coarse
> there and ugly.
>   I mind growing ugly.
>   I mind the harvest time and the hands and the wrists bound in rags
> to keep the wrists from breaking open. . . . I cannot tell about this
> time, Aunt Emily. The body will not tell. (196)

She concludes wryly by returning to the caption. " 'Grinning and
happy' . . . ? That is one telling. It's not how it was" (197). Even as
Naomi contradicts the printed facts, she provides an alternative
"telling" that makes for a truer picture of the enforced relocation.
The facts written all over Naomi's body are those that even Emily
(who moved to Vancouver with her father before the evacuation)
cannot see. By presenting Naomi's account, Kogawa counters historical manipulation of facts with novelistic record; in opposition to
the social memory she offers Naomi's personal memorial.
   The author presents divergent perspectives on the proper response to this personal and social memory. Throughout the novel
Emily and Naomi argue. Emily criticizes the narrator's fair-minded
stance: "Some people . . . are so busy seeing all sides of every
issue that they neutralize concern and prevent necessary action"
(35). She insinuates that intellectual sophistication could stymie
political activity. Though mindful of the criticism, Naomi doubts

that Emily's hard-line verbal crusade will be any more effective in remedying social evils: "Greed, selfishness, and hatred remain as constant as the human condition, do they not? Or are you thinking that through lobbying and legislation, speech-making and story-telling, we can extricate ourselves from our foolish ways? Is there evidence for optimism?" (199). Emily, Naomi implies, protests in vain; for all her efforts, few have been converted. She pictures her "erasing, rewriting, underlining, trying to find the right mix that strikes home. Like Cupid, she aimed for the heart. But the heart was not there" (40).

The implicit analogy of words and arrows brings to mind both Native American and feminist conceptions of language as weapon (cf. Basso 40; Lincoln 1983, 44; Jardine 231). But much more reveal-ing of the narrator's own poetics here is her image of the shooter as Cupid. Where Emily is content to use words to bring legislative changes, the narrator/author wishes above all to aim "for the heart" of her readers. Though it may strike some readers as insuffi-ciently "political," Kogawa's quiet style does pose a radical alter-native to political discourse. What Ramón Saldívar says of Cherríe Moraga's *Loving in the War Years* can be applied to *Obasan* as well:

> In sharp contrast to the word of the Fathers, the authoritative dis-course of the political, religious, moral world that strives to determine the very basis of the subject's interrelationships with the world and other subjects, Moraga offers the word of love. . . . This loving word is denied all privileges, backed by no authority, and not even ac-knowledged to be an ideological discourse in its own right. (197)

In this sense, the narrator who questions the efficacy of Emily's polemics is herself approximating a "right mix." Gary Willis attri-butes the "affect" of the novel to the power of narrative, "a power much greater than that of discursive argument" (249). But I believe the power derives more specifically from the author's muted rheto-ric, from her way of punctuating words with silences. Shattered imagery pervades Naomi's reminiscences, described at one point as "fragments of fragments," as "segments of stories" (53); at an-other as "dream images" (112). The reader must attend to the unar-ticulated linkages and piece together the broken parts; meaning permeates the spaces between words.

Both objects and words can unleash psychic torrents that seem disproportionate to the actual signifiers. Speaking of her inability to suppress her memory of her mother, Naomi explains: "Just a glimpse of a worn-out patchwork quilt and the old question comes thudding out of the night again like a giant moth" (26). Words can similarly unleash memory, as we see in Naomi's response to the honorific "Nesan" in Emily's journal:

> The sight of the word . . . cuts into me with a peculiar sensation of pain and tenderness. It means "older sister," and was what Aunt Emily always called Mother. Grandma Kato also called Mother "Nesan" from time to time especially if she was talking to Aunt Emily. I remember one time I called Mother "Nesan" and Grandma Kato laughed and laughed. (46)

The word agitates Naomi not because of its literal meaning but because of its association with her mother and grandmother, with a time too blissful to recall. Of all the words in Emily's journal, this one steals its way most readily into Naomi's heart. Like a metaphorical quilt, the narrator's words often enter obliquely, in the form of fables and dreams that together spin a web of verbal and emotional echoes.

Kogawa, like Kingston, deploys both Western and Eastern fables to connect past and present and to contrast fantasy and reality. Whereas Kingston's use of legendary material often turns into self-fulfilling fantasies (Cheung 1990a), Kogawa's rewriting of fairy tales brings out Naomi's yearning all the more, as in her double-telling of the tale of Goldilocks:

> In one of Stephen's books, there is a story of a child with long golden ringlets called Goldilocks who one day comes to a quaint house in the woods lived in by a family of bears. Clearly, we are that bear family in this strange house in the middle of the woods. I am Baby Bear, whose chair Goldilocks breaks, whose porridge Goldilocks eats, whose bed Goldilocks sleeps in. Or perhaps this is not true and I am really Goldilocks after all. In the morning, will I not find my way out of the forest and back to my room where the picture bird sings above my bed and the real bird sings in the real peach tree by my open bedroom window in Marpole? (126)

Naomi, unlike the primarily Anglo-Saxon audience for which the story is intended, does not readily identify with Goldilocks. In fact, what triggers her memory of the fairy tale is hearing in Slocan one of her mother's favorite records, "Silver Threads among the Gold." Naomi remarks, "It does not occur to me to wonder why Mother would have liked this song. We do not have silver threads among the gold" (126). Or Goldilocks's "long golden ringlets." Hence Naomi at first sees herself as the brown Other, the Baby Bear at whose expense Goldilocks makes herself comfortable. Yet her instinctive distaste for the role of the victim (despite her intuitive identification with it) prompts a recasting of herself as the heroine. Were she Goldilocks, she surmises, then all would be well. Then she could return to her prewar, prelapsarian home where the picture bird and the real bird mesh, where the signifier resonates with the signified. But Naomi cannot be Goldilocks any more than Pecola can have the bluest eye. The picture girl and the real girl do not and will not correspond. This impossibility presages the remoteness of her return: "No matter how I wish it, we do not go home" (126).

The story of Goldilocks most likely rubs against another sore spot in Naomi, who has been taught throughout her childhood not to be *wagamama,* not to be selfish and inconsiderate. When she is told that Mother must go to Japan to take care of Naomi's great-grandmother, who is ill, her silence masks inward protest: "My great-grandmother has need of my mother. Does my mother have need of me? In what market-place of the universe are the bargains made that have traded my need for my great-grandmother's?" (67). Not once does she verbalize or act on her own desire, however. How different from the fairy-tale girl, who has no consideration for others! And instead of being punished (at least in the version read by Naomi), she awakes in her cozy home. Meanwhile, little Naomi, who has tried scrupulously to repress her own needs, wakes in a strange bed in an outlandish place.

The Japanese fable of Momotaro, Naomi's favorite tale, speaks more truly to her life. As Kogawa retells it, the tale sets off a rippling emotional effect in Naomi and in the reader. Fujita has shown that "attendance is clearly linked to . . . the story of Momotaro" (38), which is about a boy who emerges from a peach, to the delight of an old childless couple. When Momotaro grows up, he travels to a neighboring island to fight bandits; he wins the battle and brings honor to his aged foster parents. The plot is simple enough, yet each detail summoned by the narrator is rich with allusion. The joy of the old couple at the sight of Momotaro tumbling out of a peach has parallels in Naomi's own happy prewar childhood, when all the adults lavish love and attention on her, when simply "by existing a child is delight" (55). The day Momotaro leaves his parents for the long and perilous journey is also analogous to Naomi's experience. Both the sadness of separation and the suppression of grief are delicately sketched:

> The time comes when Momotaro must go and silence falls like feathers of snow all over the rice-paper hut. Inside, the hands are slow. Grandmother kneels at the table forming round rice balls, pressing the sticky rice together with her moist fingertips. She wraps them in a small square cloth and, holding them before her in her cupped hands, she offers him the lunch for his journey. There are no tears and no touch. Grandfather and Grandmother are careful, as he goes, not to weight his pack with their sorrow.
>   Alone in the misty mountains once more, the old folk wait. (56)

This speaking picture prefigures several scenes of farewell in *Obasan:* those of Mother and Grandmother Kato when they leave for Japan, of Father when he leaves Slocan, of Grandpa and Grandma Nakane when they leave for the hospital, and of Stephen when he leaves for Toronto. No tears are shed on any of these occasions. And few words are spoken. Unlike Momotaro, however, none of these leavetakers truly returns.

It is with respect to Obasan, who is now "older than the grandmother [Naomi] knew as a child, older than any person [she knows] today" (54), that the fable has multiple bearings. Obasan and Uncle are also a childless couple. When Obasan becomes the guardian aunt of Stephen and Naomi, she too treats them as her own offspring. Emily tells Naomi's mother in the journal: "She says you entrusted them to her and they're her kids now until you return" (108). The couple's love for Momotaro is expressed neither in words nor by touch, but through the slow movement of the old woman's hands; Obasan is similarly "defined by her serving hands." The couple's considerate silence resonates in the actions of Mother, Grandpa, Uncle, and Obasan, all of whom try to shield Stephen and Naomi from grief.

But Kogawa also gives a sad twist to the tale in the relationship between Obasan and Stephen. The rice balls offered by the old

woman to Momotaro evoke a scene on the train. Obasan offers
Stephen a rice ball. "Not that kind of food," Stephen sulks, rejecting her offer (115). The episode foreshadows Stephen's rejection of
everything Japanese, including his foster mother. On the day of his
departure for a school of music, Naomi considers her brother as
"Momotaro going off to conquer the world" (214). Obasan, like the
Old Woman in the story, refrains from displaying her sorrow; instead she "kept standing in the same spot after he was gone" (214).
But the motivation of Stephen's long journey is a far cry from that
of Momotaro's. He may obtain laurels in the musical world as a
concert pianist, but he never bestows honor on his aged foster
parents. Silence in the original story expresses mutual caring, but
Stephen's increasing terseness is rebuttal. He is "irritable and is
almost completely non-communicative with Obasan" (215), who
"mends and re-mends his old socks and shirts which he never
wears and sets the table with food which he often does not eat"
(215). He ends up avoiding Obasan altogether: "Unable to bear the
density of her inner retreat . . . [he] fled to the ends of the earth"
(14). Stephen, "always uncomfortable when anything is 'too Japanese'" (217), has missed a point succinctly enunciated by Emily:
"Momotaro is a Canadian story. We're Canadian, aren't we? Everything a Canadian does is Canadian" (57).

Fujita has noted that Emily herself exemplifies the spirit of
Momotaro and that the narrator, in ending the novel with "a document like those Aunt Emily has been researching," joins Emily's
verbal warfare and "conclude[s] the Momotaro story left un-
finished in Chapter Ten" (38, 40). Like Momotaro, who leaves
home to battle bandits, Emily travels all over Canada and the States
to fight against injustice. By transferring Momotaro's courage to
Emily, Kogawa has also redefined traditional heroism in accordance with the pacifist tenor of her novel. She refuses to glorify
martial valor and omits all descriptions of physical combat in
Naomi's version of the fable. In so doing, Kogawa, like Kingston in
The Woman Warrior, has injected new meanings into a traditional
tale. Kingston grafts the legend about a male general onto her
fantasy of the woman warrior; Kogawa confers Momotaro's attributes on Emily. Kingston transforms a swordwoman into a word-
woman; Kogawa turns Momotaro's combats into Emily's "paper
battles" (189). These shifts in the script allow women to enter the

public arena without subscribing to the military ethos of patriarchal societies.

Finally, the lonely waiting of the legendary grandparents foreshadows Naomi's own pain of anticipating her mother's return: "What matters to my five-year-old mind is not the reason that she is required to leave, but the stillness of waiting. . . . After a while, the stillness is so much with me that it takes the form of a shadow which grows and surrounds me like air" (66). Little Naomi finds it much more difficult to heed the needs of others before one's own. She must come to attendance the hard way.

Kogawa thus encapsulates in less than half a page a montage of emotions that the characters hide from each other, and traces such self-restraint to a formative childhood tale. The author herself has learned the lesson well. Her evocative style provides a counterpoint to the dry official papers and Emily's effusive rhetoric. The reader must probe beneath the surface of the lapidary prose to catch the inexpressible.

Kogawa also conveys the buried emotions of the narrator—who "never spoke" as a child (57)—through "speaking dreams."[22] Three particular dreams mark Naomi's growth. The child is waylaid by a recurrent nightmare after her encounters with Old Man Gower: "In my childhood dreams, the mountain yawns apart as the chasm spreads. My mother is on one side of the rift. I am on the other. We cannot reach each other. My legs are being sawn in half" (65). The dream connects Naomi's sense of physical mutilation and her psychological alienation from her mother, who disappears "around this time" (66). The successive placement of Naomi's nightmare and her mother's disappearance suggests that the child "feels that her abandonment by Mother must be punishment for her unmentionable offence, her fall from innocence" (Gottlieb 46).

That the victim is obsessed by guilt and shame is further signified in another nightmare that recurs even after Naomi is an adult. In this dream three beautiful Oriental women, captured and guarded by several British soldiers, lie naked on a muddy road. When one of the three—"stretched between hatred and lust"— tries to seduce the soldiers, they make a sport of shooting at the women's feet. Naomi writes: "The soldiers could not be won.

[22] Gottlieb and Fujita discuss similar dreams in the novel.

Dread and a deathly loathing cut through the women" (62). This dream, which once more couples sexual overtures with punishment, highlights the dreamer's self-contempt.

The most instructive dream—one that alludes to the Grand Inquisitor in Dostoyevsky's *Brothers Karamazov*—occurs just before Naomi finally learns about her mother's ordeal in Nagasaki. In her dream the Grand Inquisitor (who resembles Old Man Gower) is prying open her eyes and her mother's mouth.

> His demand to know was both a judgement and a refusal to hear. The more he questioned [Mother], the more he was her accuser and murderer. The more he killed her, the deeper her silence became. What the Grand Inquisitor has never learned is that the avenues of speech are the avenues of silence. *To hear my mother, to attend her speech, to attend the sound of stone, he must first become silent.* Only when he enters her abandonment will he be released from his own. (228; my emphasis)

Commenting on the torture during which the Grand Inquisitor pries open Naomi's eyes, Gottlieb notes: "How different is this from traditional (Western or romantic) associations of evil with darkness. In this novel we are confronted with the mystery of evil in its most everyday manifestations and in forcibly full daylight" (41). The hierarchical opposition of speech and silence is similarly reconfigured. The coercion to speak brings to mind not only Maxine's confrontation with the mute girl in *The Woman Warrior* but also the imaginary surgery Emily performs on Naomi:

> Aunt Emily, are you a surgeon cutting at my scalp with your folders and your filing cards and your insistence on knowing all? The memory drains down the sides of my face, but it isn't enough, is it? It's your hands in my abdomen, pulling the growth from the lining of my walls, but bring back the anaesthetist turn on the ether clamp down the gas mask bring on the chloroform when will this operation be over Aunt Em? (194)

Marilyn Rose sees this operation as necessary and salutary for Naomi (1988, 223), and no doubt Emily intends only to do Naomi good. But read against the dream of the Grand Inquisitor, Naomi's pain suggests that even Emily's method may fall short. In her desperation to know all and to help Naomi speak out, Emily may be guilty of not paying sufficient attention to Naomi's inner speech, to the psychological obstacles that block articulation. One may further note that Naomi breaks her silence through her imaginary or recollected dialogue with this aunt. Face to face with the word warrior, the narrator is often outtalked or cowed into silence.

Naomi derives an epiphany from the nocturnal vision. It dawns on her that she has unwittingly assumed the role of the Grand Inquisitor, who seeks to extort an answer from her mother.[23] She now asks herself, "Did I doubt her love? Am I her accuser?" (228). The dream prompts Naomi to recognize her "culpability as Mother's accuser," to enter another's suffering, and to have faith in maternal love despite the apparent desertion (Fujita 39). At the point where Naomi decides to give up her "inquisition," she learns the truth. The avenues of silence and the avenues of speech are conjoined.

These dreams hark back to the various forms of silence discussed earlier. The first dream dramatizes what Naomi is forbidden to tell. The second traces her repression to childhood shame and guilt. The third yields a parable counseling attentive silence. The victims in the first two dreams concentrate on their own torments; in the last Naomi sees her mother as a fellow sufferer. Once she shifts focus from her own vulnerability to her mother's ordeal, she sees she has been *wagamama*—guilty of making self-centered demands. In aligning another's need with her own, in remaining solicitous of others despite her own buried grief, Naomi remains true to her Japanese upbringing and faithful to the example of Obasan.

Paradoxically, it is through Naomi's willingness to "attend the sound of stone" that the "stone bursts open." In the next chapter she is apprised of the horror of Nagasaki. Staggering as it is, the knowledge frees Naomi from her years of gnawing doubt and unspeakable guilt.

---

[23] The narrator herself expresses her impatience with excessive and intrusive questioning at the beginning of the novel, when she goes on a date with a widower: "The widower was so full of questions that I half expected him to ask for an identity card" (7).

Water and Stone

The ending of *Obasan*, like that of *The Woman Warrior*, enacts multiple reconciliations—between mother and daughter, past and present, death and life, and, above all, the nonverbal and verbal modes of expression embodied in Obasan and Emily. These reconciliations are, however, preceded by an expression of unrelenting weariness:

> I am tired, I suppose, because I want to get away from all this. From the past and all these papers, from the present, from the memories, from the deaths, from Aunt Emily and her heap of words. I want to break loose from the heavy identity, the evidence of rejection, the unexpressed passion, the misunderstood politeness. I am tired of living between deaths and funerals, weighted with decorum, unable to shout or sing or dance, unable to scream or swear, unable to laugh, unable to breathe out loud. (183)

Shortly after this jeremiad Naomi learns about her mother's fate from Grandma Kato's letters addressed to Grandpa Kato. The letters, as we saw earlier, come across to her as "skeletons" unanimated by "love." And Naomi is wont to think of love in silent terms. She quotes from a Chinese poem: "Did you not know that people hide their love / Like a flower that seems too precious to be picked?" (228).[24] The quotation conveys her own uneasiness about words, especially those that seem self-serving: "People who talk a lot about their victimization make me uncomfortable. It's as if they use their suffering as weapons or badges of some kind" (34). Grandma, too, apologizes for hers: "For the burden of these words, forgive me" (236).

But the letters themselves belie the binary opposition of stoical, protective, and considerate silence and self-lacerating, selfish, and aggressive telling. Grandma, whom Naomi remembers as "thin and tough, not given to melodrama or overstatement of any kind," describes the aftermath of the conflagration in an "outpouring"

---

[24] When one of her students teases Naomi by asking whether she has ever been "in love," she directs the class's attention to the preposition instead: "In love? Why do you suppose we use the preposition 'in' when we talk about love?" (6).

(234). Her letters show Naomi that writing unbearable thoughts, however excruciating at the time, can also release sorrow and help the writer "extricate herself from the grip of the past" (236). Such expression is surely more salutary than the "vigil of silence" observed by Mother (236), which Naomi has long misinterpreted as evidence of abandonment. Ironically, it is through Grandma's avowedly inconsiderate telling that Naomi learns of her grandmother's and mother's "deep love" (233).

For something other than horror emerges from Grandma's letters. Through them Naomi learns that as soon as Grandma regains consciousness after the blast, she focuses wholeheartedly on rescuing her niece's two children: "At no point does Grandma Kato mention the injuries she herself must have sustained" (238). Mother, totally defaced and severely wounded, is found making a pyre for a dead baby. These examples of compassion in the face of atrocity provide an affirmative answer to Naomi's earlier questioning. Though the greed, hatred, selfishness that are a part of the human condition will always exist, Naomi can now accept the evidence for optimism.

Grandma's letters thus provide Naomi with both a private reason (to "extricate herself from the grip of the past") and a public reason (through "story-telling, we can extricate ourselves from our foolish ways") to write out of her personal and family silences. Yet her (or Kogawa's) effectiveness as a "historian" lies precisely in her marked difference from many traditional historians, whose methods Barbara Omolade has sharply deplored:

> Placing the observer in an ivory tower with pen and pad, telescope or books to observe the comings and goings of the lowly is at the locus of Western thinking. . . . The function of distance is to enable the observer ostensibly to objectify, but actually to dominate the observed. In this manner, the observer-scholar has become connected to the conquistador and the slave master, for his observations became useful data for explaining and justifying the domination of the observed. (286)

By contrast, Naomi proceeds tentatively, and insists that facts alone do not history make. She traverses the historical landscape in slow motion and delivers a microscopic worm's-eye view of the muted sufferers. Her prose tracks emotional stirring unseen by the naked eye and unheard by the ordinary ear; it flashes a collage of images intimating fear and longing, and symbols from nature reflecting the contradictory human potential for cruelty and for love.

Although *Obasan* focuses on one family and on a specific period, it does have a universal quality that transcends personal and political tragedy. Like Kingston, who turns family history into national epic by giving her characters honorific titles, Kogawa endows her characters with a timeless quality by calling them Obasan, Uncle, Father, Mother, and Grandma. Obasan, in particular, is compared not only with the old woman of many Japanese legends but with "every old woman in every hamlet in the world . . . [who] stands as the true and rightful owner of the earth" (15–16). The author herself seems to have inherited from Obasan "the keys to unknown doorways and to a network of astonishing tunnels." She too is a "possessor of life's infinite personal details," accumulated, no doubt, through years of quiet absorption (16).

Toward the end of the novel, silence and speech are increasingly imaged as complementary, as in Naomi's inspection of the "two ideographs for the word 'love'. The first contained the root words 'heart' and 'hand' and 'action'—love as hands and heart in action together. The other ideograph, for 'passionate love', was formed of 'heart', 'to tell', and 'a long thread' " (228). Love may take the form of Obasan's serving hands or Emily's (and Grandma's) passionate telling: "the heart declaring a long thread knotted to Obasan's twine, knotted to Aunt Emily's package" (228).

Obasan itself unwinds as a long thread that ties the variously strong women together. The imagery of filament spreads through the entire novel, but at the beginning it is most often associated with the spider webs that ensnare Naomi, that cause her to be "caught" in the past: "We're trapped, Obasan and I, by our memories of the dead. . . . Like threads of old spider webs, still sticky and hovering, the past waits for us to submit, or depart. When I least expect it, a memory comes skittering out of the dark, spinning and netting the air, ready to snap me up and ensnare me in old and complex puzzles" (26). By the end of the story these predatory webs turn into an intricate network of supportive female relationships, a network that also gathers the seemingly disparate narrative threads into a web of verbal echoes and silences. The Japanese ideogram 系 —*kei*, as in "nikkei"—means family lineage, or

Two ideograms for "love."
Calligraphy by Shu-mei Shih.

connection; it is made up almost entirely of the "thread" 糸 radical
that also forms a part of the ideogram for "passionate love." By
untangling her past, the narrator is able symbolically to reweave a
family unraveled by the war and by extension, to restitch the scattered nikkei community into the tapestry of Canadian history.[25]

[25] For various conjugations of *kei* see Nelson 89. I thank Yukiko Kinoshita for
alerting me to the etymology of *kei*.

Silence and words couple again in the lyrical ending of the novel proper, when Naomi decides to go to the coulee she and Uncle visited every year on the anniversary of Nagasaki's bombing (though the reason for the pilgrimage was previously hidden from her). There she undergoes a symbolic baptism and enters a beatific vision: "Above the trees, the moon is a pure white stone. The reflection is rippling in the river—water and stone dancing. It's a quiet ballet, soundless as breath" (247). This epiphany, as Goellnicht observes, "holds in harmoniously negotiated tension . . . the 'stone' of silence and the 'stream' of language" (1989, 297).

Such harmony infuses the style of the novel. In recollecting and recording the past, Naomi/Kogawa answers Emily's/Kitagawa's call for public expression. In writing a quiet book, one that is attentive to image and to nuances of feeling, the author also vindicates Obasan's silence. The most trenchant passages in the novel are not the expository and explosive entries reproduced from Emily's diary but the pages of Naomi's understated prose. Kogawa suggests that open accusations and outspoken demands, while necessary, are insufficient. Emily's thundering for justice will not solve any problem until people genuinely care. By heeding the poetry in the narrative, by witnessing the quiet strength of issei such as Obasan, the reader may well experience a change of heart.

Speaking of carpentry, Naomi observes: "There is a fundamental difference in Japanese workmanship—to pull with control rather than push with force" (24). This observation implicitly contrasts nikkei and dominant Canadian modes of operation. Out of her own two-toned heritage Kogawa has carved a style that controls its force through the pull of silences.

Coda

A particular feature of the outsider's existence [is] the acquired flexibility in shifting from the mainstream construction of life to other constructions of life where she is more or
less "at home." This flexibility is necessary for the outsider
but it can also be willfully exercised by those who are at ease
in the mainstream. I recommend this willful exercise which I
call "world"-travelling.

María Lugones, "Playfulness, 'World'-Travelling,
and Loving Perception"

A small revolution has taken place in academia since *Articulate
Silences* was conceived. Many works by people of color have been
incorporated into the curriculum, so that literature by diverse ethnic minorities is sometimes studied alongside the canon. Although
I "dance to the multi-cultural piper's tune" (*Obasan* 226), I still feel
like Kogawa's Naomi responding to Emily's papers, appreciating
the sincere effort yet desiring and groping for a "right mix" (40)—
in my case of texts and pedagogy, of art and politics, and, above
all, of feminism and cultural specificity—that can be heard at the
core.

Dissenting voices have emerged in feminist and ethnic studies
stressing plurality and heterogeneity within their respective con-
stituencies. Whereas white patriarchy was formerly the common
target, rifts have now developed among marginalized groups
themselves. Debates between Third World and First World feminists and between female and male writers of color continue una-
bated. Caught in some of these divides, I have sought a more
radical approach to diversity and pointed to possible connections
across differences—in race, gender, and even discipline.

Including works by hitherto excluded writers is an important
first step toward opening up the canon. The danger lies in placing
these works in cognitive grids that bracket differences as devia-
tions. To transform the curriculum substantially, we need to unfix
mindsets and retool the critical apparatus. We must allow works by
diverse authors to re-form our deep-seated assumptions and even

pedagogies—particularly about who can speak and what is not heard. As my analyses of *The Woman Warrior* and *Obasan* suggest, not just prohibition against speech but also coercion to speak can block articulation. Not that the experiences of the two narrators are entirely parallel. Naomi's inhibition has cumulative causes—sexual, cultural, and political; Maxine's muteness is induced largely by an American schooling that fails to accommodate itself to the needs of bicultural pupils.

Although the configuration of speech and silence is not uniform in North America, many people tend to equate speech with (self-)expression and silence with passivity. The images of oppressive and expressive silence unveiled in this book destabilize these perceptions. While directing attention to the compound difficulty experienced by women who must break silences imposed by gender, culture, and race, I steer away from an unqualified endorsement of the verbally assertive First World feminism as the only viable model.

I also dispute the association of Asian quietness with femininity or inscrutability. No human culture is entirely closed to those who attempt to inhabit it, though the extent of understanding may depend on willingness to suspend received language and knowledge. The texts of the three authors chosen give voice to the voiceless and render prismatic silences. By attempting an equal intercultural dialogue in my analysis, I work toward facilitating what María Lugones calls "'world'-travelling." Such travel, as she points out, has been mandatory for the "outsider," but an insider can also get on board.

We need two-way traffic in ethnic and feminist studies as well. *Articulate Silences* explores new ways of "reading women writing" by crisscrossing between feminist and ethnic poetics (and politics). Interpretive strategies that retrieve feminist messages in women's texts also uncover other forms of subversive understatement. In "The Legend of Miss Sasagawara," for instance, the regulating mechanisms of family, community, and state mirror one another, but the three are presented with an increasing degree of muteness. In *The Woman Warrior*, the narrator's understandable anger at the immigrant community for devaluing girls conceals a strong racial self-hatred instilled by the American educational establishment.

Yamamoto, Kingston, and Kogawa resist patriarchal forces at

work in both the dominant and their own ethnic cultures. They puncture received historical, legal, or cultural "verities"; they expose language's complicity by adopting narrative strategies that circumvent traditional constraints. Through gaps, contradictions, and fragments, the three writers reinvent the past—not by reappropriating but by decentering, disseminating, and interrogating authority. "The Legend," *China Men*, and *Obasan* all violate Anglo-American generic and historiographic conventions by effacing the boundaries between private and public history and between fact and fiction. These writers refuse to act as "representatives" in any way that might deny their subjectivity or diminish their subversive energy; their characters, along with the telling testimonials, belie the homogenizing cast of official documents.

The three authors not only revise history but transfigure ethnicity. Through juxtaposing vying cultural mandates, they unsettle Asian and white American monochromatic thinking. This process is much less straightforward than the routes suggested by assimilationists, who shy away from ethnic particularities, or by cultural nationalists who call for an uncritical reclamation of a heroic Asian heritage. The painstaking path taken shuns any either/or binarism, whether in the dubious opposition of East and West, of ethnicity and feminism, or of assimilation and ethnocentrism. Though the writers are conscious of mainstream forces, they do not counter by resuscitating an "authentic" Asian mythology, especially when it sustains a patriarchal ethos. Whether they invoke haiku, Fa Mu Lan, or Momotaro, the point is never to return to the original but to tell it with a difference—chafing at the restriction of seventeen syllables while exercising the power of concision, replacing the physical weapons of the warrior with word-arrows, or suppressing the scene of battle in the tale of Momotaro to accord with the pacifist tenor of the novel. They draw freely from Asian and Anglo-American traditions but refuse to be defined or confined by either.

As a critic I also tread gingerly among these traditions. My demonstration of continuity between Japanese and Japanese American communicative styles may come across as Orientalist, as perpetuating the dichotomy of "East" and "West." My free use of Western feminist and poststructuralist theories may additionally be perceived as "imperialist" vis-à-vis the Asian American texts. I have tried to show that these disparate traditions undoubtedly inform the writing of the three women but, more important, are transformed—translated—by the writers.

My reluctance to choose between feminism and nationalism accounts in part for my use of feminist interpretive strategies to reveal male silences. Differences among men must also be acknowledged. The racist treatment of early Asian male immigrants has historically assumed a gendered form. As "represented" through American legislation and in the popular media, Asian Americans were, in Frank Chin's words, "lovable for being a race of sissies" (1972, 66). The Asian American fathers who appear in the texts straddle contradictory inscriptions of silences—as dignified Asians and effete Orientals, as oppressive patriarchs at home and submissive aliens at work, as stoic and heroic survivors and unprotesting victims. Even their wordless tenderness is often misconstrued as a lack of expression. When we explore these contradictions, we see not only cross-cultural constraints of manhood (its privileges notwithstanding) but also the peculiar predicaments faced by men whose code of masculinity differs from that of the dominant culture and whose "manly" reserve doubles their historical and political invisibility in white America. Theories that polarize the sexes and equalize all men or all women dilute the particular drama of these texts.

To focus on racial and sexual silences together is not to obliterate their differences. Attention to the interlockings of race, gender, and culture will, however, prevent the facile formulation of commanding males and silent females. More important, engagement with these intersections may bring about reciprocal empathy between women of color and white feminists, and between Asian American women and men. Instead of merely unmasking the oppression of women, feminist politics can extend its concerns to other groups that have been forcefully "feminized."

"Outlawed" groups that use what Foucault calls " 'reverse' discourse" need to exercise caution when they demand legitimacy "in the same vocabulary, using the same categories by which [they were] disqualified" (1976/1980, 101). For instance, men of color have been accused—and sometimes been guilty—of refuting effeminate stereotypes by embracing machismo, of reclaiming "manhood" by muffling women. Those who have suffered "emasculation" should know the frustration of women who have long been denied male perquisites. They could learn to dismantle white supremacy and male supremacy simultaneously.

Understanding the lives of racial and sexual others requires a commitment to travel into their worlds, which are often absent from the maps. Because there are different degrees of access, different ways of (and barriers to) communication, not all of those on the margins can or will speak. Before they can be heard in a "democracy," someone will have to learn their discourse of silence and make it audible. The three writers discussed in this book have, I believe, transported us to such other interior landscapes by their articulate—and articulations of—silences.

VERBUM SAP

Bibliography

Adachi, Ken. 1976. *The Enemy That Never Was: A History of the Japanese Canadians.* Toronto: McClelland & Stewart.

Ahmad, Aijaz. 1987. "Jameson's Rhetoric of Otherness and the 'National Allegory.'" *Social Text*, no. 17, 3–25.

Allen, Paula Gunn. 1986. *The Sacred Hoop: Recovering the Feminine in American Indian Traditions.* Boston: Beacon.

Althusser, Louis. 1971. "Ideology and Ideological State Apparatuses." In *Lenin and Philosophy and Other Essays*, trans. Ben Brewster, 127–86. New York: Monthly Review Press.

Anderson, Benedict. 1983. *Imagined Communities: Reflections on the Origin and Spread of Nationalism.* London: Verso.

Angelou, Maya. 1969. *I Know Why the Caged Bird Sings.* New York: Random House.

Anzaldúa, Gloria. 1981. "Speaking in Tongues: A Letter to Third World Women Writers." In *This Bridge Called My Back: Writings by Radical Women of Color*, ed. Cherríe Moraga and Gloria Anzaldúa, 165–73. New York: Kitchen Table Press.

———. 1987. *Borderlands/La Frontera: The New Mestiza.* San Francisco: Spinsters/Aunt Lute.

———, ed. 1990. *Making Face, Making Soul/Haciendo Caras: Creative and Critical Perspectives by Women of Color.* San Francisco: Aunt Lute Foundation Books.

Ardener, Shirley, ed. 1975. *Perceiving Women.* London: Malaby Press.

Auerbach, Nina. 1978. *Communities of Women: An Idea in Fiction.* Cambridge: Harvard University Press.

Axford, Roger W. 1986. *Too Long Silent: Japanese Americans Speak Out.* Lincoln, Neb.: Media.

Baker, Houston A., Jr. 1980. *The Journey Back: Issues in Black Literature and Criticism.* Chicago: University of Chicago Press.

Bakhtin, M. M. 1981. *The Dialogic Imagination: Four Essays by M. M. Bakhtin.* Ed. Michael Holquist. Trans. Caryl Emerson and Michael Holquist. Austin: University of Texas Press.

Basso, Keith H. 1983. "Stalking with Stories: Names, Places, and Moral Narratives among the Western Apache." In *Text, Play, and Story: The Construction and Reconstruction of Self and Society,* ed. E. Bruner and S. Plattner, 19–55. Washington, D.C.: American Ethnological Society.

Bauer, Dale M. 1988. *Feminist Dialogics: A Theory of Failed Community.* Albany, N.Y.: SUNY Press.

Bhabha, Homi. 1984. "Representation and the Colonial Text: A Critical Exploration of Some Forms of Mimeticism." In *The Theory of Reading,* Frank Gloversmith, 93–122. Totowa, N.J.: Barnes & Noble.

Blauvelt, Wm. Satake. 1989. "Hisaye Yamamoto Recalls Miss Sasagawara." *International Examiner Literary Supplement,* 19 July, 19.

Boelhower, William Q. *Through a Glass Darkly: Ethnic Semiosis in American Literature.* New York: Oxford University Press.

Bouchard, Donald F. 1977. Preface to *Language, Counter-Memory, Practice: Selected Essays and Interviews,* by Michel Foucault. Ithaca: Cornell University Press.

Broadfoot, Barry. 1977. *Years of Sorrow, Years of Shame: The Story of the Japanese Canadians in World War II.* Toronto: Doubleday Canada.

Brodzki, Bella. 1985. " 'She Was Unable Not to Think': Borges' *Emma Zunz* and the Female Subject." *MLN,* March, 330–47.

Bruchac, Joseph, ed. 1983. *Breaking Silence: An Anthology of Contemporary Asian American Poets.* Greenfield Center, N.Y.: Greenfield Review Press.

Butler, Judith. 1991. "Imitation and Gender Insubordination." In *Inside/Out: Lesbian Theories, Gay Theories,* ed. Diana Fuss, 13–31. New York: Routledge.

Cage, John. 1961. *Silence: Lectures and Writing.* Middletown, Conn.: Wesleyan University Press.

Carby, Hazel. 1987. *Reconstructing Womanhood: The Emergence of the Afro-American Woman Novelist.* New York: Oxford University Press.

Carroll, David. 1983. "The Alterity of Discourse: Form, History, and the Question of the Political in M. M. Bakhtin." *Diacritics* 13.2:65–83.

Castillo, Debra A. 1992. *Talking Back: Toward a Latin American Feminist Literary Criticism.* Ithaca: Cornell University Press.

Caudill, William, and Harry A. Scarr. 1962. "Japanese Value Orientations and Culture Change." *Ethnology* 1:53–91.

Caudill, William, and Helen Weinstein. 1969. "Maternal Care and Infant Behavior in Japan and America." *Psychiatry* 32.1:12–43.

Chan, Jeffery Paul. 1977. "Letters: The Mysterious West." *New York Review of Books,* 28 April, 41.

Chan, Jeffery Paul, Frank Chin, Lawson [Fusao] Inada, and Shawn Wong. 1981. "Resources for Chinese and Japanese American Literary Traditions." *Amerasia Journal* 8.1:19–31.

———, eds. 1991. *The Big Aiiieeeee! An Anthology of Asian American Writers.* New York: New American Library/Meridian.

Chan, Sucheng. 1986. *This Bittersweet Soil: The Chinese in California Agri-culture, 1860–1910*. Berkeley: University of California Press.

———. 1989, "On the Ethnic Studies Requirement," pt. 1: "Pedagogical Implications." *Amerasia Journal* 15.1:267–80.

———. *Asian Americans: An Interpretive History*. Boston: Twayne-Hall.

Chen, Jack. 1981. *The Chinese of America*. San Francisco: Harper & Row.

Chesler, Phyllis. 1973. *Woman and Madness*. New York: Avon.

Cheung, King-Kok. 1988. " 'Don't Tell': Imposed Silences in *The Color Pur-ple* and *The Woman Warrior*." *PMLA*, March, 162–74.

———. 1990a. "Self-fulfilling Visions in *The Woman Warrior* and *Thousand Pieces of Gold*." *Biography: An Interdisciplinary Quarterly*, Spring, 143–53.

———. 1990b. "The Woman Warrior versus the Chinaman Pacific: Must a Chinese American Critic Choose between Feminism and Heroism?" in Hirsch and Keller, 234–51.

———. 1991. "Double-Telling: Intertextual Silence in Hisaye Yamamoto's Fiction." *American Literary History* 3.2:277–93.

———. 1991–92. "Thrice Muted Tale: Interplay of Art and Politics in Hisaye Yamamoto's 'The Legend of Miss Sasagawara.' " *MELUS* 17.3:109–25.

———. Forthcoming. "Attentive Silence in Joy Kogawa's *Obasan*." In *Listen to "Silences": New Essays in Feminist Criticism*, ed. Shelley Fisher Fishkin and Elaine Hedges. New York: Oxford University Press.

Chin, Frank 1972. "Confessions of the Chinatown Cowboy." *Bulletin of Concerned Asian Scholars* 4.3:58–70.

———. 1984. "The Most Popular Book in China." *Quill* 4.6–12.

———. 1985. "This Is Not an Autobiography." *Genre* 18:109–30.

———. 1991. "Come All Ye Asian American Writers of the Real and The Fake." In Chan et al. 1–92.

Chin, Frank, and Jeffery Paul Chan. 1972. "Racist Love." In *Seeing through Shuck*, ed. Richard Kostelanetz, 65–79. New York: Ballantine.

Chin, Frank, Jeffery Paul Chan, Lawson Fusao Inada, and Shawn Wong, eds. 1974/1983. *Aiiieeeee! An Anthology of Asian-American Writers*. Wash-ington, D.C.: Howard University Press.

Ching, Frank, and Frank Chin. 1972. "Who Is Afraid of Frank Chin, or Is It Ching?" *Bridge* 2.2:29–34.

Christ, Carol P. 1980. *Diving Deep and Surfacing: Women Writers on Spiritual Quest*. Boston: Beacon.

Christian, Barbara. 1987. "The Race for Theory." *Cultural Critique* 6 (Spring):51–64.

Chu, Louis. 1961/1979. *Eat a Bowl of Tea*. Seattle: University of Washington Press.

Chua, C. Lok. 1981. "An Exorcism: Two Asians in America." *Massachusetts Review* 22.2:361–67.

———. 1991. "Mythopoesis East and West in *The Woman Warrior*." In Lim 1991, 146–50.

Cihai: The Encyclopaedic Chinese Dictionary. 1979. 3 vols. Shanghai: [Ci Shu]; Hong Kong: Joint.

Cisneros, Sandra. 1988. *The House on Mango Street*. Houston: Arte Público Press.

Cixous, Hélène, and Catherine Clément. 1986. *The Newly Born Woman*. Trans. Betsy Wing. Minneapolis: University of Minnesota Press.

Clément, Catherine. 1980. "Enslaved Enclave." In Marks & Courtivron, 130–36.

Crow, Charles L. 1984. "Home and Transcendence in Los Angeles Fiction." In *Los Angeles in Fiction: A Collection of Original Essays*, ed. David Fine, 189–205. Albuquerque: University of New Mexico Press.

——. 1986. "The *Issei* Father in the Fiction of Hisaye Yamamoto." In *Opening Up Literary Criticism: Essays on American Prose and Poetry*, ed. Leo Truchlar, 34–40. Salzburg. Wolfgang Neugebauer.

——. 1987. "A *MELUS* Interview: Hisaye Yamamoto." *Melus* 14.1:73–84.

Daniels, Roger, 1981. *Concentration Camps, North America: Japanese in the U.S. and Canada during World War II*. Malabar, Fla.: R. E. Krieger.

Danuenhauer, Bernard P. 1980. *Silence: The Phenomenon and Its Ontological Significance*. Bloomington: Indiana University Press.

Davis, Angela Y. 1983. *Women, Race & Class*. New York: Vintage/Random House.

Dearborn, Mary V. 1986. *Pocahontas's Daughters: Gender and Ethnicity in American Culture*. New York: Oxford University Press.

Delgado, Richard. 1982. "Words That Wound: A Tort Action for Racial Insults, Epiphets, and Name-Calling." *Harvard Civil Rights–Civil Liberties Law Review* 17.1:133–81.

Diamond, Irene, and Lee Quinby, ed. 1988. *Feminism & Foucault: Reflections on Resistance.*Boston: Northeastern University Press.

Dostoyevsky, Fyodor. 1958/1982. *The Brothers Karamazov*. Trans. David Magarshack. New York: Viking.

Douglas, Mary. 1973. *Natural Symbols: Explorations in Cosmology*. London: Barrie & Jenkins.

DuPlessis, Rachel Blau. 1981/1985. "For the Etruscans." In *The New Feminist Criticism: Essays on Women, Literature, and Theory*, ed. Elaine Showalter, 271–91. New York: Pantheon.

——. 1985. *Writing beyond the Ending: Narrative Strategies of Twentieth-Century Women Writers*. Bloomington: Indiana University Press.

Eagleton, Terry. 1976. *Marxism and Literary Criticism*. Berkeley: University of California Press.

Eakin, Paul John. 1985. *Fictions in Autobiography: Studies in the Art of Self-invention*. Princeton: Princeton University Press.

Felman, Shoshana. 1991. "Women and Madness: The Critical Phallacy." In *Feminisms: An Anthology of Literary Theory and Criticism*, ed. Robyn R. Warhol and Diane Price Herndl, 6–19. New Brunswick, N.J.: Rutgers University Press.

Fischer, Michael M. J. 1986. "Ethnicity and the Post-modern Arts of Memory." In *Writing Cultures: The Poetics and Politics of Ethnography*, ed. James Clifford and George E. Marcus, 194–233. Berkeley: University of California Press.

Fishkin, Shelley Fisher. 1991. "Interview with Maxine Hong Kingston." *American Literary History* 3.4:782–91.

Foucault, Michel. 1976/1980. *The History of Sexuality.* Trans. R. Hurley. New York: Vintage.

——. 1977/1980. *Language, Counter-memory, Practice: Selected Essays and Interviews.* Ed. Donald F. Bouchard. Ithaca: Cornell University Press.

——. 1979. *Discipline and Punish: The Birth of the Prison.* Trans. Alan Sheridan. New York: Vintage/Random House.

Friedman, Susan Stanford. 1989. "The Return of the Repressed in Women's Narratives." *Journal of Narrative Technique* 19.1:141–56.

Fujita, Gayle K. 1985. " 'To Attend the Sound of Stone': The Sensibility of Silence in *Obasan*'" *MELUS* 12.3:33–42.

Gates, Henry Louis, Jr. 1991. " 'Authenticity,' or the Lesson of Little Tree." *New York Times Book Review,* 24 November, 1, 26–30.

——, ed. 1984. *Black Literature and Literary Theory.* New York: Methuen.

Gibson, Donald B. 1989. "Text and Countertext in Toni Morrison's *The Bluest Eye.*" *LIT: Literature Interpretation Theory* 1.1–2:19–32.

Gilbert, Sandra M., and Susan Gubar. 1979. *The Madwoman in the Attic: The Woman Writer and the Nineteenth-Century Literary Imagination.* New Haven: Yale University Press.

Gilman, Charlotte Perkins. 1892/1973. *The Yellow Wallpaper.* New York: Feminist Press.

Glissant, Edouard. 1989. *Caribbean Discourse: Selected Essays.* Trans. J. Michael Dash. Charlottesville: University Press of Virginia.

Goellnicht, Donald C. 1989. "Minority History as Metafiction: Joy Kogawa's *Obasan.*" *Tulsa Studies in Women's Literature,* Fall, 287–306.

——. 1991. "Father Land and/or Mother Tongue: The Divided Female Subject in Kogawa's *Obasan* and Hong Kingston's *The Woman Warrior.*" In *Redefining Autobiography in Twentieth-century Women's Fiction: An Essay Collection,* ed. Janice Morgan and Colette T. Hall, 119–34. New York: Garland.

——. 1992. "Tang Ao in America: Male Subject Positions in *China Men.*" In *Reading the Literatures of Asian America,* ed. Shirley Geok-Lin Lim and Amy Ling, 191–212. Philadelphia: Temple University Press.

Gottlieb, Erika. 1986. "The Riddle of Concentric Worlds in *Obasan.*" *Canadian Literature* 109 Summer: 34–53.

Gould, Stephen Jay. 1981. *The Mismeasure of Man.* New York: Norton.

Griffin, Susan. 1981. *Pornography and Silence: Culture's Revenge against Nature.* New York: Colophon/Harper.

Gubar, Susan. 1981. " 'The Blank Page' and the Issues of Female Creativity." *Critical Inquiry* 8:243–63.

Hall, Edward T. 1959. *The Silent Language.* New York: Doubleday.

Henderson, Mae Gwendolyn. 1989. "Speaking in Tongues: Dialogics, Dialectics, and the Black Woman Writer's Literary Tradition." In *Changing Our Own Words: Essays on Criticism, Theory, and Writing by Black Women,* ed. Cheryl A. Wall, 16–37. New Brunswick, N.J.: Rutgers University Press.

Herman, Judith Lewis. 1992. *Trauma and Recovery.* New York: Basic Books.

Hirsch, Marianne, and Evelyn Fox Keller. 1990. *Conflicts in Feminism*. New York: Routledge.

Hom, Marlon, K. 1984. "A Case of Mutual Exclusion: Portrayals by Immigrant and American-Born Chinese of Each Other in Literature." *Amerasia Journal* 11.2:29–45.

——, trans and ed. 1987. *Songs of Gold Mountain: Cantonese Rhymes from San Francisco Chinatown*. Berkeley: University of California Press.

Homans, Margaret. 1983. "'Her Very Own Howl': The Ambiguities of Representation in Recent Women's Fiction." *Signs* 9.2:186–205.

——. 1986. *Bearing the Word: Language and Female Experience in Nineteenth-Century Women's Writing*. Chicago: University of Chicago Press.

hooks, bell. 1984. *Feminist Theory from Margin to Center*. Boston: South End Press.

Houston, Jeanne Wakatsuki. 1985. *Beyond Manzanar: Views of Asian-American Womanhood*. Santa Barbara, Calif.: Capra.

Hsu, Kai-yu, and Helen Palubinskas, eds. 1972/1976. *Asian-American Authors*. Boston: Houghton Mifflin.

Hutcheon, Linda. 1980. *Narcissistic Narrative: The Metafictional Paradox*. Waterloo, Ont.: Wilfrid Laurier University Press.

——. 1987. "Beginning to Theorize Postmodernism." *Textual Practice* 1.1:10–31.

——. 1988. *A Poetics of Postmodernism: History, Theory, Fiction*. New York: Routledge.

Hwang, David Henry. 1983. *FOB*. In *Broken Promises: Four Plays*, 3–57. New York: Avon.

——. 1989. "Afterword." In *M. Butterfly*, 94–100. New York: Plume/Penguin.

Ichioka, Yuji. 1980. "*Amerika Nadeshiko:* Japanese Immigrant Women in the United States, 1900–1924." *Pacific Historical Review* 59.2:339–57.

——. 1988. *The Issei: The World of the First Generation Japanese Immigrants, 1885–1924*. New York: Free Press.

Irigaray, Luce. 1985a. *Speculum of the Other Woman*. Trans. Gillian C. Gill. Ithaca: Cornell University Press.

——. 1985b. *This Sex Which Is Not One*. Trans. Catherine Porter with Carolyn Burke. Ithaca: Cornell University Press.

Islas, Arturo. 1983. "Maxine Hong Kingston: From an Interview between Kingston and Arturo Islas." In *Women Writers of the West Coast Speaking of Their Lives and Careers*, ed. Marilyn Yalom, 11–19. Santa Barbara, Calif.: Capra.

Iwata, Edward. 1990. "Word Warriors." *Los Angeles Times*, 24 June, E1.

Jameson, Fredric. 1981. *The Political Unconscious. Narrative as a Socially Symbolic Act*. Ithaca: Cornell University Press.

——. 1986. "Third-World Literature in the Era of Multinational Capitalism." *Social Text*, no. 15, 65–88.

JanMohamed, Abdul R., and David Lloyd, eds. 1990. *The Nature and Context of Minority Discourse*. New York: Oxford University Press.

Jardine, Alice. 1981. "Pre-texts for the Transatlantic Feminist." *Yale French Studies* 62:220–36.

Jehlen, Myra. 1981. "Archimedes and the Paradox of Feminist Criticism." *Signs* 6.4:575–601.

Jensen, J. Vernon. 1973. "Communicative Functions of Silence." *ETC.: A Review of General Semantics* 30.3:249–57.

Johnson, Barbara. 1978. *The Critical Difference: Essays in the Contemporary Rhetoric of Reading.* Baltimore: Johns Hopkins University Press.

Johnson, Diane. 1977. "Ghosts." Review of *The Woman Warrior,* by Maxine Hong Kingston. *New York Review of Books,* 3 February, 19.

———. 1982. "Anti-autobiography: Maxine Hong Kingston, Carobeth Laird, and N. Scott Momaday," In *Terrorists and Novelists,* 3–13. New York: Knopf.

Jones, Manina. 1990. "The Avenues of Speech and Silence: Telling Difference in Joy Kogawa's *Obasan.*" In *Theory between the Disciplines: Authority/Vision/Politics,* ed. Martin Kreiswirth and Mark A. Cheetham, 213–29. Ann Arbor: University of Michigan Press.

Juhasz, Suzanne. 1985. "Maxine Hong Kingston: Narrative Technique and Female Identity." In Rainwater & Scheick, 173–89.

Kammer, Jeanne. 1979. "The Art of Silence and the Forms of Women's Poetry." In *Shakespeare's Sisters: Feminist Essays on Women's Poetry,* ed. Sandra Gilbert and Susan Gubar, 153–64. Bloomington: Indiana University Press.

Kennedy, Colleen, and Deborah Morse. 1991. "A Dialogue with(in) Tradition: Maxine Hong Kingston's *The Woman Warrior.*" In Lim, 1991, 121–30.

Kikumura, Akemi. 1981. *Through Harsh Winters: The Life of a Japanese Immigrant Woman.* Novato, Calif.: Chandler & Sharp.

Kikumura, Akemi, and Harry H. L. Kitano. 1981. "The Japanese American Family." In *Ethnic Families in America: Patterns and Variations,* ed. Charles H. Mindel and Robert W. Habenstein, 2d ed., 49–60. New York: Elsevier.

Kim, Elaine H. 1982. *Asian American Literature: An Introduction to the Writings and Their Social Context.* Philadelphia: Temple University Press.

———. 1987. "Defining Asian American Realities through Literature." *Cultural Critique* 6:87–111.

———. 1990. " 'Such Opposite Creatures': Men and Women in Asian American Literature." *Michigan Quarterly Review,* Winter, 68–93.

Kingston, Maxine Hong. 1976/1989. *The Woman Warrior: Memoirs of a Girlhood among Ghosts.* New York: Vintage/Random House.

———. 1978. "San Francisco's Chinatown: A View from the Other Side of Arnold Genthe's Camera." *American Heritage,* December, 35–47.

———. 1980/1989. *China Men.* New York: Vintage/Random House.

———. 1980. *Du juan xiu xian er bian ti* [a Chinese edition of *China Men*]. Trans. Zhang Shi. Taibei shi, Taiwan: Huang Guan chu ban she. [The edition in which Kingston's father wrote commentary in the margins.]

———. 1982. "Cultural Mis-readings by American Reviewers." In *Asian and*

Western Writers in Dialogue: New Cultural Identities, ed. Guy
Amirthanayagam, 55–65. London: Macmillan.
——. 1983. "Imagined Life." *Michigan Quarterly Review* 22.4 (Fall):561–70.
——. 1987. *Hawai'i One Summer.* San Francisco: Meadow.
——. 1989/1990. *Tripmaster Monkey: His Fake Book.* New York: Vin-
tage/Random House.
——. 1991. "Personal Statement." In Lim 1991, 23–25.
Kitagawa, Muriel. 1985. *This Is My Own: Letters to Wes & Other Writings on
Japanese Canadians, 1941–1948.* Ed. Roy Miki. Vancouver: Talonbooks.
Kitano, Harry H. 1969. *Japanese Americans: The Evolution of a Subculture.*
Englewood Cliffs, N.J.: Prentice-Hall.
Kogawa, Joy. 1981. *Obasan.* Toronto: Lester & Orpen Dennys; Boston:
David R. Godine, 1982.
——. 1984. Preface to *Issei: Stories of Japanese Canadian Pioneers,* by Gordon
G. Nakayama. Toronto: NC Press.
——. 1985. "The Japanese-Canadian Dilemma." *Toronto Life,* December,
29–33, 58, 60.
——. 1988. Excerpt from a sequel to *Obasan. Seattle Review* 11.1:115–25.
——. 1992. *Itsuka.* Toronto: Viking.
Kolodny, Annette. 1975. "Some Notes on Defining a 'Feminist Literary
Criticism.'" *Critical Inquiry* 2.1:75–92.
——. 1980. "A Map for Rereading; or, Gender and the Interpretation of
Literary Texts." *New Literary History* 11.3:451–67.
Kondo, Dorinne K. 1990. *Crafting Selves: Power, Gender, and Discourses of
Identity in a Japanese Workplace.* Chicago: University of Chicago Press.
Koppelman, Susan, ed. 1985. *Between Mothers and Daughters.* New York:
Feminist Press.
Kristeva, Julia. 1980. *Desire in Language: A Semiotic Approach to Literature and
Art.* Ed. Leon S. Roudiez. New York: Columbia University Press.
——. 1981. "Women's Time." Trans. Alice Jardine and Harry Blake. *Signs:
Journal of Women in Culture and Society* 7.1:13–35.
Krupat, Arnold. 1989. *The Voice in the Margin: Native American Literature and
the Canon.* Berkeley: University of California Press.
Kunihiro, Masao. 1976. "The Japanese Language and Intercultural Com-
munication." In *The Silent Power: Japan's Identity and World Role,* ed. Japan
Center for International Exchange, 51–73. Tokyo: Simul Press.
Lacan, Jacques. 1977. *Écrits: A Selection.* Trans. Alan Sheridan. New York:
Norton.
LaCapra, Dominick. 1985. *History & Criticism.* Ithaca: Cornell University
Press.
Lai, Him Mark, Joe Huang, and Don Wong, eds. 1980. *The Chinese of
America, 1785–1980.* San Francisco: Chinese Culture Foundation.
Lakoff, Robin. 1975. *Language and Woman's Place.* New York: Harper & Row.
Lambertson, Michiko. 1982. Review of *Obasan,* by Joy Kogawa. *Canadian
Woman Studies* 4.2:94–95.
Lanser, Susan Sniader. 1981. *The Narrative Act.* Princeton: Princeton Uni-
versity Press.

——. 1989. "Feminist Criticism, 'The Yellow Wallpaper,' and the Politics of Color in America." *Feminist Studies* 15.3:415–441.

Lauter, Paul. 1985. "Race and Gender in the Shaping of the American Literary Canon: A Case Study from the Twenties." In *Feminist Criticism and Social Change: Sex, Class, and Race in Literature and Culture,* ed. Judith Newton and Deborah Rosenfelt, 19–44. New York: Methuen.

Lebra, Takie Sugiyama, and William P. Lebra. 1984. "Nonconfrontational Strategies for Management of Interpersonal Conflicts." In *Conflict in Japan,* ed. E. S. Kraus, T. P. Rohlen, and P. G. Steinhoff, 41–60. Honolulu: University of Hawaii Press.

Lee, Robert G. 1991. "*The Woman Warrior* as an Intervention in Asian American Historiography." In Lim 1991, 52–63.

Leighton, Alexander H. 1945. *The Governing of Men: General Principles and Recommendations Based on Experience at a Japanese Relocation Camp.* Princeton: Princeton University Press.

Lentricchia, Frank. 1983. *Criticism and Social Change.* Chicago: University of Chicago Press.

Li, David Leiwei. 1990. "*China Men:* Maxine Hong Kingston and the American Canon." *American Literary History* 2.3:482–502.

Li Fang et al., comps. 1974. *T'ai-p'ing kuang chi,* vol. 1. Taiwan: T'ai-nan p'ing p'ing ch'u-pan-she.

Li, Ju-Chen. 1965. *Flowers in the Mirror.* Trans. Lin Tai-yi. Berkeley: University of California Press.

Lim, Shirley Geok-lin. 1990. "Japanese American Women's Life Stories: Maternality in Monica Sone's *Nisei Daughter* and Joy Kogawa's *Obasan.*" *Feminist Studies* 16.2:289–312.

——. ed. 1991. *Approaches to Teaching Kingston's "The Woman Warrior."* New York: Modern Language Association.

Lincoln, Kenneth. 1983. *Native American Renaissance.* Berkeley: University of California Press.

——. 1993. *Indi'n Humor: Bicultural Play in Nature America.* New York: Oxford University Press.

Ling, Amy. 1990. *Between Worlds: Women Writers of Chinese Ancestry.* New York: Pergamon.

Lionnet, Françoise. 1989. *Autobiographical Voices: Race, Gender, Self-portraiture.* Ithaca: Cornell University Press.

Low, David. 1983. Review of *Obasan,* by Joy Kogawa. *Bridge* 8.3:22, 28.

Lowe, Lisa. 1991. "Heterogeneity, Hybridity, Multiplicity: Making Asian American Differences." *Diaspora* 1.1:24–43.

Lu Xun. 1972. *Selected Stories of Lu Hsun.* Trans. Gladys Yang and Yang Hsien-yi. Beijing: Foreign Languages Press.

Lugones, María. 1990. "Playfulness, 'World'-Travelling, and Loving Perception." In Anzaldúa 1990, 390–402.

Lyman, Stanford M. 1971. "Generation and Character: The Case of the Japanese Americans." In *Roots: An Asian American Reader,* ed. Amy Tachiki et al., 48–71. Los Angeles: UCLA Asian American Studies Center.

——. 1988a. "On Nisei Interpersonal Style: A Reply to S. Frank Miyamoto." *Amerasia Journal* 14.2:105–8.

——. 1988b. "'American' Interpersonal Style and Nikkei Realities: A Rejoinder to S. Frank Miyamoto." *Amerasia Journal* 14.2:115–23.

Lyotard, Jean-François. 1984. *The Postmodern Condition: A Report on Knowledge.* Trans. Geoff Bennington and Brian Massumi. Minneapolis: University of Minnesota Press.

McCaffery, Larry. 1982. *The Metafictional Muse: The Works of Robert Coover, Donald Barthelme, and William H. Gass.* Pittsburgh: University of Pittsburgh Press.

McDonald, Dorothy Ritsuko, and Katharine Newman. 1980. "Relocation and Dislocation: The Writings of Hisaye Yamamoto and Wakako Yamauchi." *MELUS* 7.3:21–38.

McDowell, Deborah E. 1988. "'That Nameless . . . Shameful Impulse': Sexuality in Nella Larsen's *Quicksand* and *Passing.*" In *Black Feminist Criticism and Critical Theory,* ed. Joe Weixlmann and Houston A. Baker, Jr., 139–67. Greenwood, Fla.: Penkevill.

——. 1989. "Negotiating between Tenses: Witnessing Slavery after Freedom—*Dessa Rose.*" In *Slavery and the Literary Imagination,* ed. Deborah E. McDowell and Arnold Rampersad, 144–63. Baltimore: John Hopkins University Press.

Macherey, Pierre. 1978. *A Theory of Literary Production.* Trans. Geoffrey Wall. New York: Routledge.

Magnusson, A. Lynne. 1988. "Language and Longing in Joy Kogawa's *Obasan.*" *Canadian Literature/Littérature Canadienne* 116 (Spring):58–66.

Marks, Elaine. 1978. "Women and Literature in France." *Signs* 3.4:832–42.

Marks, Elaine, and Isabelle de Courtivron, eds. 1980. *New French Feminisms.* New York: Schocken.

Masuda, Koh, ed. 1974. *Kenkyusha's New Japanese-English Dictionary.* 4th ed. Tokyo: Kenkyusha.

Matsuda, Mari J. 1989. "Public Response to Racist Speech: Considering the Victim's Story." *Michigan Law Review* 87.8:2320–81.

Matsumoto, Michihiro. 1988. *The Unspoken Way* [*Haragei: Silence in Japanese Business and Society*]. Tokyo and New York: Kodansha International.

Matsumoto, Valerie. 1991. "Desperately Seeking 'Deirdre': Gender Roles, Multicultural Relations, and Nisei Women Writers of the 1930s." *Frontiers* 12.1:19–32.

Matsuura, Shinobu. 1986. *Higan: Compassionate Vow.* Trans. Matsuura family. Berkeley, Calif.: Privately printed.

Merivale, P[atricia]. 1988. "Framed Voices: The Polyphonic Elegies of Hébert and Kogawa." *Canadian Literature/Littérature Canadienne* 116 (Spring):68–82.

Miller, Nancy K. 1981. "Emphasis Added: Plots and Plausibilities in Women's Fiction." *PMLA* 96:36–48.

——. 1986. "Arachnologies: The Woman, the Text, and the Critic." In *The Poetics of Gender,* ed. Nancy K. Miller, 270–95. New York: Columbia University Press.

Milton, Edith. 1982. Review of *Obasan*, by Joy Kogawa. *New York Times Book Review,* 5 September, 8, 17.

Mirikitani, Janice. 1981. *Shedding Silence: Poetry and Prose.* Berkeley: Celestial Arts.

Mistri, Zenobia Baxter. 1990. " 'Seventeen Syllables': A Symbolic Haiku." *Studies in Short Fiction* 27.2:197–202.

Miyamoto, S. Frank, 1986–87. "Problems of Interpersonal Style among the Nisei." *Amerasia Journal* 13.2:29–45.

——. 1988. "Miyamoto Reply to Stanford Lyman." *Amerasia Journal* 14.2:109–13.

Miyoshi, Masao. 1974. *Accomplices of Silence: The Modern Japanese Novel.* Berkeley: University of California Press.

Mohanty, Chandra Talpade. 1984. "Under Western Eyes: Feminist Scholarship and Colonial Discourses." *Boundary 2* 12.3/13.1:333–58.

Mori, Toshio. 1949/1985. "The Woman Who Makes Swell Donuts." In *Yokohama, California,* 22–25. Seattle: University of Washington Press.

Morita, J. R. 1983. Review of *Obasan*, by Joy Kogawa. *World Literature Today* 57.3:516.

Morrison, Toni. 1970. *The Bluest Eye.* New York: Washington Square Press.

Nakayama, Gordon G. 1984. *Issei: Stories of Japanese Canadian Pioneers.* Preface by Joy Kogawa. Toronto: NC Press.

Naylor, Gloria. 1982. *The Women of Brewster Place.* New York: Penguin.

Nee, Victor G., and Brett de Bary Nee. 1973/1981. *Longtime Californ': A Documentary Study of an American Chinatown.* New York: Pantheon.

Nelson, Andrew Nathaniel, comp. 1974. *The Modern Reader's Japanese-English Character Dictionary.* 2d rev. ed. Rutland, Vt.: Charles E. Tuttle.

Neubauer, Carol E. 1983. "Developing Ties to the Past: Photography and Other Sources of Information in Maxine Hong Kingston's *China Men.*" *MELUS* 10.4:17–36.

Niiya, Brian T. 1990. "Open-Minded Conservatives: A Survey of Autobiographies by Asian Americans." M.A. thesis, University of California, Los Angeles.

Nishida, Tsukasa. 1979. "Comparing Japanese-American Person-to-Person Communication: A Third Culture Approach." Ph.D. diss., University of Minnesota.

Nomura, Gail M., Russell Endo, Stephen H. Sumida, and Russell C. Leong, eds. 1989. *Frontiers of Asian American Studies: Writing, Research, and Commentary.* Pullman: Washington State University Press.

O'Barr, William M., and Bowman K. Atkins. 1980. " 'Women's Language' or " 'Powerless Language'?" In *Women and Language in Literature and Society,* ed. Sally McConnell-Ginet, Ruth Borker, and Nelly Furman, 93–110. New York: Praeger.

Ogawa, Dennis M. 1978. *Kodomo no tame ni* [For the sake of the children]. Honolulu: University Press of Hawaii.

Okada, John. 1957/1984. *No-No Boy.* Seattle: University of Washington Press.

Olsen, Tillie. 1965/1972. *Silences.* New York: Dell.

Omi, Michael, and Howard Winant. 1986. *Racial Formation in the United States: From the 1960s to the 1980s*. New York: Routledge.

Omolade, Barbara. 1990. "The Silence and the Song: Toward a Black Woman's History through a Language of Her Own." In *Wild Women in the Whirlwind: Afra-American Women and the Contemporary Literary Renaissance*, ed. Joanne M. Braxton and Andrée Nicola McLaughlin, 282–95. New Brunswick, N.J.: Rutgers University Press.

Orenstein, Gloria Feman. 1990. *The Deflowering of the Goddess*. New York: Pergamon.

Osajima, Keith. 1988. "Asian Americans as the Model Minority: An Analysis of the Popular Press Image in the 1960s and 1980s." In *Reflections on Shattered Windows: Promises and Prospects for Asian American Studies*, ed. Gary Y. Okihiro et al., 165–74. Pullman: Washington State University Press.

Ostriker, Alicia Suskin. 1986. *Stealing the Language: The Emergence of Women's Poetry in America*. Boston: Beacon.

Palumbo-Liu, David. 1990. "Discourse and Dislocation: Rhetorical Strategies of Asian-American Exclusion and Confinement." *LIT: Literature Interpretation Theory* 2:1–7.

Petersen, William, Michael Novak, and Philip Gleason, eds. 1982. *Concepts of Ethnicity*. Cambridge: Belknap/Harvard University Press.

Pfaff, Timothy. 1980. "Talk with Mrs. Kingston." *New York Times Book Review*, 15 June, 1.

Picard, Max. 1948/1952. *The World of Silence*. Trans. Stanley Godman. Chicago: Henry Regnery.

Portch, Stephen R. 1985. *Literature's Silent Language: Nonverbal Communication*. New York: Peter Lang.

Pratt, Annis. 1976. "The New Feminist Criticisms." In *Beyond Intellectual Sexism*, ed. Joan Roberts, 175–95. New York: David McKay.

Pryse, Marjorie, and Hortense Spillers, eds. 1985. *Conjuring: Black Women, Fiction, and Literary Tradition*. Bloomington: Indiana University Press.

Rabine, Leslie W. 1987. "No Lost Paradise: Social Gender and Symbolic Gender in the Writings of Maxine Hong Kingston." *Signs* 12:471–92.

Rabinowitz, Paula. 1987. "Eccentric Memories: A Conversation with Maxine Hong Kingston." *Michigan Quarterly Review* 26.1:177–87.

Radhakrishnan, R. 1990. "Ethnic Identity and Post-structuralist Differance." In JanMohamed & Lloyd, 50–71.

Radner, Joan, and Susan Lanser. 1987. "The Feminist Voice: Coding in Women's Folklore and Literature." *Journal of American Folklore* 100:412–25.

Rainwater, Catherine. 1985. "Anne Redmon: The Fugal Procedure of *Music and Silence*." In Rainwater & Scheick, 69–83.

Rainwater, Catherine, and William J. Scheick, eds. 1985. *Contemporary American Women Writers: Narrative Strategies*. Lexington: University Press of Kentucky.

Rayson, Ann. 1987. "Beneath the Mask: Autobiographies of Japanese-American Women." *MELUS* 14.1:43–57.

Redekop, Magdalene. 1989. "The Literary Politics of the Victim." *Canadian Forum*, November, 14–17.

Rich, Adrienne. 1979. *On Lies, Secrets, and Silence: Selected Prose, 1966–1978.* New York: Norton.

Rodriguez, Richard. 1983. *Hunger of Memory: The Education of Richard Rodriguez.* New York: Bantam.

Rose, Marilyn Russell. 1987. "Hawthorne's 'Custom House,' Said's *Orientalism,* and Kogawa's *Obasan:* An Intertextual Reading of an Historical Fiction." *Dalhousie Review* 67.2/3:286–96.

———. 1988. "Politics into Art: Kogawa's *Obasan* and the Rhetoric of Fiction." *Mosaic* 21 (Spring):215–26.

Rose, Mike. 1989/1990. *Lives on the Boundary: A Moving Account of the Struggles and Achievements of America's Educational Underclass.* New York: Penguin.

Rowe, Karen E. 1986. "To Spin a Yarn: The Female Voice in Folklore and Fairy Tale." In *Fairy Tales and Society: Illusion, Allusion, and Paradigm,* ed. Ruth B. Bottigheimer, 53–74. Philadelphia: University of Pennsylvania Press.

Rubenstein, Roberta. 1987. *Boundaries of the Self: Gender, Culture, Fiction.* Urbana: University of Illinois Press.

Russ, Joanna. 1983. *How to Suppress Women's Writing.* Austin. University of Texas Press.

Said, Edward W. 1979. *Orientalism.* New York: Vintage/Random House.

———. 1983. *The World, the Text, and the Critic.* Cambridge: Harvard University Press.

St. Andrews, B. A. 1986. "Reclaiming a Canadian Heritage: Kogawa's *Obasan.*" *International Fiction Review* 13.1:29–31.

Saldívar, Ramón. 1990. *Chicano Narrative: The Dialectics of Difference.* Madison: University of Wisconsin Press

San Juan, E., Jr. 1991. "Beyond Identity Politics: The Predicament of the Asian American Writer in Late Capitalism." *American Literary History* 3.3:542–65.

Schenck, Celeste. 1988. "All of a Piece: Women's Poetry and Autobiography." In *Life/Lines: Theorizing Women's Autobiography,* ed. Bella Brodzki and Celeste Schenck, 281–305. Ithaca: Cornell University Press.

Schueller, Malini. 1989. "Questioning Race and Gender Definitions: Dialogic Subversions in *The Woman Warrior.*" *Criticism* 31.4:421–37.

Schweik, Susan. 1989. "The 'Pre-Poetics' of Internment: The Example of Toyo Suyemoto." *American Literary History* 1:89–109.

Showalter, Elaine. 1982. "Feminist Criticism in the Wilderness." In *Writing and Sexual Difference,* ed. Elizabeth Abel, 9–35. Chicago: University of Chicago Press.

Sledge, Linda Ching. 1980. "Maxine Hong Kingston's *China Men:* The Family Historian as Epic Poet." *MELUS* 7.4:3–22.

Smith, Sidonie. 1987. "Maxine Hong Kingston's *Woman Warrior:* Filiality and Women's Autobiographical Storytelling." In *A Poetics of Women's*

Autobiography: Marginality and the Fictions of Self-representation, 150–73. Bloomington: Indiana University Press.

Smith, Valerie. 1987. *Self-discovery and Authority in Afro-American Narrative.* Cambridge: Harvard University Press.

Sollors, Werner. 1986. *Beyond Ethnicity: Consent and Descent in American Culture.* New York: Oxford University Press.

Sone, Monica. 1953/1979. *Nisei Daughter.* Seattle: University of Washington Press.

Sontag, Susan. 1966. *Styles of Radical Will.* New York: Farrar, Straus.

Spelman, Elizabeth V. 1988. *Inessential Woman: Problems of Exclusion in Feminist Thought.* Boston: Beacon.

Spivak, Gayatri Chakravorty. 1988. *In Other Worlds: Essays in Cultural Politics.* New York: Routledge.

Stout, Janis P. 1990. *Strategies of Reticence: Silence and Meaning in the Works of Jane Austen, Willa Cather, Katherine Anne Porter, and Joan Didion.* Charlottesville: University Press of Virginia.

Sue, Diane M., and David Sue. 1988. "Asian Americans." In *Experiencing and Counseling Multicultural and Diverse Populations*, ed. Nicholas A. Vacc, Joe Wittmer, and Susan B. DeVaney, 2d ed., 241–62. Muncie, Ind.: Accelerated Development.

Sumida, Stephen H. 1989. "Asian American Literature in the 1980s: A Sampling of Studies and Works." In Nomura et al., 151–58.

——. 1991. *And the View from the Shore: Literary Traditions of Hawai'i.* Seattle: University of Washington Press.

Sunahara, Ann Gomer. 1981. *The Politics of Racism: The Uprooting of Japanese Canadians during the Second World War.* Toronto: James Lorimer.

Sundquist, Eric J. 1988. "The Japanese American Internment: A Reappraisal." *American Scholar* 58:529–47.

Suzuki, Bob H. 1977. "Education and the Socialization of Asian Americans: A Revisionist Analysis of the 'Model Minority' Thesis." *Amerasia Journal* 4.2:23–51.

Tajiri, Vince. 1990. Review of *Seventeen Syllables and Other Stories*, by Hisaye Yamamoto. *Amerasia Journal* 16.1:255–57.

Takaki, Ronald. 1989. *Strangers from a Different Shore: A History of Asian Americans.* Boston: Little, Brown.

Talbot, Stephen. 1990. "Talking Story: Maxine Hong Kingston Rewrites the American Dream." *Image* [magazine of the *San Francisco Examiner*], 24 June, 6–17.

Tannen, Deborah, and Muriel Saville-Troike, eds. 1985. *Perspectives on Silence.* Norwood, N.J.: Ablex.

Tate, Claudia. 1986. "On Black Literary Women and the Evolution of Critical Discourse." *Tulsa Studies in Women's Literature* 5.1:111–23.

tenBroek, Jacobus, Edward N. Barnhart, and Floyd W. Matson. 1954. *Prejudice, War, and the Constitution: Japanese American Evacuation and Resettlement.* Berkeley: University of California Press.

Tong, Benjamin R. 1971. "The Ghetto of the Mind: Notes on the Historical Psychology of Chinese America." *Amerasia Journal* 1.3:1–31.

———. 1977. "Critic of Admirer Sees Dumb Racist." *S.F. Journal*, 11 May, 20.

Trinh T. Minh-ha. 1989. *Woman, Native, Other: Writing Postcoloniality and Feminism*. Bloomington: Indiana University Press.

———. 1991. *When the Moon Waxes Red: Representation, Gender, and Cultural Politics*. New York: Routledge.

Tsai, Shih-shan Henry. 1986. *The Chinese Experience in America*. Bloomington: Indiana University Press.

Tsushima, Yuko. 1989. "The Silent Trader." Trans. Geraldine Harcourt. In *The Graywolf Annual Six: Stories from the Rest of the World*, ed. Scott Walker, 1 11. Saint Paul, Minn.: Graywolf Press.

Uchida, Yoshiko. 1982. *Desert Exile. The Uprooting of a Japanese-American Family*. Seattle: University of Washington Press.

Ueda, Makoto, ed. and trans. 1976. *Modern Japanese Haiku: An Anthology*. Toronto: University of Toronto Press.

Venant, Elizabeth. 1990. "Atypically English." Review of *The Remains of the Day*, by Kazuo Ishiguro. *Los Angeles Times*, 8 November, E1, E18–19.

Wakeman, Frederic, Jr. 1980. "Chinese Ghost Story." Review of *China Men*. *New York Review of Books*, 14 August, 42–45.

Wald, Alan. 1987. "Theorizing Cultural Difference: A Critique of the 'Ethnicity School.'" *MELUS* 14.2:21–33.

Walker, Alice. 1970. *The Third Life of Grange Copeland*. New York: Harcourt Brace Jovanovich.

———. 1982/1983. *The Color Purple*. New York: Washington Square.

———. 1983. *In Search of Our Mothers' Gardens*. New York: Harcourt Brace Jovanovich.

Walker, Nancy. 1989. "Language, Irony, and Fantasy in the Contemporary Novel by Women." *LIT: Literature Interpretation Theory* 1.1–2:33–57.

Wang, Alfred S. 1988. "Maxine Hong Kingston's Reclaiming of America: The Birthright of the Chinese American Male." *South Dakota Review* 26.1:18–29.

Ward, J. A. 1985. *American Silences: The Realism of James Agee, Walker Evans, and Edward Hopper*. Baton Rouge: Louisiana State University Press.

Ward, Peter W. 1982. *The Japanese in Canada*. Ottawa: Canadian Historical Association.

Washington, Mary Helen. 1984. " 'Taming All That Anger Down': Rage and Silence in Gwendolyn Brooks's *Maud Martha*." In Gates 1984, 249–62.

Watts, Alan W. 1957. *The Way of Zen*. New York: Pantheon.

Wayne, Joyce. 1981. "*Obasan*: Drama of Nisei Nightmare." *RIKKA* 8.2:22–23.

Weglyn, Michi. 1976. *Years of Infamy: The Untold Story of America's Concentration Camps*. New York: William Morrow.

Wetzel, Patricia J. 1988. "Are 'Powerless' Communication Strategies the Japanese Norm?" *Language in Society* 17.4:555–64.

White, Hayden. 1978. *Tropics of Discourse*. Baltimore: John Hopkins University Press.

Willis, Gary. 1987. "Speaking the Silence: Joy Kogawa's *Obasan*." *Studies in Canadian Literature* 12.2:239–49.

Wittig, Monique. 1969/1985. *Les Guérillères*. Trans. David Le Vay. Boston: Beacon.

Wong, Jade Snow. 1945/1989. *Fifth Chinese Daughter*. Seattle: University of Washington Press.

Wong, Sau-ling Cynthia. 1988. "Necessity and Extravagance in Maxine Hong Kingston's *The Woman Warrior:* Art and the Ethnic Experience." *MELUS* 15.1:3–26.

———. 1991. "Kingston's Handling of Traditional Chinese Sources." In Lim 1991, 26–36.

———. Forthcoming. *From Necessity to Extravagance: Contexts and Intertexts in Asian American Literature*. Princeton: Princeton University Press.

Woo, Deborah. 1990. "Maxine Hong Kingston: The Ethnic Writer and the Burden of Dual Authenticity." *Amerasia Journal* 16.1:173–200.

Yaeger, Patricia. 1988. *Honey-Mad Women: Emancipatory Strategies in Women's Writing*. New York: Columbia University Press.

Yalom, Marilyn. 1985. *Maternity, Mortality, and the Literature of Madness*. University Park: Pennsylvania State University Press.

Yamamoto [DeSoto], Hisaye. 1941. "Et Ego in America Vixi." *Current Life*, June, 13.

———. 1976a. ". . . I Still Carry It Around." RIKKA 3.4:11–19.

———. "Writing." 1976b. *Amerasia Journal* 3.2:126–33.

———. 1988. *Seventeen Syllables and Other Stories*. Latham, N.Y.: Kitchen Table Press.

Yamauchi, Wakako. 1966/1983. "And the Soul Shall Dance." In Chin et al., 232–39.

———. 1976. "Songs My Mother Taught Me." *Amerasia Journal* 3.2:63–73.

———. 1977. "Handkerchief." *Amerasia Journal* 4.1:143–50.

———. 1979. "The Poetry of the Issei on the American Relocation Experience." In *CALAFIA: The California Poetry*, ed. Ishmael Reed, lxxi–lxxviii. Berkeley: Y'Bird Books.

Yanagisako, Sylvia Junko. 1985. *Transforming the Past: Tradition and Kinship among Japanese Americans*. Stanford: Stanford University Press.

Yarborough, Richard. 1986. "Breaking the 'Codes of Americanness.'" *American Quarterly* 38.5:860–65.

Yasuda, Kenneth. 1957. *The Japanese Haiku: Its Essential Nature, History, and Possibilities in English, with Selected Examples*. Rutland, Vt.: Charles E. Tuttle.

Yim, Susan. 1984. "In a Hailstorm of Words." *Honolulu Star-Bulletin*, Evening ed., 20 September, D1, D8.

Yogi, Stan. 1988. "Legacies Revealed: Uncovering Buried Plots in the Stories of Hisaye Yamamoto and Wakako Yamauchi." M.A. thesis, University of California, Berkeley.

———. 1989. "Legacies Revealed: Uncovering Buried Plots in the Stories of Hisaye Yamamoto." *Studies in American Fiction* 17.2:169–81.

Index

190   Index

Broadfoot, Barry, 130n
Brodzki, Bella, 23n
Buddhism, 7n, 19, 20, 55–57, 68–70, 129n, 132
Butler, Judith, 13n

Camps, internment, 62–69. See also Japanese American internment
Carby, Hazel, 15
Carrasco, Jesus ("Seventeen Syllables"), 38, 40–42, 48n
Carroll, David, 13n
Carter, Forrest: The Education of Little Tree, 12n
Castillo, Debra A., 4n, 16n
Caudill, William, 148n
Censor/censorship, 4, 27, 71–72, 140. See also Self-censorship
Chan, Jeffery Paul, 3n, 28, 69, 78n. See also Aiiieeeee; Big Aiiieeeee
Chan, Sucheng, 6n, 48n, 107n
Chaucer, Geoffrey, 110n
Chen, Jack, 103, 107n
Chesler, Phyllis, 58
Chin, Frank, 3n, 7n, 9n, 17n, 19, 78n, 171. See also Aiiieeeee; Big Aiiieeeee
"Chinamen," connotations of, 101n
Ching, Frank, 17n
Chop Chop (China Men), 119
Christ, Carol P., 4n
Christian, Barbara, 23
Christianity, 7n, 17n, 19, 20, 42–43, 45–46, 68, 129n, 132, 145
Chu, Louis: Eat a Bowl of Tea, 9, 48n
Chua, C. Lok, 22, 121
Cisneros, Sandra: The House on Mango Street, 100n
Cixous, Hélène, 4n, 100
Class, 40, 48n, 50, 129n
Clément, Catherine, 4n
Coding strategies, 15, 27, 33n. See also Appropriation; Distraction; Indirection; Juxtaposition; Narrative strategies; Trivialization
Colonialism, discursive, 25–26, 125, 127–28, 149. See also Domination
Communication: empathic and telepathic, 146, 150, 152, 162; between issei and nisei, 29, 37, 46; between issei spouses, 29, 37, 46; nonverbal, 2–4, 18, 28, 31, 42, 127n, 128, 146–47, 150, 152, 162; problems of, 33–34, 52, 81–84, 108–9, 159; styles of, 8–9, 30–32, 48, 172; visual, 127n, 146–48
Confucianism, 6–7n, 47
Connection: between ancestral culture and ethnic culture, 31, 94–96, 127n;

between ethnic groups, 22, 120, 125; between mothers and children, 39–42, 45–46, 94–99, 148–49, 152, 163; between past and present, 13, 75, 154, 156, 163; between self and community, 19, 99–100, 153–54; between strangers, 119–20, 148; between women, 99–100, 124–25, 130, 147–48, 166; between women and men, 101, 124–25. See also Gender and ethnicity
Context: and history, 13–14, 29, 46–53, 65–73, 90–91, 104, 129–30; of speech, 32, 138. See also History
Counterinvestment, 86, 103
Counter-memory, 15, 102–3
Crow, Charles L., 12, 45, 49n, 55n
Cultural interplay, 15–17, 19–21, 121–22, 125, 128–29, 132, 149–51, 156–62, 165–67, 170–71. See also Bicultural idiom; Literary sources
Culture(s): Cantonese/Chinese, 6, 7n, 22, 24–25, 82, 83, 87; differences in, 1–9, 16–19, 91–92, 97; Japanese/nikkei, 6, 22, 46–49, 132, 139–52, 157–60, 166–67; negotiation and transformation of, 21, 79, 85, 94–98, 121–22, 170; polarization of, 16–18, 91–93, 170–71; women as transmitters of, 10, 98–100, 112, 147–51; and writing, 15–16, 30–33, 94–100, 152–67. See also Cultural interplay; Decorum; Heritage

Daniels, Roger, 130n
Dauenhauer, Bernard P., 2
Davis, Angela Y., 107n
Decorum: feminine, 3–4, 83; Japanese/nikkei, 8n, 30–33, 46–54, 147–48, 157, 163
Defoe, Daniel: Robinson Crusoe, 122
Delgado, Richard, 128n
Derrida, Jacques, 2, 89n
Dew, imagery of, 145–46
DeWitt, John, 65n
Dialogism, 5, 15, 19, 21, 74, 76, 77, 79, 97, 124, 152–55
Diamond, Irene, 13n
Discourse. See Double-voiced discourse; Language
Distraction, 27n, 37, 109n. See also Coding strategies
Domination, 3, 7, 9, 21, 68, 78, 99, 164; through education, 5–6, 11n, 81–92, 149; ideological, 90–91. See also Colonialism; Racism
Dostoyevsky, Fyodor: The Brothers Karamazov, 161–62